*The Enabling State*

# The Enabling State

Modern Welfare Capitalism
in America

NEIL GILBERT
BARBARA GILBERT

New York    Oxford
OXFORD UNIVERSITY PRESS
1989

Oxford University Press

Oxford   New York   Toronto
Delhi   Bombay   Calcutta   Madras   Karachi
Petaling Jaya   Singapore   Hong Kong   Tokyo
Nairobi   Dar es Salaam   Cape Town
Melbourne   Auckland
and associated companies in
Berlin   Ibadan

Library of Congress Cataloging-in-Publication Data
Gilbert, Neil, 1940–
The enabling state : modern welfare capitalism
in America / Neil Gilbert, Barbara Gilbert.
p.   cm. Includes index.
ISBN 0-19-505894-1
1. Public welfare—United States.   2. Human services—United States.
3. Welfare state.   I. Gilbert, Barbara.   II. Title.
HV91.G45   1989   361.6'5'0973—dc19   89-31085   CIP

9 8 7 6 5 4 3 2 1

Printed in the United States of America
on acid-free paper

*For Evan and Jesse*

# Acknowledgments

Our work on this book was sustained by generous support from several sources and benefitted from the good advice of a number of colleagues. Many thanks are due to the Japanese Social Welfare Activity Research and Development Fund and its chairman Dr. Hideo Ibe for sponsoring a survey of the American social welfare system out of which *The Enabling State* emerged. As the study grew beyond initial expectations, Dr. Ibe encouraged our efforts and patiently awaited the results. We could not have completed this book without his thoughtful assistance. A Western European Fulbright Fellowship in 1986 provided an opportunity to examine current social welfare developments in England and Sweden as a backdrop to the American experience. Several examples of these developments are included in this book. Sven Olsson at the University of Stockholm, Institute for Social Research and Howard Glennerster at the London School of Economics and Political Science helped greatly to create a congenial atmosphere for research and writing during this period. The work on comparative methodology in the last chapter was supported, in part, by a grant from the Committee on Research at the University of California at Berkeley.

We are especially grateful to Harry Specht who read the entire manuscript, taking the opportunity to exercise his critical faculties without restraint. A number of helpful comments were also received from colleagues when part of the manuscript was presented at a meeting of the International Study Group on Modern Welfare States, sponsored by the McCormack Institute. An initial version of chapter 1 was published in the edited proceedings of this conference.* While these and other re-

*Robert Morris (ed.), *Testing the Limits of Social Welfare: International Perspectives on Policy Changes in Nine Countries* (Hanover, NH: University Press of New England, 1989).

sponses helped us to rethink and sharpen this work, in the final analysis we must claim full responsibility for any deficiencies that remain.

In preparing this book we were favored by the excellent support facilities of the School of Social Welfare at Berkeley. Jim Steele, the administrative officer, held down the daily bureaucratic impositions of University life, while Lorretta Dodson typed several drafts of the manuscript with painstaking care and unfailing good humor. Finally we should thank our sons, Evan and Jesse, who politely suffered many dinner table conversations on the recondite elements of social welfare with a stoicism beyond their years.

# Contents

# *Foreword*

The less government we have, the better.
Ralph Waldo Emerson
*Essays: Prudence*

It is perfectly true that that government is best which governs least. It is
equally true that that government is best which provides the most.
Walter Lippmann
*A Preface to Politics*

One summer's afternoon at the Empire City Race Track in 1938, Harry
Hopkins is said to have remarked, "We shall tax and tax, and spend and
spend, and elect and elect." A social worker who came to be one of
Franklin D. Roosevelt's intimate advisors and an influential planner of
the New Deal, Hopkins denied ever uttering these words. Whatever was
actually said that afternoon, the comment attributed to Hopkins brim-
med with anticipation of the federal government's emerging role in
social welfare. From the New Deal to the early 1970s, the American
welfare state rose on the twin pillars of taxing and spending. As a
percentage of the gross national product, direct public expenditures for
social welfare climbed from 4 percent in 1929 to 9 percent in 1940 to 20
percent in 1975. And, as in other advanced nations, the rapid expansion
of the American welfare state in the postwar decades came to a halt in
the early 1970s. After 1975, direct public expenditures on social welfare leveled off at about 18 percent of the gross national product. The
declining rate of growth in direct public expenditures has been variously

described as a "crisis" for the welfare state or a sign of its "maturation." Something has clearly occurred, but neither of these metaphors
captures the event.

During the last two decades a complex array of social transfers and
public/private interactions have evolved, which changed the character
and reshaped the boundaries of social welfare. Since the mid-1960s
there has been a trend away from direct expenditures for benefits provided by public agencies toward the use of more diverse measures to
finance and deliver welfare provisions. On the finance side, indirect
measures such as tax deductions and government lending have introduced new dimensions to the standard method of social transfer through
taxing and spending. On the delivery side, private enterprise has entered
the realm of social services, competing with increasing frequency in
what was once the main preserve of public and voluntary providers.
These changes represent something other than a decline or maturation of
the welfare state—it has been transformed into the *enabling state*.

In the enabling state, social welfare transfers are interlaced throughout the fabric of modern capitalist society. Some benefits are more
visible than others. Some costs are easier to calculate than others. Some
recipients have more public approval than others.

Studies of social welfare frequently address such questions as: Is it
enough? Are we losing ground? How can it improve? But to answer
these questions one must first have a reasonably clear picture of what
exists. In this regard, the conventional image of the welfare state offers
a distorted picture, focusing largely on direct expenditures and disadvantaged populations. It is a view that unwittingly conceals numerous
beneficiaries of social transfers in the areas of health, housing, income
maintenance, asset maintenance, personal care, and education. Percep-
tions are so narrow and some of these benefits so difficult to appraise
that many recipients decry the rising costs of welfare without realizing
the extent to which their own subsidies add to the bill.

In analyzing the emergent character of the enabling state, this book
examines a range of activities that have altered the structure of public
and private contributions to the finance and delivery of social transfers
for health, housing, and the other major welfare provisions. Our immediate aim is to heighten the visibility of these arrangements, their costs,
and their beneficiaries. The larger purpose of this book is to clarify the
dynamics of modern welfare capitalism and to broaden the analytic
foundation for the scientific study of social welfare. Whether in the test

and control groups of classic experimental design or in the careful plotting of the positions of the stars, science is a process of learning by methodical comparison. The scientific study of social welfare rests on the ability to distinguish the boundaries of this resource allocation system and to identify the various types of transfer mechanisms through which it operates. In the absence of such knowledge there can be no methodical comparisons of how social welfare arrangements develop over time or vary among nations. We explore the boundaries of the enabling state and how it functions to form a synoptic view that goes beyond the conventional image of social welfare. It is a view that, hopefully, will offer scholars a more precise analytic perspective on social welfare and at the same time open fresh avenues of thought and action to policymakers.

*The Enabling State*

# 1

# *The Structure of Social Welfare*

When one thinks about social welfare, the image that immediately comes to mind is that of what might be called the "direct public expenditure model." From this viewpoint, social welfare is identified with a range of health, housing, income maintenance, education, and personal social service provisions directly financed by government. Although these government-financed goods and services account for a major portion of social welfare provisions, they represent only part of the picture, conveying a somewhat distorted view of welfare benefits and beneficiaries. It is a view that concentrates on one form of welfare transfer directed largely, though not exclusively, toward the poor and dependent members of society. This narrow frame of reference neglects alternative forms of public and private transfer that are spread over a wider beneficiary population and considerably enhance the overall level of provision for social welfare.

For a more accurate picture of the scope and structure of social welfare, we must expand the conventional purview to include a range of "indirect" public transfers that are delivered by way of tax preferences and credit subsidies. Arguing for this broader view in a classic statement over thirty years ago, Richard Titmuss observed that whether income is provided to individuals through direct government payments or indirectly as a savings on taxes is mainly a difference in administrative methods; in both cases, provisions for financial support are made, in effect, through transfer payments.[1] But the public sector is not the only source of social welfare transfers. To render a full account of social welfare efforts, we must also consider the extent to which social provisions are financed and delivered through voluntary and private channels.

During the last decade a paradigm of social welfare has emerged, embracing what is termed the "mixed economy of welfare," which incorporates direct and indirect measures from both public and private sources.[2] From this perspective, it is the nature and purpose of the transaction rather than direct government financing that defines the provision of social welfare. As T. H. Marshall put it, in these transactions "the market value of an individual cannot be the measure of his right to welfare."[3] Indeed, one of the primary functions of social welfare in a capitalist society is the allocation of benefits from sources other than the economic marketplace, bringing about a distribution of resources that would not have occurred had the society relied solely on a market economy. But to observe that allocations for social welfare derive mainly from outside the market economy offers an elusive conceptual boundary for the analysis of these transfers.

The study of social welfare is often conducted within the conceptual borders of the "welfare state." This construct has several connotations, which emphasize the state or public sector role in administering welfare provisions.[4] As that role has changed in recent times, conventional views of the welfare state provide an inadequate perspective on the range and complexity of social welfare transactions. Moving beyond the direct public expenditure activities of the welfare state, a new role for government is taking shape under welfare capitalism—that of the enabling state, which joins public and private efforts through diverse arrangements for the finance and delivery of social welfare. To sharpen the boundaries and identify the basic features of these diverse arrangements for social welfare, we must draw a distinction between social markets and economic markets as mechanisms for allocating resources. It is the interaction between social and economic markets and their division of responsibility for the financing and delivery of social provisions that form the contemporary model of welfare capitalism.

## The Welfare–Capitalism Paradigm

Transactions in social and economic markets differ in both form and purpose. The social market distributes resources through unilateral transfers. These transfers are unilateral in the sense that they do not immediately create an economic obligation to compensate providers for the cash value of the goods and services obtained. However, these transfers do create social obligations that are more diffuse, implicit, and less easily discharged than the quid pro quo of economic exchange. Unlike transfers, the exchange between buyer and seller in the economic market is a fairly discrete interaction that creates no lingering ties or social obligations between the parties. Transfers and exchanges are the characteristic forms through which transactions are conducted in social and economic markets, respectively.[5]

These markets differ not only in the way transactions are conducted, but also in the motives and functions that drive them. Transactions in the economic market are influenced by desires to achieve growth, profit, and the satisfaction of consumer wants. Some would say that in the pursuit of growth and profit, the market economy creates many of the consumer wants it then seeks to satisfy.[6] With neither profit nor growth as an explicit motive, the social market is typically seen as performing three important functions.

First, it is viewed as a mechanism for social integration. Unilateral transfers from the state, the local community, and the family create a web of social obligations that bond the individual to these larger units in society. Entitlement to benefits and the social obligations that accompany it exert a force that draws members of society together and enhances one's sense of belonging to the community. Second, it provides goods and services to meet basic needs that people cannot fulfill through purchase in the economic market for reasons of financial hardship, dependency, incompetence, or the economic market's inability to produce these social provisions. In this respect, the social market functions as a "safety net," protecting against the contingencies and flaws of resource allocation through the economic market. It provides a minimum standard of material support below which members of society are not allowed to fall. Third, the social market modifies the distribution of resources generated by the market economy. The function here is to reduce inequality and the sense of social injustice that is bred by extreme disparities in living conditions.

The extent to which social markets serve each of these functions in capitalistic societies is a matter of degree. In different societies, one function such as meeting a minimal level of need may be emphasized over another such as reducing inequality. This is certainly the case in the United States, much less so in Scandinavian countries. There are those who would argue that this functional perspective is an ideological screen that masks the true purpose of the social market, which is to regulate the poor.[7] The Marxist's view of the social market is that it serves less as a safety net for people in need than as a "safety valve" for capitalism, mitigating the discontent and oppression of the poor and working classes just enough to reduce pressures for basic structural reform. No doubt the social market allocations reduce discontent and oppression that might stem from extreme material deprivation. Whether this reflects the quest for integration, security, and redistribution or the less estimable motives of a capitalist elite trying to keep the poor and working classes healthy and docile may be seen, in part, as a question of interpretation. We say "in part" because the poor and working classes are not the only beneficiaries of the social market. In fact, when both direct and indirect government expenditures are included in the conceptual boundaries of the social market, the magnitude of social welfare transfers to the middle classes is substantial.[8]

The boundaries of the social market encompass both a public and a private sector. As shown in Fig. 1.1, transfers in the public sector are accomplished through direct expenditures by federal, state, and local units of government as well as through tax expenditures and credit subsidies, which are less direct but produce the same transfer effects as direct government outlays. For example, a government-subsidized child care service provides the same kind of financial assistance to eligible families as a refundable tax credit for child care expenses. And a publicly insured student loan at an interest rate 10 percent below market rates benefits the recipients as much as a direct grant for the 10 percent difference.

The private sector of the social market contains three branches through which goods and services are provided, namely, informal networks of families and friends, voluntary nonprofit agencies, and profit-oriented agencies. As the latter is also the basic vehicle for exchange in the economic market, the distinction between social and economic mar-

THE SOCIAL MARKET        THE ECONOMIC MARKET

| Public Sector | Private Sector | | | |
|---|---|---|---|---|
| Direct provision of transfers by federal, state, and local governments | Provisions through informal networks of family and friends | Provisions by voluntary (nonprofit) agencies | Provisions by profit-oriented agencies and private practitioners | Goods and services produced and distributed by profit-oriented enterprises |
| Indirect transfers through tax expenditures and credit-subsidy mechanisms | | | | |

*Figure 1.1.* Social and Economic Markets of Welfare Capitalism

kets becomes a bit ill-defined at this point. The role of profit-oriented agencies in the social market involves more the delivery than the financing of welfare provisions. However, there are instances in which profit-making enterprises actually subsidize transfers as, for example, when a private-housing developer will price several units below their market value for rent or sale to low-income households. These are not so much private acts of charity as responses to standards and incentives created by the public sector; housing units are usually set aside to satisfy local regulations or to take advantage of government loan requirements.

The involvement of profit-oriented agencies reveals the permeable character of the border between social and economic markets. This is to say that whereas theoretically, these markets distribute resources through different modes of allocation and for different reasons, in practice they overlay and interact in ways that yield more complexity than can be represented in neat theoretical distinctions. For example, the transfer of resources in the social market involves both the financing and delivery of goods and services, two functions that are not always performed by the same unit. Thus, a public agency may hire its own staff to provide day-care service for low-income mothers, or it may use purchase-of-service arrangements to have the day care delivered by members of the client's family, voluntary agencies, or for-profit enterprises. Purchase of service is one of the main channels through which profit-oriented agencies are involved in the delivery of provisions in the social market. But it is not always clear how these for-profit enterprises should be categorized in the conceptual framework of social and economic markets. If half of the families using a day-care center pay for the service as a market exchange out of their income and the other half receive the service free of charge as a transfer subsidized by public purchase of service, is the day-care center in the social or economic market? What if the paying customers have a major part of their costs refunded through child care tax credits?

Tax expenditures and credit subsidies open a line of influence that affects the operation of both social and economic markets. These indirect subsidies may influence not only the way welfare services are delivered in the social market but also the structure of financial compensation in the economic market. In England, for example, the chancellor's budget for 1987 included a scheme for tax relief on profit-related pay. This scheme provides incentives for employees to take up to 20 percent of their basic compensation in the form of profit-linked pay. Because it applies only to profit-making enterprises, an interesting twist to this scheme is the secondary incentive it provides to shift the delivery of social services from the public sector to private enterprise.[9]

In addition to financing goods and services produced by profit-making enterprises directly through purchase-of-service contracts and indirectly through tax expenditures and credit subsidies, the public sector of the social market intersects with the economic market on other levels. Public agencies employ the regulatory powers of the state to set standards and conditions for private providers. By tightening or loosening regulations, the public sector creates incentives for private involvement in the delivery of social welfare. Reducing the stringency of building-code standards for day-care centers, for instance, can stimulate an increase in the number of individual providers who care for groups of children in their own homes, usually at a lower cost than is charged in larger centers. And, as previously noted, zoning and building regulations can be used to encourage private development of low-income housing units. As the role of profit-making enterprises in the delivery of social welfare expands, the regulatory functions of public agencies gain importance (a point that we will take up later in more detail). Public agencies can also engage private organizations in collaborative relationships sharing information and material resources. For example, this type of partnership might involve the donation of unsalable surplus foods to community food banks, or the loan of private facilities for public purposes.[10] Although the potential for collaborative arrangements covers a broad range of activities, in practice they are still quite limited.

In the roles of funder, regulator, and partner, the social market interacts and overlaps with the economic market. The expansion and contraction of these roles influence the boundaries and fundamental character of the social market. In this sense the social market is not a static construct, but an allocative mechanism in a continual state of evolution. If the boundaries are more fluid and less precise than depicted in Fig. 1.1, they serve nevertheless as a useful paradigm within which to survey the material scope of social welfare provisions and to analyze the changing character of public responsibility in the larger framework of welfare capitalism.

## Scope of Social Welfare Transfers

Social welfare has always been characterized by a mixture of public, self-help, charitable, and profit-making activities. In the United States prior to 1945, however, these activities were highly restricted, providing income and service assistance primarily to those viewed as the most needy. Others were left to fend for themselves or to get such help as they could from family, friends, local associations, and the market economy. While the Great Depression and the introduction of the social insurance system in 1935 set the moral and financial groundwork for expanding the public sector of the social welfare system, initially the number of beneficiaries and levels of aid were quite limited. It was not until the postwar period that direct government expenditures on social insurance and noncontributory public aid, and indirect expenditures via tax deductions and credit subsidies for social welfare purposes underwent significant growth. Public social insurance expanded to include almost all workers and moved into new areas of need such as disability, survivorship, medical care, and unemployment. Entitlements to free public aid broadened to include more of the population through liberalized group and geographic eligibility qualifications, and increased provision of universal benefits.

Following the growth of direct public expenditures, the American tax system has been enlarged to provide a range of transfers through tax preferences for social welfare purposes. These tax expenditures have partially subsidized the vast expansion of employee benefits programs and private pension schemes. Moreover, partly in response to tax incentives, individuals and businesses increased their voluntary contributions to charity, thereby augmenting this traditional source of social welfare funds. Along with the growth of tax expenditures, but even more elusive, has been the proliferation of credit-subsidy mechanisms for a wide variety of social welfare transfers—most notably in health, housing, education, and agriculture. These transfers operate through direct government loans, government-guaranteed loans, direct and subsidized insurance, and government-"sponsored" supposedly autonomous credit institutions and insurance pools. The true cost and scope of these transfer mechanisms is only now beginning to be examined. Through these mechanisms government becomes involved not only in additional expenditures (until 1986 largely "off-budget"), but also in hidden costs relating to the difference between subsidized and market rates, as well as incurring a vast reservoir of contingent public liability in the case of default, calamity, or collapse. Thus, during the last few decades, there has been both an expansion of funds for social welfare purposes and a diffusion in the sources, mechanisms, purpose, and clientele.

The public sector is the largest source of funds for the transfer of income, goods, and services in the social market. Since 1960, both direct and indirect public expenditures have increased dramatically.

### Direct Public Transfers

Total direct public expenditure for social welfare purposes between 1960 and 1980 (including all levels of government and compulsory public insurance) rose from $52.3 billion to $492.7 billion, and from 10.3 to 18.1 percent of the gross national product (GNP); by 1984, these expenditures had climbed to $671.9 billion or 18.0 percent of the GNP. As shown in Table 1.1, personal social services under the public assistance category, combined with all the personal social services included in the category of "other social welfare," amount to almost $16.2 billion. Though not a trivial sum, this is nevertheless only 2.4 percent of the total direct social welfare expenditures under public programs in 1984. In contrast, cash benefits provided by social insurance, public assistance, supplemental security income, and veterans' pension programs amount to approximately $365 billion or 54 percent of the 1984 expenditures. Education accounted for $151.9 billion or 23 percent of the total, and $148.3 billion or 22.1 percent was spent on health benefits and programs. In 1960, these expenditures constituted 38.4 percent of all governmental outlay, and by 1984, about 53 percent of all governmental outlay. On a per capita basis (in 1984 dollars), expendi-

*Table 1.1.* Social Welfare Expenditures, by Source of Funds and Public Program; 1975–1984[a]

| | 1975 | | 1980 | | 1983 | | 1984, prel. | |
|---|---|---|---|---|---|---|---|---|
| Program | Federal | State and local | Federal | State and local | Federal | State and local | Federal | State and local |
| Total | 167,426 | 122,654 | 302,616 | 190,180 | 398,792 | 243,285 | 419,264 | 252,707 |
| Social insurance | 99,715 | 23,298 | 191,162 | 38,592 | 274,212 | 56,846 | 289,884 | 52,381 |
| Old-age, survivors, disability, health | 78,430 | (x)[s] | 152,110 | (x) | 224,709 | (x) | 239,395 | (x) |
| Health insurance (Medicare) | 14,781 | (x) | 34,992 | (x) | 56,930 | (x) | 62,481 | (x) |
| Public employee retirement[b] | 13,339 | 6,780 | 26,983 | 12,507 | 36,920 | 17,914 | 38,587 | 20,300 |
| Railroad employee retirement | 3,085 | (x) | 4,769 | (x) | 6,082 | (x) | 6,144 | (x) |
| Unemployment insurance and employment services[c] | 3,429 | 10,407 | 4,408 | 13,919 | 3,144 | 22,206 | 2,529 | 13,575 |
| Other railroad employee insurance[d] | 75 | (x) | 224 | (x) | 448 | (x) | 230 | (x) |
| State temporary-disability insurance[e] | (x) | 990 | (x) | 1,377 | (x) | 1,767 | (x) | 1,821 |
| Workers' compensation[f] | 1,357 | 5,122 | 2,668 | 10,789 | 2,909 | 14,959 | 2,999 | 16,684 |
| Hospital and medical benefits | 50 | 2,420 | 130 | 3,596 | 264 | 4,818 | 282 | 5,729 |
| Public aid | 27,186 | 14,122 | 48,666 | 23,133 | 55,895 | 29,935 | 57,666 | 32,206 |
| Public assistance[g] | 14,529 | 12,832 | 23,542 | 21,346 | 28,796 | 27,824 | 30,838 | 30,162 |
| Medical vendor payments (Medicaid)[h] | 7,056 | 6,445 | 14,550 | 12,844 | 18,828 | 17,499 | 20,212 | 19,251 |
| Social services | 1,963 | 660 | 1,757 | 586 | 1,881 | 627 | 2,092 | 697 |
| Supplemental security income | 4,802 | 1,290 | 6,440 | 1,787 | 8,683 | 2,111 | 9,094 | 2,043 |
| Food stamps | 4,694 | (x) | 9,083 | (x) | 11,727 | (x) | 11,561 | (x) |
| Other[i] | 3,162 | (x) | 9,601 | (x) | 6,689 | (x) | 6,173 | (x) |
| Health and medical programs | 8,521 | 9,267 | 12,688 | 15,231 | 15,594 | 20,382 | 16,496 | 21,368 |
| Hospital and medical care | 4,045 | 5,175 | 6,451 | 6,042 | 8,737 | 7,781 | 9,082 | 8,259 |
| Civilian programs | 1,231 | 5,175 | 2,391 | 6,042 | 2,254 | 7,781 | 2,392 | 8,259 |
| Defense Department[j] | 2,814 | (x) | 4,060 | (x) | 6,483 | (x) | 6,690 | (x) |
| Maternal and child health programs | 271 | 296 | 351 | 519 | 428 | 672 | 352 | 679 |
| Medical research | 2,642 | 286 | 4,414 | 422 | 4,984 | 583 | 5,497 | 606 |
| Medical facilities construction | 413 | 1,391 | 223 | 1,954 | 164 | 1,930 | 212 | 1,930 |
| Other | 1,150 | 2,119 | 1,250 | 6,294 | 1,281 | 9,416 | 1,354 | 9,894 |
| Veterans programs | 16,570 | 449 | 21,254 | 212 | 25,561 | 265 | 25,822 | 305 |
| Pensions and compensation | 7,579 | (x) | 11,306 | (x) | 13,895 | (x) | 13,949 | (x) |
| Health and medical programs | 3,517 | (x) | 6,204 | (x) | 8,388 | (x) | 8,855 | (x) |

*(continued)*

*Table 1.1. (Continued)*

| Program | 1975 Federal | 1975 State and local | 1980 Federal | 1980 State and local | 1983 Federal | 1983 State and local | 1984, prel. Federal | 1984, prel. State and local |
|---|---|---|---|---|---|---|---|---|
| Hospital and medical care | 3,287 | (x) | 5,750 | (x) | 7,763 | (x) | 8,141 | (x) |
| Hospital construction | 137 | (x) | 323 | (x) | 474 | (x) | 527 | (x) |
| Medical and prosthetic re-search | 93 | (x) | 131 | (x) | 152 | (x) | 186 | (x) |
| Education | 4,434 | (x) | 2,401 | (x) | 1,708 | (x) | 1,413 | (x) |
| Life insurance[k] | 556 | (x) | 665 | (x) | 744 | (x) | 746 | (x) |
| Welfare and other | 485 | 449 | 679 | 212 | 827 | 265 | 860 | 305 |
| Education | 8,629 | 72,205 | 13,452 | 107,597 | 12,397 | 129,416 | 12,979 | 139,046 |
| Elementary and secondary | 4,563 | 55,183 | 7,430 | 79,720 | 6,140 | 96,512 | 6,659 | 103,359 |
| Construction[m] | 21 | 5,725 | 41 | 6,483 | 77 | 7,112 | 28 | 7,230 |
| Higher | 2,864 | 13,521 | 4,468 | 21,708 | 5,052 | 25,416 | 5,028 | 27,616 |
| Construction | 274 | 1,239 | 42 | 1,486 | 85 | 1,974 | 35 | 2,236 |
| Vocational and adult[m] | 940 | 3,501 | 1,207 | 6,169 | 898 | 7,488 | 1,046 | 8,072 |
| Housing | 2,541 | 631 | 6,608 | 601 | 8,087 | 1,003 | 9,068 | 1,306 |
| Other social welfare | 4,264 | 2,683 | 8,786 | 4,813 | 7,046 | 5,438 | 7,349 | 6,096 |
| Vocational rehabilitation | 814 | 222 | 1,006 | 245 | 1,008 | 326 | 1,109 | 338 |
| Medical services and re-search | 174 | 44 | 237 | 56 | 269 | 100 | 277 | 83 |
| Institutional care[n] | 20 | 276 | 74 | 408 | 107 | 553 | 118 | 753 |
| Child nutrition[o] | 2,064 | 454 | 4,209 | 643 | 4,099 | 882 | 4,270 | 928 |
| Child welfare[p] | 50 | 547 | 57 | 743 | 160 | (NA)[t] | 165 | (NA) |
| Special CSA and ACTION programs[q] | 638 | (x) | 2,303 | (x) | 475 | (x) | 479 | (x) |
| Welfare, not elsewhere classified[r] | 677 | 1,184 | 1,137 | 2,774 | 1,197 | 3,677 | 1,207 | 4,076 |

[a]Given in millions of dollars.

[b]Excludes refunds to those leaving service. Federal data include military retirement.

[c]Includes compensation for federal employees and ex-servicemen, trade adjustment and cash training allowance, and payments under extended, emergency, disaster, and special unemployment insurance programs.

[d]Unemployment and temporary-disability insurance.

[e]Cash and medical benefits in five areas. Includes private plans where applicable.

[f]Benefits paid by private insurance carriers, state funds, and self-insurers. Federal includes black-lung benefit programs.

[g]Includes payments under state general assistance programs and work incentive activities, not shown separately.

[h]Medical vendor payments are those made directly to suppliers of medical care.

[i]Refugee assistance, surplus food for the needy, and work experience training programs under the Economic Opportunity Act and the Comprehensive Employment and Training Act. Beginning 1983, includes low-income energy assistance program.

[j]Includes medical care for military dependent families.

[k]Excludes servicemen's group life insurance.

[l]Includes federal expenditures for administrative costs (Department of Education) and research, not shown separately.

*Table 1.1. (Continued)*

<sup>a</sup>Construction costs of vocational and adult education programs included under elementary–secondary expenditures.

Federal expenditures represent primarily surplus foods for nonprofit institutions.

Surplus food for schools and programs under National School Lunch and Child Nutrition Acts.

Represents primarily child welfare services under Title V of the Social Security Act.

Includes domestic volunteer programs under ACTION and community action and migrant workers programs under Community Services Administration.

Federal expenditures include administrative expenses of the Secretary of Health and Human Services; Indian welfare and guidance; and aging and juvenile delinquency activities. State and local include antipoverty and manpower programs, child care and adoption services, legal assistance, and other unspecified welfare services.

Not applicable.

Not available

*Source*: U.S. Bureau of Census, *Statistical Abstract of the United States, 1987* (Washington, D.C.: U.S. Government Printing Offices, 1986), p. 341.

tures rose from $937 per capita in 1960 to $2801 in 1984. Between 1970 and 1981, the number of benefit recipients increased 13 percent while the overall population increased 11.5 percent. Between 1965 and 1983, non-means-tested public benefits rose from 24.3 percent to 43 percent of social expenditures, and means-tested benefits rose from 5.9 to 11 percent.[11]

In addition to the direct social welfare expenditures noted in Table 1.1, there is another category of public transfers that serves a significant welfare function and should be included as such in the national accounting of welfare expenditures. That is the category of government aid to farmers, which consists of both direct and indirect expenditures. In the category of direct aid, farm income stabilization payments increased from approximately $1.5 billion in 1980 to $20 billion in 1986. This amounted to an average of $535 per farm in 1980 and $6787 per farm in 1986. Because not all farmers receive these direct payments, the average cash aid per recipient farmer is substantially higher.[12]

### Indirect Transfers through Tax Expenditures

Although the classification of tax expenditures is a complex and evolving process, such expenditures may be defined roughly as revenue losses generated by special exceptions to the normal tax structure, which are directed to particular types of activities or groups of taxpayers. These tax reliefs are justified in terms of public objectives such as enhancing human welfare, strengthening the economy, and preserving endangered national resources. In reality, tax expenditures are revenue "losses" only insofar as they are not replacing revenue that might otherwise be spent in pursuit of these public objectives; in this sense, they may be viewed as partial compensation to taxpayers for privately undertaking activity that might otherwise require direct public spending. Although tax expenditures in fact affect all levels of government, they are currently calculated only with reference to national income taxation.[13]

Tax expenditures are a function of the benchmark tax structure against which they are measured, of all income on which taxes are assessed, of total dollars spent on a tax-preferenced activity, and of the applicable tax rate. There are six basic types of tax preferences: exclusions, deductions, credits, refundable credits, preferential tax rates, and tax liability deferrals. Their calculation is complicated by the interactive effects of different taxes and the fact that preferences can generate benefits from federal, state, and local taxes. There are also different methods to estimate the value of tax expenditures. The "revenue-foregone" approach, for example, simply counts the amount actually shielded from taxation, which requires no assumptions about how taxpayers would behave in the absence of tax preferences. In contrast, the "revenue gain" approach estimates the increase in revenue expected if tax relief provisions were abolished.[14]

It is only during the last two decades that tax expenditures have gained substantial recognition as a form of government support. The idea that special deductions and exemptions in the tax code are equivalent to government expenditures gathered support in 1967 when Stanley Surrey, the assistant secretary to the treasury, proposed that these "tax expenditures" be counted as federal revenue losses. This idea won formal acceptance in the Congressional Budget Act of 1974.[15] As shown in Table 1.2, in recent years total tax expenditures have ranged between 46 and 49 percent of federal tax revenues and equaled about 36 percent of direct expenditures.

The question of which tax expenditures address social welfare purposes and which address other economic purposes is not easy to answer. The standard tax expenditure categories are unclear in this regard, because some items simultaneously serve several purposes and constituencies. Table 1.3 divides tax expenditures into three groups: those that do not serve social welfare purposes as generally reflected by the direct

*Table 1.2.* Federal Revenue, Direct Expenditure, and Tax Expenditure (Selected Years)[a]

| Year | Revenue | Direct Expenditure | Tax Expenditure | Tax Expenditure as Percentage of Revenue | Tax Expenditure as Percentage of Direct Expenditure |
|------|---------|--------------------|-----------------| ----------------------------------------|-----------------------------------------------------|
| 1982 | 617.8 | 745.7 | 281.3 | 45.5 | 37.7 |
| 1983 | 600.6 | 808.3 | 292.4 | 48.7 | 36.3 |
| 1984 | 666.5 | 851.8 | 314.6 | 47.2 | 36.9 |
| 1985 | 734.1 | 946.3 | 340.6 | 46.3 | 35.9 |
| 1986 | 769.1 | 989.8 | 380.7 | 49.5 | 38.4 |

[a]Given in billions of dollars.

*Source*: U.S. Bureau of the Census, *Statistical Abstract of the United States, 1986*, p. 310; *Statistical Abstract of the United States, 1987*, p. 297; Committee on Fiscal Affairs, OECD, *Tax Expenditures: A Review of Issues and County Practices*, 1984, pp. 80–83; Office of Management and Budget, *Budget of the United States Government FY 1988, Supplement*, 1987, p. 6c–45.

expenditures identified in Table 1.1, those that are clearly related to social welfare, and those that appear at least partially or indirectly to support a broadly defined concept of social welfare.

The data in Table 1.3 may be used to calculate several estimates of total social welfare expenditures. Focusing on the second group of items—those most directly related to the welfare of individuals—is an approach that suggests $163 billion or about 48 percent of all tax expenditures is minimally devoted to social welfare. Adding the third group of items—those partially related to social welfare—is an approach that yields a maximal revenue loss of $256 billion or about 75 percent of all tax expenditures. Of course, a variety of intermediate approaches is possible, depending on one's purposes, welfare ideology, and interpretation of any items in the last category that tend to benefit wealthier individuals and the business community.

Under the tax reform commencing in 1987, overall tax expenditures have declined, with most business tax preferences being substantially decreased or eliminated. The core social welfare tax expenditures, though pared down, have remained quite sizeable, with the middle class continuing to be major beneficiaries. The intention of Congress was to keep overall federal revenues equivalent, while creating a simpler and fairer tax structure through the reconfiguration of tax liabilities. To this end, nonessential and mainly business tax preferences and expenditures were greatly reduced, the alternative minimum tax was strengthened

*Table 1.3.* Revenue Loss Estimates for Selected Tax Expenditures[a]

| Sources | Revenue Loss Estimates |
|---|---|
| *Nonwelfare Tax Expenditures* | |
| International Affairs | $ 2,250 |
| General Science | 5,330 |
| Energy | 3,480 |
| Natural Resources and Environment | 2,330 |
| General Commerce | 70,970 |
| SUBTOTAL | $84,360 |
| *Welfare Tax Expenditures Directly Benefiting Individuals* | |
| Housing | $38,030 |
| Employment | 9,245 |
| Health | 24,675 |
| Education | 1,775 |
| Income Security | 89,305 |
| SUBTOTAL | $163,030 |
| *Partial and Indirect Welfare Tax Expenditures* | |
| Income Enhancement | $68,495 |
| Agricultural Income Enhancement | 1,280 |
| Housing and Community Development | 6,895 |
| Health | 3,450 |
| Education | 1,565 |
| Employment | 415 |
| Other Charity | 11,135 |
| SUBTOTAL | $93,235 |

[a]Given in millions of dollars: for year ending September 30, 1985.
*Source*: U.S. Bureau of the Census, *Statistical Abstract of the United States, 1986*, p. 310. (For a detailed breakdown of tax expenditures in each category, see Appendix Table A.1.)

(thereby lessening the utility of tax preferences for wealthy individuals), many lower-income persons were removed from the tax rolls, and individual tax rates fell for most people.

### Indirect Transfers through Credit-Subsidy Mechanisms

Like tax expenditures, only more so, public credit-subsidy mechanisms are amorphous, poorly understood, and hard to measure. By the end of 1986, the federal government was involved in over $1.1 trillion of federally assisted loan financing: it held $252 billion in direct loans and guaranteed or insured $450 billion in other loans; furthermore, government-sponsored but ostensibly autonomous financial enterprises had loaned another $453 billion using federally subsidized credit.[16]

The federal budget measures only the immediate net outlay for this credit system (until 1986, much of which was even "off-budget"). It accounts for neither the cost to government of borrowing money on the market and relending it at lower rates, nor the cost of federal loan guarantees. Furthermore, there is no way to budget for defaults on direct loans until they occur, whereas defaults on guaranteed loans do not even show up as a loss. Although loans by the autonomous financial agencies are theoretically not the public's responsibility (unless they are guaranteed loans), there is an implicit degree of public commitment to these agencies and their investors. This commitment poses the likelihood of massive public bailouts. In the late 1980s, for example, both the independent farm credit banks and the Federal Savings and Loan Insurance Corporation (FSLIC) were in financial difficulty—the former system requesting a $6 billion public bailout.

Considering the size of the farm population, the lion's share of federal credit system benefits goes to farmers. Of the 1986 total of $41.3 billion in new direct loans, $26.7 billion (65 percent) was for agriculture, $2 billion (5 percent) was for housing and community development, $1.6 billion (4 percent) was for education, and the remaining $11 billion (11 percent) was for assorted commercial, military, and infrastructure purposes.[17] Of five major federally sponsored independent agencies, accounting for $246 billion in outstanding loans by 1984, 29 percent of the total was for farmers, 2.2 percent for student loans, and 68.8 percent for housing.[18] By the early 1980s, about 25 percent of the nation's entire nonfarm residential mortgage debt was publicly guaranteed.[19]

Social welfare transfers financed by credit subsidies derive from the differences between interest rates charged by government and market rates for similar loans, the costs of loan defaults, and other benefits of public guarantees. Because of complexities in credit-subsidy accounting, a meaningful dollar figure for the total amount of indirect public social welfare transfers attributable to this source is unattainable. In analyzing specific areas of social welfare activity, however, we will sort out some of the relevant figures at hand in an effort to convey the scope and functions of this mechanism.

In general, the core public system of social welfare financing has proved to be politically impregnable and practically irreplaceable. Direct public expenditures increased dramatically between 1960 and the late 1970s, with the rate of growth tapering off in the 1980s except for farm aid. Since the mid-1970s the most striking expansion has been in the realm of indirect public expenditure for individual and employer-sponsored retirement accounts, child care, the earned income credit, and credit relief, measures that encourage consumer choice and the delivery of social welfare provisions through the private sector.

## *Private Transfers through Informal Networks, Family, and Philanthropic Contributions*

In 1986, total philanthropic spending by individuals, charities, foundations, and corporations amounted to $87.2 billion, up from $20.7 billion in 1970 and $47.7 billion in 1980. The proportion of the charitable dollar spent on secular social welfare activities (as opposed to religious, artistic, and civic activities) declined in the high-public-spending decade 1970–1980, leveled off in the early 1980s, and began to climb in the mid-1980s. As shown in Table 1.4, approximately $34.7 billion or 40 percent of all philanthropic contributions went to social welfare programs in 1986. This figure is probably somewhat below the real level of outlay, because much of the spending in the category of religious activity is very likely devoted to social welfare purposes. Despite warnings by various interest groups, there is no evidence indicating that overall charitable giving has abated as a result of economic events and tax changes.

In addition to charitable donations, private sector cash transfers also include financial assistance provided within families, mostly between generations. The magnitude of these transfers varies according to different estimates. Lampman calculates that interfamily transfers of cash, food, and housing amounted to $86 billion in 1978.[20] A 1985 survey by the Census Bureau found that $18.9 billion in cash transfers were provided mainly by parents assisting children who no longer live with them and children aiding elderly parents. These providers numbered about 6.3 million people and helped almost 10 million of their family members with an average payment of $3006.[21]

Whereas the monetary value of charitable donations and financial assistance within families can be estimated with a fair amount of precision, it is more difficult to calculate the total dollar value of in-kind

*Table 1.4.* Private Charitable Expenditure

|  | 1970 | 1980 | 1984 | 1986 |
|---|---|---|---|---|
| Total Spent[a] | 20.75 | 47.74 | 74.25 | 87.2 |
| Total Social Welfare Spending (Health, Education, and Social Services)[a] | 9.52 | 17.9 | 28.53 | 34.7 |
| Social Welfare Spending as Percentage of Total | 46 | 38 | 38 | 40 |

[a]Given in billions of dollars.

*Source*: U.S. Bureau of the Census, *Statistical Abstract of the United States, 1986*, p. 385; *Wall Street Journal*, June 15, 1987, p. 25.

transfers in the private sector. The problem, in part, is one of deciding what range of activities to include here; for example, does changing a light bulb or preparing a meal for one's family constitute an in-kind transfer? To include every conceivable family chore as in-kind social welfare transfers somehow distorts the personal affection invested in the division of labor and interdependence that people implicitly agree to assume when creating a family. Although it contains elements of both market exchange and social transfers, the modern "marriage contract" has rested principally on mutual devotion. A more limited definition of in-kind transfers in family life might be confined to circumstances that place an extraordinary demand on family resources such as social care and support of elderly and disabled members. These demands are regularly met through public sector provisions when families are unable to carry the burden. But families still provide a major portion of the social care and support for these groups. The National Center for Health Statistics estimates that approximately 80 percent of home health care services for the elderly are provided by family members,[22] and 67 percent of severely mentally handicapped children live at home with their parents.[23] Along with these family care activities, the classification of private sector in-kind transfers would also include voluntary community service activities. In 1985 about 48 percent of the population fourteen years old and older worked in some way to help others without compensation.[24] Much of this voluntary work is devoted to social welfare services. These estimates of family care and voluntary community service provide at best a rough picture of the scope of in-kind transfer activity in the private sector on which it is currently infeasible to pin a dollar value.

While it is difficult to determine the precise value of family care for dependent members, there is reason to believe that activities in this realm have declined in recent decades. Certainly, the pool of female labor that traditionally performed these caring services receded as the rate of employment for married women with children under six rose from 30 percent to 50 percent between 1970 and 1983.[25] With the rate of divorce to marriage almost doubling from 1960 to 1980, there are generally fewer parents at home to look after children and fewer intact families with the time and energy to assist elderly parents. As mothers' labor has shifted from the household to the market economy, public and private agencies have moved in to assume greater responsibility for personal care services. Thus, for example, between 1977 and 1986 according to a liberal estimate, the number of child care centers increased by 77 percent to 235,000 facilities.[26]

## Private Transfers by For-Profit Enterprises

While national income and wage income rose approximately 500 percent between 1965 and 1984, supplemental employer income contribution to workers rose by more than 1000 percent. Between 1970 and 1984, this supplemental income went from 7.8 to 12.5 percent of national income. In 1984 nonwage compensation to employees was $369 billion, or 20 percent of wages (and when paid time off is added to nonwage compensation, the average fringe benefit package came to about 37 percent). Private pension schemes form a major component of these fringe benefits. From 1970 to 1984, the assets of private pension funds, at book value, soared from $151.4 billion to $948.2 billion; about 56 percent of workers were covered and 32.5 percent vested in these schemes by 1983.[27]

Fringe benefits of private employment are not primarily social welfare transfers. They form part of the basic package of compensation that workers accept, often bargain for, in lieu of income. As such, these benefits are an integral feature of the labor/capital exchange in the market economy; yet they are not entirely an exchange. The tax-preferred treatment and partial public regulation of fringe benefits lends the transaction an element of social transfer, the amount of which is reflected in the data on tax expenditures. This transfer is thus, in part, financed and mandated by the public sector rather than by private enterprise. The tax treatment of fringe benefits in the United States is among the most liberal in the industrialized West. An analysis of practices in twenty-three member countries of the Organisation for Economic Co-operation and Development (OECD) reveals that just five of the sixteen most popular fringe benefits are taxed in the United States; this figure represents slightly more than one-half the average number of fringe benefits taxed by the entire group; furthermore, only Switzerland, Italy, and Greece taxed a lower number of fringe benefits than the United States.[28]

For obvious reasons, private enterprise is rarely a direct source for financing social welfare transfers. The business of business, as the Fords and Mellons might have said, is to make money, not to give it away. Of course, the Fords, Mellons, Rockefellers, and many others have generously given of their own fortunes to philanthropic causes. However, such charitable activity usually functions quite apart from the operation of private enterprise. The range of this activity is incorporated in the charitable expenditures (shown in Table 1.4).

Though limited in scope, there are various cases in which social welfare transfers are financed by private enterprises in the course of their operations. These transfers are usually spurred by public regulations and incentives that encourage private enterprise to partially subsidize consumers in return for license to operate in certain areas. Rent control and the designation of a number of units for low-income tenants in new middle-income and upper-income housing developments are major examples of market transactions in which goods are provided for less than the value they would otherwise command in the absence of public restrictions and incentives. In a similar vein, building regulations that stipulate the construction of access facilities for the handicapped induce or force private enterprise to invest in provisions that are often not dictated by normal business concerns for growth and profit. In medicine there was a time in the recent past when family doctors charged fees for services on a sliding scale based on estimates of their patients' financial circumstances rather than on an established market value of the medical service.

Reliable data on the magnitude of private enterprise financing of social welfare activities are scarce for several reasons. Most important-ly, perhaps, the types of activities just illustrated are not clearly per-ceived as social welfare transfers. The precise value of these transfers is hard to calculate. And though one might argue that ultimately social welfare is highly dependent on the surplus produced in the market economy, direct transfers through the activities of private enterprise are in fact still rather limited. While private enterprise contributes minimally to the direct financing of social welfare provisions, during the last decade it has come to play an increasing role in the production and delivery of these benefits. This development has advanced the changing structure of public and private responsibility under welfare capitalism.

### Decentralization, Privatization, and Commercialization: Shifting Responsibilities[29]

After two decades of almost continuous expansion, in the late 1970s the welfare systems in most industrial societies entered a period of fiscal restraint and political reappraisal, with fundamental questions being raised about their proper scope and functions.[30] In response to social, political, and economic pressures (which are examined in Chapter 2), new structural arrangements to finance and produce social welfare benefits have emerged. One of the prominent changes in the structure of modern welfare systems involves the related movements toward decentralization, privatization, and commercialization of the social market.

In analyzing the trend toward decentralization, there are three considerations to bear in mind: geographic context, form of benefits provided, and range of allocative functions. As a practical matter, decentralization has both geographic and demographic dimensions. Thus, comparisons between changing levels of responsibility for social welfare in the United States and other countries may be somewhat deceptive. California, for example, is three times as large as England geographically and has twice the population of Sweden. In the United States a shift in decision-making authority over social programs from the federal government to the state level constitutes a significant degree of decentralization. Yet the administrative units at the state level often serve huge populations and cover great distances. In terms of bureaucratic span of control, the increased authority over social welfare administration by state governments in California and other large states (while representing a considerable step toward decentralization in the American context) would be comparable in many operational characteristics to a highly centralized system of welfare administration in, for example, Sweden, Italy, and Israel.

How one looks at decentralization is also relative to the form in which benefits are provided. Benefits in kind, such as day care and counseling, are consumed at the point of distribution. Thus, the administrative arrangements to provide these benefits pertain simultaneously to distribution and to consumption. Cash benefits, vouchers, and credit subsidies present a different case. The distribution of cash benefits may be administered by a highly centralized unit of government, but the consumption is highly decentralized because the locus of decisions on how to translate the cash into consumer products rests in the hands of the individual recipients.[31] Thus, social welfare programs that provide cash benefits, vouchers, or credit relief, regardless of how they are administered by the state, may be thought to represent a "market model" of decentralization, which is as Rivlin puts it, "the most extreme form of decentralization."[32] The trend toward decentralization in the United States is expressed both in changing allocative arrangements for services and the introduction of new mechanisms, such as tax credits, to extend the provision of benefits in cash.

Finally, in the process of decentralization there are several roles that may be devolved from central to local levels. These roles include that of funder, owner, provider, and regulator.

FUNDER

To the extent that direct public tax revenues are used to pay for social welfare activity, a transfer of this role from central to local government represents one line of decentralization. By shifting funding costs to consumers through user charges (though partially subsidized), decentralization can be carried a step farther. Another approach to decentralization that joins government and consumer payments involves the use of indirect public support through mechanisms such as tax credits and subsidies.

OWNER

Ownership entails legal or constructive title to the land, facilities, equipment, contracts, and treasury of a given activity. In a totally statist society, the central government would own the hospitals, the schools, the service centers, the housing, and the treasury. Devolution of ownership involves the transfer to or the initial location of the ownership function in local government or the private sector. Within the private sector, it is possible and increasingly common to have joint-venture ownership by several profit-motivated entities or by a combination of profit-oriented and nonprofit entities.

## PROVIDER

Provision is related to though not synonymous with ownership. Usually, goods and services are provided by the owners of an enterprise. It is possible, and increasingly common in social welfare activities, to have public ownership and private provision through management and independent contractor arrangements; it is also common to have private ownership with provision by other private entities, including various combinations of for-profit and nonprofit enterprises.

## REGULATOR

The function of regulation, in the broadest sense, is to impose order, coherence, and standards on public interest activities; with regard to social welfare activities, regulation may focus on issues of cost, quality, and access. In a truly statist system there is no independent regulation per se, because there is no independent judiciary and the state itself embodies regulation in its roles of owner, funder, and provider. In a classical capitalist system external regulation is extremely limited, because the market is seen as providing necessary and sufficient self-regulation; sometimes this market self-regulation may take the collective form of trade association regulation, which, however, almost always operates to serve trade rather than public interests. An independent regulatory system (whether in judicial, administrative, or combined format) is a key feature of progressive capitalism, democratic socialism, and the mixed economy. In the United States, regulatory independence (and confusion) is enhanced by the separation of legislative, executive, and judicial powers, and by multilayered government, creating a built-in system of regulation through competing sources of authority and alternative channels of recourse. The ideal function of regulation is to promote the public interest, to counterbalance the excesses of government and the excesses of capitalism, and to enforce rational standards in the numerous activities that impinge on personal, business, and national well-being. Whereas those who advocate the decentralization of welfare activity often envision a lessening of public regulatory and judicial interference, it is likely that as more social welfare activities move toward diffuse private implementation with some form of public subsidy and universal entitlement, the regulatory function will be increasingly strengthened and rationalized. At the same time, the emergence of centralized corporate entities engaged in the provision of social welfare services will make public regulation somewhat easier to implement.

## Why Decentralization?

Of the several reasons usually put forth in support of decentralized arrangements for the delivery of social services, the benefits of greater effectiveness, diversity, and accountability are among those most often cited. On the question of effectiveness, whether a social service program is best administered through centralized or decentralized units depends in part on the types of activities and specific character of the service. This point is colorfully illustrated by Moynihan's assessment of proposals to organize a centralized rat control program and a decentralized poison control information service in New York City. Criticizing these proposed arrangements, Moynihan notes that "the urban rat is preeminently a neighborhood type, preferring when possible, never even to cross the street. As for rodent control, opinion is universal (as best I know) that the fundamental issue is how individual humanoids maintain their immediate surroundings." The solution, he suggests, "comes down, alas, to the question of keeping lids on garbage cans," which is most conveniently handled at the neighborhood level. In contrast, a poison control information service requires a level of expertise and resources unlikely to be found in city neighborhoods. These services are designed to provide information about the chemical nature of possibly harmful substances ingested by persons. This type of service appears exceedingly well suited to a centralized delivery system. A national center with laboratory and computer resources capable of rapidly generating accurate information and accessible through one telephone number from anywhere in the county, for example, would seem to offer an effective arrangement.[33]

In addition to a critical mass of resources that may be necessary for producing certain types of services, there are other technical considerations that may favor centralization, such as the economies of scale that can accrue to a large central unit, particularly if it is producing and delivering a standardized benefit. However, many of the personal social services that deal with therapy, counseling, and giving advice employ an intensive form of technology under which the treatment plans vary in light of constant feedback about clients' conditions. Tailored to individual cases, these types of services do not lend themselves to standardized production.[34]

The enhancement of accountability that presumably results from decentralization of decision-making authority is closely aligned to the issue of impact on program effectiveness. By their very nature, decentralized programs tend to be more responsive to local preferences and hence more disposed to shape their efforts and define effectiveness according to local criteria. Public opinion in the United States would seem generally in support of decentralization, as state government is viewed as being closer to the people, more sensitive to their needs, and less impersonal than the federal government.[35] Those who emphasize the accountability of decentralized administration often view this movement as a remedy for bureaucratic alienation fostered by large central units. In recent time, antipathy toward the bureaucratic apparatus of central government has grown—an antipathy that joins people of otherwise highly divergent political ideology in support of decentralization. Both, the traditional ''free-market'' conservatives on the right and liberals of a syndicalist socialist bent on the left, extol the virtues of decentralized arrangements that would restrict the scope and power of central government.

Concerns for accountability are most pressing when public opinion is strongly divided in regard to the perceived value of a program's benefits and the worthiness of its recipients. Thus, in morally controversial programs such as Aid to Families with Dependent Children (AFDC), public disagreement about what benefits should be given to whom creates political pressures for decentralized administration that will be responsive to local preferences. While the proximity of decentralized arrangements increases the likelihood of direct accountability and responsiveness to local jurisdictions, the consequences of this proximity cuts in two directions. In matters of social welfare, localism can be intrusive, parochial, and potentially oppressive, with community members and local officials taking too close an interest in the personal affairs of program recipients.

Decentralization is also seen as a movement that stimulates innovation. Experimentation among decentralized units allows for a pooling of risks whereby the losses suffered through the failure of one unit's innovation may be balanced against the successful experiments of other independent units. Thus, under the banner of the "New Federalism" in the early 1970s, President Nixon encouraged the devolution of decision-making authority from the federal to the state level as a process that would "set states and localities free—free to set new priorities, free to meet unmet needs, free to make their mistakes, yes, but also free to score splendid successes which otherwise would never be realized."[36]

Whereas effectiveness, accountability, and innovation are often submitted as reasons for decentralization, in times of severe fiscal constraint the devolution of decision-making authority performs a latent function, which is not widely publicized by its political supporters. That is, under the banner of enhanced local accountability, decentralization serves to shift the unpleasant task of making politically difficult decisions on how to cut public spending. In the United States, for example, the Social Services Block Grant authorized by the Omnibus Budget Reconciliation Act of 1981 gave states unprecedented authority for planning and implementation of social services at the same time that federal support for these services was being reduced.[37]

In addition to the various manifest and latent functions of decentralization, support for this movement can be seen in a broader context as part of the philosophical debate about the proper locus of responsibility for social welfare. The issue here concerns the extent to which social welfare should be financed and produced by government, voluntary agencies, the family, and the private market. The Reagan administration in the 1980s has emphasized self-help through family and voluntary units and use of the private sector for the production of social welfare, while seeking a reduction of government effort and responsibility in this realm. Along similar lines, discussions of social policy in the United States recently have turned from a preoccupation with the scale of welfare entitlements to analyses of the social obligations that should adhere to these entitlements.[38]

### Privatization and Commercialization

In this broader context, the movement toward decentralization involves not only the dispersal of administrative authority from central to local government, but also a shift in responsibility from public to voluntary and private units. The privatization of social welfare thus is often a corollary of decentralization. In a similar vein, the commercialization of social welfare is also seen as closely related to privatization and de-

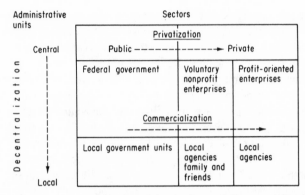

*Figure 1.2.* Decentralization, Privatization and Commercialization

centralization. However, decentralization, privatization, and commercialization of social welfare are developments that can be distinguished, as illustrated in Fig. 1.2, along two conceptual dimensions: central/local administrative units and public/private sectors.

Privatization occurs when functions related to ownership, funding, regulation, management, and provision are removed from the public domain. In primary education for example, although most functions are carried out by local public units, there also exists a small, diffuse, and well-entrenched domain of private education in which only minimal regulatory and funding functions (through institutional and philanthropic, though not consumer, tax preferences) remain in the public sphere. Primary education is thus characterized by a mix of local public monopolies with essentially no consumer choice, and an expensive, small, and marginally regulated private domain that offers meaningful choice only to those few able to afford it. The monopolistic structure of public education is somewhat at odds with the current climate of devolution and choice; it is an arrangement that is ripe for change. If consumer choice and private education should be expanded under some form of public subsidy, as is the case in most developed nations, it is likely that public regulation of private activities in this area would also increase.

Privatization may be implemented by either nonprofit or for-profit units. When they move into the profit-oriented branch of the private sector, social welfare activities take on the spirit of commerce. Commercialization then is one type of privatization. In its broadest sense, however, the commercialization of social welfare is a more diffuse and interactive process. It involves not only the penetration of profit-motivated providers, but also an infusion of the ethos and method of the economic market into all branches of the social market. The noncompetitive service culture traditionally associated with the social market emphasizes concern for adequacy of provision over cost, status rather than contract relationships between consumer and provider, and transfer rather than exchange as the basic mode of allocation. During the last decade, the commercialization of the social market has emerged as a major force in reshaping not only the noncompetitive service culture, but also the essential nature of public responsibility for social welfare.

## Notes

1. Richard Titmuss, *Essays on "The Welfare State"* (London: Unwin University Books, 1958), pp. 34–55.

2. In recent years, several studies have begun to examine the nature of social welfare from an analytic perspective much broader than the direct-expenditure model. See, for example, Robert J. Lampman, *Social Welfare Spending* (Orlando, Fl.: Academic Press, 1984); Howard Glennerster, *Paying for Welfare* (Oxford: Basil Blackwell, 1985); Martin Rein and Lee Rainwater, eds., *Public/Private Interplay in Social Protection: A Comparative Study* (Armonk, N.Y.: M. E. Sharpe, 1986); Neil Gilbert "How to Rate a Social-Welfare System," *Wall Street Journal*, January 13, 1987, p. 30; Richard Rose, "Common Goals But Different Roles: The State's Contribution to the Welfare Mix," in *The Welfare State East and West*, eds. Richard Rose and Rei Shiratori (New York: Oxford University Press, 1986); Alex Inkeles, "Rethinking Social Welfare: U.S. and U.S.S.R. in Comparative Perspective," Working Papers in Economics E-86-34, Domestic Studies Program, Hoover Institution, Stanford University, July 1986; and Norman Johnson, *The Welfare State in Transition* (Amherst, Ma.: University of Massachusetts Press, 1987).

3. T. H. Marshall, "Value Problems of Welfare Capitalism," *Journal of Social Policy*, 1:1 (January 1972), pp. 19–20.

4. John Carrier and Ian Kendall, "Categories, Categorization, and the Political Economy of Welfare," *Journal of Social Policy*, 15:3 (January 1986), pp. 315–35.

5. For further discussion of the distinction between transfers and exchange see Lampman, *Social Welfare Spending*, pp. 10–39.

6. For the classic statements here, see John K. Galbraith, *The Affluent Society* (New York: Mentor Books, 1958), p. 205, and the response by Friedrick Hayek, "The Non Sequitur of the 'Dependence Effect,'" in *Private Wants and Public Needs*, ed. Edmund S. Phelps (New York: W. W. Norton, 1962), pp. 37–42.

7. Frances Fox Piven and Richard Cloward, *Regulating the Poor: The Functions of Public Welfare* (New York: Pantheon Books, 1971).

8. Julian Le Grand, *The Strategy of Equality* (London: Allen and Unwin, 1982); Julian Le Grand and David Winter, "The Middle Classes and the Welfare State," discussion

paper No. 14, March 1987, The Welfare State Program, Suntory–Toyota International Center for Economics and Related Disciplines, London School of Economics; Neil Gilbert, *Capitalism and the Welfare State* (New Haven, Conn.: Yale University Press, 1983).

9. Graham Mather, "Profits—Everyone's Incentive," *The Times*, March 18, 1987, p. 10.

10. For more detail, see Gilbert, *Capitalism and Welfare State*, pp. 29–31; Michael Hill and Glen Bramley, *Analysing Social Policy* (Oxford: Basil Blackwell, 1986), pp. 102–17.

11. Robert Morris, "Rethinking Welfare in the United States: The Welfare State in Transition," in *Modern Welfare States*, eds. Robert Friedmann, Neil Gilbert, and Moshe Sherer (New York: New York University Press, 1987).

12. A detailed account of the scope of direct and indirect farm transfers is presented in Chapter 5.

13. The calculation of national tax expenditures is complicated. For some purposes requiring great exactitude, separate categories of tax expenditures may not simply be summed up into a grand total because of overlapping and the interactive nature of their revenue impact within the tax structure. However, the differences between an additive summary of tax expenditure and a summary that controls for interactive effects are not large. For the purposes of this book, the additive summary is an adequate representation of total tax expenditures. Issues concerning the definition and calculation of tax expenditures are discussed in Richard Goode, "The Economic Definition of Income," in *Comprehensive Income Taxation,* ed. Joseph Pechman (Washington, D.C.: The Brookings Institution, 1977), pp. 1–36, and Committee on Fiscal Affairs, Organisation for Economic Co-operation and Development, *Tax Expenditures: A Review of the Issues and Country Practices* (Paris: OECD, 1984), pp. 9–23.

14. Committee on Fiscal Affairs, OECD, *Tax Expenditures: A Review,* pp. 16–23.

15. Goode, "Economic Definition," p. 26.

16. Office of Management and Budget, *Budget of the United States Government FY 1988, Supplement, Part 3B* (Washington, D.C.: U.S. Government Printing Office, 1988).

17. Ibid., Table 14.2.

18. U.S. Bureau of the Census, *Statistical Abstract of the United States, 1986* (Washington, D.C.: U.S. Government Printing Office, 1985), p. 500.

19. Ibid., p. 738.

20. Lampman, *Social Welfare Spending,* pp. 27–28.

21. U.S. Bureau of the Census, *Who's Helping Out? Support Networks Among American Families* (Washington, D.C.: U.S. Government Printing Office, 1988).

22. National Center for Health Statistics, U.S. Department of Health, Education, and Welfare, "Home Health Care for Persons 55 Years and Over," *Vital and Health Statistics: Statistical Publication Series 10* (1972).

23. Bonnie Brown Morell, "Deinstitutionalization: Those Left Behind," *Social Work,* 24 (November 1979), p. 528.

24. U.S. Bureau of the Census, *Statistical Abstract of the United States, 1988* (Washington, D.C.: U.S. Government Printing Office, 1987), p. 359.

25. Sheila Kamerman, "The Child-Care Debate: Working Mothers vs. America," *Working Woman* (November 1983), pp. 131–35.

26. Jeanne Saddler, "Low Pay, High Turnover Plague Day-Care Industry," *Wall Street Journal*, February 2, 1987, p. 25. For alternative estimates of day-care facilities see Chapter 4.

27. U.S. Bureau of the Census, *Statistical Abstracts of the United States, 1986* (Washington, D.C.: U.S. Government Printing Office, 1985), pp. 368, 369, 436, 510.

28. Organisation for Economic Co-operation and Development, *The Taxation of Fringe Benefits* (Paris: OECD, 1988), pp. 49–57.

29. The following discussion draws on material originally presented by Neil Gilbert "Changing Structures for the Delivery of Social Benefits in the United States," paper delivered at the 2nd Conference on the Study of Trends in the Welfare State, University of Massachusetts, McCormack Institute of Public Affairs, September 24, 1986.

30. Friedmann et al., *Modern Welfare States*.

31. Gilbert, *Capitalism and the Welfare State*, p. 178.

32. Alice Rivlin, *Systematic Thinking for Social Action* (Washington, D.C.: The Brookings Institution, 1971), p. 122.

33. Daniel P. Moynihan, "Comments on 'Restructuring' the Government of New York City," in *The Neighborhoods, the City and the Region: Working Papers on Jurisdiction and Structure*, State Study Commission for New York City, 1973, p. 15.

34. Neil Gilbert and Harry Specht, *Dimensions of Social Welfare Policy* (Englewood Cliffs, N.J.: Prentice-Hall, 2nd edition, 1986), p. 96.

35. Martin Anderson, *Welfare: The Political Economy of Welfare Reform* (Palo Alto, Calif.: Hoover Institution Press, 1981), p. 165.

36. Richard Nixon, "Message to Congress on General Revenue Sharing," *Weekly Compilation of Presidential Documents*, 7 (February 8, 1977), p. 170.

37. George E. Peterson et al., *The Reagan Block Grants* (Washington, D.C.: The Urban Institute, 1986), pp. 1–67.

38. See, for example, Lawrence Mead, *Beyond Entitlement: The Social Obligations of Citizenship* (New York: Free Press, 1986) and James Q. Wilson, "The Rediscovery of Character: Private Virtue and Public Policy," *The Public Interest* (Fall 1985), pp. 3–16.

# 2

# *Commercialization of the Social Market*

> The atmosphere of hostility to capitalism which we shall have to explain presently makes it much more difficult than it otherwise would be to form a rational opinion about its economic and cultural performance. The public mind has by now so thoroughly grown out of humor with it as to make condemnation of capitalism and all its works a foregone conclusion—almost a requirement of the etiquette of discussion. Whatever his political preference, every writer or speaker hastens to conform to this code and to emphasize his critical attitude, his freedom from "complacency," his belief in the inadequacies of capitalist achievement, his aversion to capitalist and his sympathy to anti-capitalist interests, Any other attitude is voted not only foolish, but anti-social and looked upon as an indication of immoral servitude.[1]

So wrote Joseph Schumpeter in 1942, describing the popular disdain toward capitalism in that era. No enemy of capitalism, Schumpeter believed nevertheless that it was unlikely to survive. According to his analysis, it was not failure as an economic system that would lead to the demise of capitalism, but rather its commercial success that would eventually undermine the attitudes, values, and entrepreneurial behavior that imbued the system with vitality and moral force. By 1949, events in England seemed only to confirm Schumpeter's prognosis. "The ethos of capitalism," he declared, "is gone."[2]

But what Schumpeter perceived as an inevitable march into socialism, forty years later appears more as a cyclical alteration between emphases on conservative and liberal tendencies in public life. Observing the widespread liberal mood in the 1940s, Arthur Schlesinger, Sr., predicted that the cycle of liberalism would recede by the early 1960s, with the next conservative epoch commencing around 1978—a prediction not far from the mark as events have indicated.[3] In the late 1980s many developed nations, including socialist and communist examples, are in the midst of creating or revitalizing an economic market-oriented approach to the production and distribution of material resources. Margaret Thatcher's historic election to a third term was the second largest conservative victory since World War II and the first consecutive three-term winning streak by a British prime minister since the 1820s. Thatcher gained the day on a platform of privatization, which pledged to supplant democratic socialism with popular capitalism. Her efforts toward this end are reflected in social welfare initiatives such as the sale of council housing, the contracting out of ancillary hospital services, and the Enterprise Allowance Scheme that allows unemployed people to start their own businesses without the immediate loss of unemployment compensation.[4] In response to the evident popularity of a market-oriented approach to public policy, the Fabian Socialists even started to rethink the merits of market forces coming up with "market socialism," a new label for the old idea of worker-owned cooperatives functioning in a competitive market.[5] Meanwhile, on the other side of the Iron Curtain, popular humor depicts socialism as a long and grueling road from capitalism to capitalism. Although private enterprise is not exactly flourishing in the Soviet Union, the Gorbachev government endorsed the loosening of central controls, the development of private business activities limited to family-run operations, and the establishment of "enterprise centers" in twenty to thirty ministries, with a mandate to generate profit-oriented activities.[6] The reasons for this renewed interest in the economic market stem, in part, from the failures of statist institutions to achieve adequate levels of growth, efficiency, and effectiveness in a world where comparative results are apparent and consumer demands difficult to control.

The United States, for reasons relating to its history and traditions, has been in the forefront of this market rebirth, putting into extensive practice both market and tax reforms, and encouraging their emulation abroad. The social welfare system, including the large component traditionally devoted to providing collective support and care for the poor, the vulnerable, and the dependent, is actively involved in this resurgence of market forces. Hospitals that have been nonprofit charitable institutions for more than 100 years are being sold to the highest bidder; nursing homes for the elderly are overwhelmingly in commercial hands, as are day-care centers and preschools for children. Social workers are increasingly employed by corporations or functioning as independent professionals. Other public activities are moving in the same direction. City garbage collection services are being contracted out to newly formed private companies; there have been serious proposals to sell off metropolitan airports, the postal system, and national parks; even a few jails are being run by private corporations.

But the commercialization of the social market encompasses more than public contracting with private enterprise for the delivery of in-kind welfare provisions. It represents a larger configuration of ideas and activities that include a renewed emphasis on the work ethic reflected mainly in the "workfare" programs in conjunction with public assistance and, some might say, in extending the age of retirement at which one is eligible for social security, for example, from sixty-five to sixty-seven during the next twenty years; there is also increasing use of indirect cash transfers that subsidize private consumption through tax expenditures in support of, for example, individual retirement accounts, child care services, low-income taxpayers, and health insurance. Finally, on a more philosophical plane, there is an infusion of the capitalist ethos with its zeal for efficiency, consumer choice, and entrepreneurial activity.[7]

This movement toward commercialization of the social market is supported by several basic assumptions:

> The cost, quality, and accessibility of social welfare services will be beneficially affected by the introduction of competition, choice, the entrepreneurial spirit, profit making, and business methods.

> The tax system is a desirable vehicle for the transfer of income that may be applied toward the private purchase of social welfare provisions in the economic market.

> There are limits to the affordability of desirable social welfare services and no limit to the demand for them, so that the mode of financing, delivery, and usage of the recent past must be restructured to maintain fiscal health, to refine demand, and to maintain reasonable overall service levels.

> In a capitalist society that has moved from an industrial and manufacturing to a technology and service–oriented economy, the growing production of services in the social market present a ready outlet for investment-hungry capital as well as opportunities for employment.

Employment patterns of American workers, including those of traditional social service workers, must accommodate themselves to these new trends even if it means moving into the more volatile and rootless mode of entrepreneurship and corporate life.

The commercialization of the social market involves a variety of public, voluntary, and profit-oriented service providers. The latter include individual professionals and groups selling their services, small family enterprises, and large corporations operating on a regional, national, and even multinational basis. Except for the larger corporations, these profit-oriented providers have always been, to some extent, participants in the mixed economy of welfare. In colonial times, the public authorities "contracted out" with individuals to provide housing, food, and medical care to the poor. Furthermore, nursing homes typically have been started as small family businesses. Since the mid-1960s, the structure of this mixed economy has undergone notable changes as responsibility for the delivery of social provisions has shifted to units in the private sector.[8] This shift represents a movement toward commercialization of the social market, the impetus for which can be traced to several underlying trends.

**Impetus for Commercialization**

Because American society is open, vital, diverse, and full of opportunity, it is subject to instability. Release from the constricting social bonds of tradition also loosens the social supports of traditional institutional arrangements. During the last two decades there has been a significant disintegration of traditional family, neighborhood, and religious institutions. This is not to say that it was a unique era of social and economic turmoil. Measured against the devastation of the Black Plague in the fourteenth century or even the Great Depression of the 1930s, the decades from the late 1960s to the present would seem rather quiescent. However, most people assess their circumstances with a historical gaze that extends back no further than their early memories of childhood. Thus, for the ordinary American between the ages of approximately twenty-five and fifty, the norms and expectations of today tend to be measured against the relatively prosperous and stable postwar period of 1945–1965. With that period as a benchmark, the American middle class has experienced an era of growing needs and heightened insecurity during the past two decades.

This plight of the middle class flows in large part from the disintegration of traditional family life. Between 1960 and the late 1980s, the rates of divorce to marriage rose from 26 percent to almost 50 percent. During the same period the proportion of births to unwed mothers multiplied more than threefold from 5 percent to more than 17 percent.[9] It is estimated that 70 percent of all children born in 1980 will spend at least part of their first eighteen years in a single-parent household.[10]

There is less time and energy available for domestic life and community service. Many housewives who once invested huge amounts of voluntary labor in caring for their families and supporting community service institutions have been transformed into paid full-time employees. Between 1960 and 1985 the rate of employment for married women with children under six grew from 19 percent to 53 percent.[11] Of all women employed in nonagricultural industries, approximately 28 percent held part-time jobs. In more than 30 percent of two-income families, either the husband or wife works the night shift.[12] Not only are more family members employed, but they are also working longer than many of their European counterparts. A four- to five-week vacation, seven to ten public holidays, and six months to one year of paid maternity leave are guaranteed by law to most western Europeans. Most Americans receive only two- to three-week vacations and seven to ten other days off. Between 1950 and 1980, the average number of working hours per week in manufacturing remained almost constant in the United States, while declining between 20 and 30 percent in most western European countries.[13] Only in Japan do workers enjoy as little leisure time as in the United States, and this is balanced in family life by the relative absence of mothers in the labor force.

The significant shift of family labor from the household to the market economy has not been coupled with a corresponding gain in economic security.[14] The median income of a two wage-earner family in 1984 provided only 39 percent more purchasing power than the median income of a single wage-earner family in 1970. For all married couples, the median family income adjusted for inflation actually declined almost 1 percent from 1970 to 1982.[15] A thirty-year-old man in 1949 saw his real earnings rise by 63 percent by the time he was forty, whereas a thirty-year-old man in 1973 saw his real earnings fall by 1 percent in ten years. There are signs that this trend is starting to reverse, as median family income in 1986 was up 4 percent over the previous year.[16]

The tenuous state of economic security is perhaps most sharply illustrated in the savings rate for American households, which is among the lowest of the developed nations. However, international comparisons ignore the relatively high rate of home ownership among American households, which represents a form of savings. Comparative figures notwithstanding, savings as a percentage of personal disposable income declined from 8.1 percent to 5.1 percent between 1970 and 1985. By 1986 the savings rate had dropped to 3.9 percent, the lowest rate since 1947, and the average American consumer owed approximately 20 percent more than he earned.[17]

The erosion of marital stability and economic security in family life is intensified by physical mobility and the decline of neighborhood life. On the average, American families move once every six years and, given the country's size, tend to move farther from family and friends than do other nationals.[18] Nondescript commuter suburbs abound, which are empty during daytime of women and children and inhabited during evenings and weekends by rootless transients. Once a focal point of community life, neighborhood public schools no longer serve this function as parental interests are dispersed by the busing of students across urban areas. Neighborhood shops that were once long-standing family or local enterprises—such as barbers, butchers, laundries, book-shops, and pharmacies—are giving way to corporate chains and franchises that seek younger, childless, and more free-spending clientele. Traditional community-based service institutions, such as hospitals, are also being replaced by distantly headquartered corporate enterprises. In this busy, diffuse, and demanding environment, the automobile—with its socially isolating effects—is ubiquitous, replacing the more leisurely and social transport of pedestrian life.

Religion as an institutional source of personal and family security is also on the wane. While 60 percent of Americans profess to a religious affiliation, and there are some well-publicized signs of a fundamentalist religious revival among the less-educated and less-affluent Protestant denominations, actual church attendance declined from 47 percent in 1957 to between 40 and 42 percent in the 1980s.[19] The Catholic church, once a mainstay of urban neighborhood life and educational and social services, is finding its financial and human resources shrinking. Fewer and older nuns, for example, are available to run the parochial schools and to care for the most elderly members of their orders. As the older ethnic and religious groups have become assimilated into the mass society, their familial bonds and obedience to the traditional church tend to diminish. A 1986 Gallup Poll, for example, reveals a substantial loss of public confidence in organized religion.[20]

There are other influences that heighten middle-class insecurity. America is known as the land of opportunity, but the corollary of opportunity for upward mobility is the risk of downward mobility. Based on a representative sample of 5000 American families, findings from the Panel Study of Income Dynamics reveal that less than half of the families in the top fifth of the income distribution in 1971 remained in that position in 1978, with more than one-fifth having fallen into the lower three quintiles. Overall, 23 percent of the sample moved at least two quintile positions in either direction during a period of seven years.[21] Trying at least to hold their own amid all this movement, the wage-earning middle class is being squeezed by demography as the proportion of elderly is increasing along with the costs to sustain them, which must be borne by the working population. In the background, the mass media continually exposes Americans to a bewildering array of products, ideas, life-styles, and temptations, which fuel the trend to acquire more material goods and debt at the expense of less tangible benefits such as leisure, family life, and financial security. All the while the legal system, notable for its cost and its inability to protect the law-abiding, fails to provide a coherent sense of social order and justice.

The insecurities attendant upon the decline of social institutions and the vagaries of the market economy have created a growing middle-class constituency for social welfare provisions. Since the mid-1960s there has been a significant expansion of entitlements for social services. This movement toward the universal provision of services was fed by several programs, including such legislation as Title XX (later converted to the Social Services Block Grant under the Omnibus Budget Reconciliation Act of 1981), the Older Americans Act, and the Community Mental Health Centers Act, which made social services available to many people with incomes well above the poverty level.[22] In addition to direct expenditures on social services, middle-class transfers also expanded through tax expenditures for child care, individual retirement accounts (IRAs), and employee fringe benefits.

During the early 1980s, eligibility requirements for social services began to tighten as cutbacks in federal spending were initiated. Although the total volume of cutbacks is difficult to calculate, one estimate suggests that at the height of contraction the overall decrease in federal spending was relatively modest, amounting to about 5 percent of baseline expenditures for 1982.[23] The brunt of these cutbacks was apparently not borne by the middle class but by social programs serving the poor.

Middle-class consumers differ from the traditional low-income clientele of social services insofar as their expectations are higher, their personal resources greater, and their needs more temporal. Middle-class consumers are accustomed to choice; they tend to prefer cash benefits and in-kind services delivered through a variety of providers, including profit-oriented agencies that allow the middle class to distance themselves psychologically and even physically from hard-core problem groups, from the shabbiness of many public service facilities, and from any notion that they are charity or welfare recipients.

During the last two decades the broadening middle-class base of welfare recipients has exerted a force for the commercialization of social welfare from the consumer side of social transfers. At the same time, increasing disenchantment with the bureaucratic apparatus of central government has opened the way to commercialization from the finance and delivery side of the transaction. Reaching a rhetorical apex in the Reagan years, the pledge to reduce the activities and costs of federal government has been a conspicuous theme in the campaign of every successful presidential candidate since the Nixon administration's New Federalism in the early 1970s. Heclo draws an interesting parallel between the Reagan administration's restricted view of central government's role and earlier protests against bureaucratic regimentation. In the 1980s, Heclo observes,

> a number of former campus radicals can be found actively involved in politics carrying forward the Reagan revolution. The Reagan vision of a nation for like-minded individuals, each doing their own thing unfettered by bureaucratic hierarchies, is not too distant from the hopes of campus youths in the 1960s.[24]

The United States is not the only western democracy in which the public's discontent with government bureaucracy is evident. Sweden's size and homogeneity lend an intimacy to the relationship between the individual and state that demography precludes in the United States. Yet a Swedish survey in 1984 shows 81 percent of the respondents agreeing that "the state has become increasingly despotic at the expense of individual rights."[25] In Britain the debate among Fabian Socialists on the merits of "market socialism" is animated by a sense of resentment and frustration with the big bureaucracies of the welfare state.[26] In 1982 the Mitterrand government enacted legislation designed to shift responsibility for social services in France from the central government to local jurisdictions.[27]

Although the United States is not unique in its dissatisfactions with the bureaucratic monoliths of central government, its response in the realm of social welfare has been, perhaps, the most extreme. American society has always held, as Glazer puts it,

> a remarkably strong sentiment that problems should be taken care of by autonomous, independent institutions, and even by profit-making businesses, rather than by the state. That one can handle social problems, such as the problem of the poor, through profit making might seem bizarre; yet this is widely believed to be a reasonable approach and not only by Republicans.[28]

To limit the size and role of government bureaucracy in social welfare activities, the American approach has come to emphasize the private production and delivery of welfare provisions. There are two paths to this approach. First, and most preferred, is the allocation of benefits in the form of cash through direct and tax expenditures, which allow recipients to purchase welfare provisions from private sources; with this approach, the role of government is restricted essentially to writing checks for individual grants and tax refunds. Since the mid-1960s, the largest expansion of cash benefits outside of social security (a special case of indexed benefits and a rapidly growing population of elderly) has involved the combination of tax expenditures for day care, low-income workers, retirement schemes, and employee benefits.

For benefits provided in kind, the second path involves public financing of services produced and delivered by private agencies. Over the last two decades, there has been a dramatic increase in these purchase-of-service arrangements. Prior to the 1960s, the private sector of the social market made only limited use of public funds to finance social services for delivery by private agencies. For example, in 1962 governmental grants to Jewish social service agencies accounted for only 11 percent of the total income received by these agencies; however, barely a decade later, governmental payments to these agencies accounted for 51 percent of their income.[29] By 1980, federal funds provided more than 50 percent of all the financial support for private, nonprofit social service agencies.[30] At the same time, this sector has been increasingly penetrated by proprietary entities dedicated to profiting from service delivery. By the mid-1980s, profit-oriented agencies had become firmly established in many program areas such as homemaker services, employment training, transportation, and meals-on-wheels. Profit-oriented agencies are most prominently represented in nursing home care, day care, child welfare, and health care (a presence examined in greater detail in Chapters 3 and 6). This influx of profit-motivated providers has lent momentum to the commercialization of the social market, pressing its modus operandi into closer conformity to that of the economic market.

## Does It Work? Issues of Cost, Care, and Preference

The increasing involvement of profit-oriented agencies in the delivery of services and the allocation of cash benefits through tax expenditures are two notable developments underlying the commercialization of the social market. Several questions arise in the wake of these developments. How do profit and nonprofit agencies perform as service providers in the social market? Will the profit incentive drive up cost? Does the service ethos of traditional nonprofit organizations ensure better care? And what are the effects of transfers conducted through the tax mechanism?

On the question of for-profit versus nonprofit service providers, the largest body of research focuses on nursing homes and hospitals. There are, however, scattered findings in other areas.[31] Wooden's survey of children's institutions, for example, documents numerous abuses by proprietary agencies in this field; it also uncovers many frightful practices by public agencies across the country and by voluntary nonprofit agencies such as Brother Lester Roloff's infamous Rebekeh Home for Girls; even Father Flanagan's Boys Town does not emerge unscathed![32]

The evidence on nursing homes is considerably more elaborate, but no more decisive. Regarding the comparative costs of profit-oriented versus nonprofit providers, there is a fair degree of agreement. Summarizing the results of more than a dozen studies, Marmor, Schelsinger, and Smithey note that "these studies have reached a common conclusion—controlling for characteristics of patients, range of services provided, and other attributes of the facility, for-profit homes have average costs five to fifteen percent lower than their nonprofit counterparts."[33]

Similarly, in a large-scale econometric analyses of nursing home data, Birnbaum and colleagues consistently found that "non-profit voluntary and governmental organizations have higher costs than for-profit nursing homes by at least several dollars per day."[34] Further confirmation of these cost differences is reported in a British survey of 456 residential homes for the elderly; in this study, Judge and Knapp found that the weekly cost per resident in local public authority homes was 17 percent higher than in the average private accommodations. After controlling for differences in home design, occupancy, location, and other variables, private home charges remained clearly lower than local authority costs.[35]

However, differences in the cost alone do not testify to the greater efficiency of for-profit providers. The question remains of what is being delivered in the way of nursing home care under for-profit and nonprofit auspices. Measuring the quality of nursing home care is a formidable task. Do we examine the warmth, attentiveness, and qualifications of staff, the taste and presentation of meals, the ambience and comfort of the physical plant, or the mundane details of how many times a week the sheets are changed? And how does one calculate the relationship between quality and access? As in other social services (see Chapter 8), the qualitative experience of nursing home care is to some extent shaped by the characteristics of its clientele. The daily routine in a facility with a high proportion of disoriented, incontinent, and severely disabled residents will be more messy and complicated than in one that limits access to a group with less debilitating problems.

Despite the difficulties of measuring the quality of services, there is evidence to suggest that profit-oriented nursing home facilities are over-represented among providers offering very low-quality care.[36] A study of forty-three profit-oriented nursing homes in southern California, for example, reveals that the most profitable facilities offered the lowest quality of patient care as operationally defined by the hours of skilled nursing care available to patients on a daily basis.[37] Measuring quality from another angle, Weisbrod compares for-profit and nonprofit services according to what he terms "type II" attributes. These are the hard-to-monitor aspects of service that offer agencies seeking to maximize profit the greatest incentive to 'shave' on quality. Examining the use of sedatives in nine nursing homes, he reports that whereas there was very little difference between the percentages of patients in proprietary and nonprofit homes who received drug prescriptions at the time of admission, there was a huge difference in the dosage of sleeping medication administered to these patients, with those in proprietary homes receiving an average of 12.5 units per month compared to 3 units in the church-owned nonprofit homes. Consistent with the findings in southern California, Weisbrod also discovered that profit-oriented nursing homes employed fewer full-time registered nurses and full-time maintenance workers per patient than nonprofit facilities. It would appear from these data that proprietary homes use relatively inexpensive drugs rather than the more costly labor that would be needed to care for patients if they were sedated less.[38] What the data do not tell us is whether this represents the "best" medical practice dictated by true needs for medication or a cost-cutting procedure that takes advantage of vulnerable patients. The vulnerability of nursing home patients raises an important question about the extent to which these facilities provide information about their services to family members and others who represent the patients' interests. On this issue, the evidence reveals that nonprofit providers are more willing to share information and more open to surveillance by patient representatives.[39]

There are, however, other views and findings that lend alternative interpretations to the differences between profit-oriented and nonprofit nursing facilities. Judge and Knapp made a coherent case explaining the lower costs of profit-oriented facilities in terms of the high degree of proprietorial involvement in the daily operations of owner-managed homes and the noneconomic motivations that prompt the establishment of these businesses in the first place.[40] The Moreland Commission found that government-sponsored nursing homes had significantly higher costs than either profit-oriented or voluntary nonprofit facilities due in large measure to employee fringe benefits in government nursing homes that averaged $3.44 per day compared to $1.76 for nonprofit and $1.18 for proprietary facilities.[41] From a less academic perspective, Mendelsohn's exposé of inadequacies in nursing home service offers bleak testimony on the quality of care in both profit-making and nonprofit facilities.[42]

In the area of hospital care, estimates vary on the relative costs of proprietary and nonprofit facilities. Several studies have found that profit-oriented hospitals charge between 15 and 24 percent more per patient than their nonprofit counterparts, with the highest cost differences concentrated in lab fees, supplies, medication, and other ancillary services.[43] Other studies reveal only small inconsistent differences.[44]

Posing the question of hospital costs in a broader analytic framework,

Herzlinger and Krasker examine the return on investment for both proprietary and nonprofit organizations. Their premise is that society benefits most from the hospitals in which resources invested earn the highest return. Analyzing a range of variables, they found that nonprofit institutions have a lower turnover per hospital bed and defer replacing their plants and equipment for longer periods than their proprietary counterparts. Nonprofit hospitals are publicly subsidized by exemptions from most income, sales, and sometimes, real estate taxes; they also benefit from the ability to borrow money at the lower interest rates of tax-exempt bonds. In comparing per-patient costs, the price of public subsidies for nonprofit hospitals must be weighed into the balance. Moreover, the shorter lengths of stay in profit-oriented facilities alter the results if one calculates cost per admission rather than per day. Considering these and other variables, these authors conclude that profit-oriented hospitals cost less and produce better results for society than nonprofit providers.[45]

The various findings on cost and care in proprietary and nonprofit hospitals do not yield a clear preference. Assessing the research findings during a three-year inquiry into these issues, a 1986 report from the Committee on Implications of For-Profit Enterprise in Health Care under the auspices of the National Academy of Science's Institute of Medicine concludes "that available evidence on differences between for-profit and not-for-profit health care organizations is not sufficient to justify a recommendation that investor ownership of health care organizations be either opposed or supported by public policy."[46]

Comparative research on other publicly financed services delivered by for-profit providers—such as day care, meals-on-wheels, transportation for the elderly, residential treatment for children, and various types of counseling—is limited. The problem of empirically evaluating the quality of service in these areas is fraught with complexity, and the results are likely to be as indeterminate as in the area of health care.[47] Given the diversity of social services, the many criteria that might be employed to assess quality and determine costs, the importance of intervening variables such as organizational size and location, and the large differences within the categories of profit-oriented and nonprofit providers, no general conclusion can be drawn about the superior form of organization.

However, one might recast the issue and inquire into the particular conditions under which profit-oriented or nonprofit providers may be advantageous for the delivery of a specific type of service. After all, there are differences between profit-motivated and nonprofit organizations at least at the extremes—for example, between the traditional church-sponsored nonprofit and the transient profit-oriented institution that operates under the motto of caveat emptor. These differences fall into the categories of public accountability, incentive structure, and organizational ethos. Theoretically, nonprofit organizations have a higher degree of public accountability than profit-oriented organizations because their boards of directors are composed of people expected to represent the broad interests of the community rather than the financial interests of the ownership group. Compared to profit-motivated firms, the members of nonprofit organizations have less incentive to exploit vulnerable consumers for financial gain because of the legal prohibition against the distribution of the net earnings of nonprofit organizations. Finally, there is a charitable ethos traditionally associated with nonprofit social service organizations that is at variance with the capitalist spirit of profit-making enterprises. This ethos is reflected in greater concern for the adequacy than the efficiency of services and for access according to need rather than ability to pay. These differences, of course, are more a matter of degree than kind, and they all but disappear as we move from the traditional religious and/or ethnic-based voluntary nonprofit service provider to newly created nonprofit agencies that are essentially profit-motivated in disguise. To the extent that these differences exist, the following conditions offer some guidelines for assessing the preferability of nonprofit versus profit-motivated service providers.[48]

CLIENT COMPETENCE

Many social services deal with groups of clients—such as children, mentally disabled, and emotionally upset people—who are not well equipped to exercise choice and defend their self-interests. To the extent that public accountability and the charitable ethos influence nonprofit agencies more than profit-making agencies, the nonprofit form is a better service delivery mechanism to accommodate the needs of immobile, ill-informed, and highly vulnerable consumers.

COERCIVENESS OF SERVICE

Services invested with coercive powers, such as protective services for children and work with parolees, pose a threat to personal liberty. In these cases a high degree of public accountability is essential for the protection of clients' rights. The greater emphasis on private accountability to owners and stockholders in profit-making organizations would appear to make them less inclined to offer adequate protection for clients' rights than nonprofit service providers; moreover, the profit motive might encourage holding back on provisions to consumers who are virtually in the custody of the service provider. In this regard, the most extreme and undesirable case would involve public contracting with private enterprise to operate prisons. (In such a market one could even imagine private companies developing a lobby for more prisons and longer sentences to keep them full.) Despite these misgivings, in recent years an increasing number of private companies have been engaged to manage and provide services for federal and state prisons. In 1987, more than thirty state detention centers were owned and operated by profit-oriented firms. Although favorable reports have appeared on the preliminary experiences of these "prisons for profit," the final verdict on the cost and quality of their operations awaits more probing systematic investigation.[49] Initial experiences may reflect the outcomes of a "loss-leader strategy" employed to gain a foothold in the prison market.

POTENCY OF DIRECT PUBLIC REGULATION

Services that involve uniform procedures and standard products—such as public health vaccinations—readily lend themselves to monitoring and regulation. Profit-oriented and nonprofit providers appear equally desirable when the services they deliver are subject to public regulations strong enough to ensure high quality and client protection.

FEASIBILITY OF INDIRECT METHODS OF REGULATION

Many social services are not highly standardized. The costs of obtaining information and problems associated with measurement of quality severely complicate attempts at direct public regulation of numerous services purchased from private providers. An indirect method of regulation, however, known as "proxy shopping," uses paying customers to monitor service quality and to verify whether purchase prices are reasonable. Taking advantage of the discipline and accountability imposed by competition and consumer choice, this method allows those handling public funds to identify the providers of social services who can attract paying customers—people who, after shopping, have chosen a specific provider because it offers the best quality for the price charged. Public funds can then be used to purchase services from this provider for clients of social welfare, at the same price paid by unsubsidized customers—the proxy shoppers. The utility of this scheme depends on several supplementary conditions, such as the existence of enough suppliers to form a competitive market and the providers' inability to distinguish unsubsidized customers from those who are subsidized. Proxy shopping can be used to select providers from among the profit-oriented and nonprofit agencies.[50]

Two or more of the conditions just noted may affect the provision of a particular service. Depending upon the combination of these conditions, they lend varying degrees of support to the choice between for-profit or nonprofit service providers. To deliver a standardized service to competent clients under conditions of potent regulatory controls, for example, one may select from among service providers with little concern for characteristic differences between for-profit and nonprofit status. Were the circumstances reversed, however—calling for the provision of customized service to incompetent clients in the absence of regulatory devices—nonprofit providers would appear to be the prudent choice. Overall, the relative merits of profit-oriented and nonprofit service providers remain to be judged on a case-by-case basis, examining the conditions related to the service and the extent to which conventional assumptions about for-profit and nonprofit status apply to the firms under consideration.

## Indirect Subsidies: Who Benefits?

The increasing allocation of cash benefits through tax expenditures raises an issue that is different from nonprofit versus profit-oriented delivery mechanisms, but it is not completely unrelated. This issue concerns the distribution of benefits among income groups. It relates to questions about the role of profit-motivated providers in the sense that they are frequently criticized for assigning differential access to services according to income.[51]

The cash subsidies that individuals receive through tax expenditures are income-tested rather than means-tested benefits. In means-tested programs, such as Aid to Families with Dependent Children (AFDC), applicants must disclose the value of both their income and assets; they are usually required to sell off almost all of their significant assets before they qualify for assistance; finally, they must also submit to probing investigations. Income-tested programs are concerned only with the applicant's current income and permit both application and verification through tax returns.[52] The nature and degree of income-testing for tax expenditures and the extent to which they benefit different income groups vary according to the type of fiscal mechanism employed. Four of these mechanisms most frequently employed for social welfare-related subsidies are deductions, credits, declining credits, and refundable credits.

Deductions are sums of money subtracted from taxable income and as such provide the greatest benefits to those in the highest tax brackets. Deductions are available for many purposes including the encouragement of private retirement schemes. Under the Economic Tax Recovery Act of 1981, for example, workers were allowed to establish private individual retirement accounts (IRAs) to which they could contribute up to $2000 that would be excluded from their taxable income.

As shown in Table 2.1, the degree of IRA participation is directly related to income. People in the higher income groups not only have more surplus funds available to invest in IRAs, but also gain the largest tax return on these deductions. For these reasons, the general pattern of IRA participation increasing with income will no doubt continue. However, the range of incomes to which this pattern applies has been reduced by the ceiling for participation introduced under the 1986 Tax Reform Act. Starting in 1987, tax-deductible IRAs were available only to families in which neither partner is covered by another retirement plan or their adjusted gross income is less than $50,000. Under the new regulations, families earning up to $40,000 (single people up to $25,000) may continue to make a maximum IRA deduction of $2000 from each partner's earned income; for joint-return filers in the $40,000 to $50,000 range ($25,000 to $35,000 for singles), the IRA deduction is phased out under a formula in which the maximum is limited to 20 percent of the difference between $50,000 ($35,000 for singles) minus the adjusted gross income. Thus, the main beneficiaries of the IRAs have shifted from upper to middle-income groups.

In contrast to deductions, tax credits are subtracted not from taxable income but from the tax liability. Thus, the dollar value of a tax credit is the same regardless of one's marginal tax bracket. The declining tax credit modifies the basic credit by introducing a formula designed to

*Table 2.1.* Distribution of IRAs, by Income Groups, 1983

| Income (dollars) | IRAs, Percentage of All Workers Covered in Each Group |
|---|---|
| 1–4,999 | 7.1 |
| 5,000–9,999 | 8.5 |
| 10,000–14,999 | 11.1 |
| 15,000–19,999 | 17.3 |
| 20,000–24,999 | 20.1 |
| 25,000–29,999 | 28.4 |
| 30,000–49,999 | 38.7 |
| 50,000 and over | 57.7 |
| Not Reported | 18.8 |

*Source*: U.S. Bureau of the Census, *Statistical Abstract of the United States, 1987*, p. 353.

yield higher benefits for low-income taxpayers than for those in the middle-income and upper-income groups. Thus, for example, the child care tax credit permits taxpayers with adjusted incomes of $10,000 or less to take a credit of up to $1440 for child care expenses, while those earning more than $28,000 may only qualify for a maximum of $960. However, as with tax deductions, there is no benefit for those who earn too little to pay taxes and only limited benefits to those whose taxes are very low.

The working poor, those earning too little to pay income taxes, receive no benefits from deductions, credits, and declining credits. The refundable tax credit is a mechanism designed to serve this group, as illustrated by the Earned-Income Tax Credit (EITC) scheme. Introduced as a temporary provision in the Tax Reduction Act of 1975 and later made permanent in 1978, EITC is restricted to working families with children. This credit was aimed to offset the increasing charge of social security taxes on the working poor and to provide financial assistance to those who had no tax liability. In regard to the latter objective, a special feature of this scheme is that if the tax credit is larger than the worker's tax liability the difference is refunded to the taxpayer in cash. The credit is available to those with an earned income less than $15,000. It is calculated at 14 percent of the first $6080 of earned income and is decreased by 10 percent of income over $6920, dropping to zero at an income level of approximately $15,000.[53]

As a mechanism for the centralized financing of cash benefits, the refundable tax credit has gained considerable interest among social welfare policy analysts in recent years. It is seen as a way of reducing welfare dependency by the delivery of cash benefits outside of the traditional public welfare system. While these cash benefits would be income-tested, this involves the benign, impersonal kind of disclosure that all citizens make annually in filling out their income tax forms, rather than the probing means test associated with public assistance programs. A number of proposals for this approach have been developed in varying degrees of detail.[54] Alvin Schorr, for example, suggests replacing the EITC and the personal tax exemption with a $400-per-person refundable tax credit, which would be reduced by 5 percent of income over $10,000.[55] Estimates indicate that this scheme would financially benefit about 60 percent of those who currently file a tax return and would be particularly advantageous to the 5.5 million people with incomes so low that they do not file tax returns; the latter group would be eligible for a refundable tax credit amounting to $5 billion. Overall, the cost of this scheme would be approximately $7 billion a year, more than two-thirds of which would go to those with incomes below the tax threshold.

The growing use of both profit-oriented agencies to deliver publicly financed services and tax expenditures to allocate cash transfers open fresh avenues of thought and action around the provision of social welfare. Well-worn questions about access, cost, distribution, and quality of social provisions are thrown into bold relief by the employment of these allocative mechanisms in the social market. And new issues emerge as these mechanisms take diverse forms in health care, housing, personal social services, income maintenance, and education, the basic areas subsidized by social welfare transfers. The following chapters examine how each of these areas function under the contemporary system of welfare capitalism.

## Notes

1. Joseph Schumpeter, *Capitalism, Socialism, and Democracy* (New York: Harper and Row, 3rd edition, 1950), p. 63.

2. Ibid., p. 410.

3. Arthur M. Schlesinger, *Paths to Progress,* 1949, cited in Arthur M. Schlesinger, Jr., *The Cycles of American History* (Boston: Houghton-Mifflin, 1986), pp. 24–25.

4. Julian LeGrand and David Winter, "The Middle Classes and the Welfare State," discussion paper No. 14, March 1987, The Welfare State Program, Suntory–Toyota International Center for Economics and Related Disciplines, London School of Economics; Carol Steinbach, "Eight Lessons from Europe," *The Entrepreneurial Economy*, 3:7 (January 1985), pp. 4–14.

5. Raymond Plant, "The Market: Needs, Rights, and Morality," *New Statesman*, 113 (March 6, 1987), pp. 14–15; Julian LeGrand, "The Market: Workers, Capital, and Consumers," *New Statesman*, 113 (March 6, 1987), pp. 16–18; and Alan Ryan, "Socialism's Great Rethink," *The Times*, March 25, 1987, p. 14.

6. Peter Peterson, "Gorbachev's Bottom Line," *New York Review of Books*, January 25, 1987, pp. 29–33.

7. For further discussion see Neil Gilbert, *Capitalism and the Welfare State* (New Haven, Conn.: Yale University Press, 1983), pp. 3–44.

8. Ibid.

9. U.S. Bureau of the Census, *Statistical Abstract of the United States, 1986* (Washington, D.C.: U.S. Government Printing Office, 1985).

10. Daniel Patrick Moynihan, "Children and Welfare Reform," *The Journal of the Institute for Socioeconomic Studies* (Spring 1981), pp. 1–20.

11. U.S. Bureau of the Census, *Statistical Abstract, 1986*, p. 399.

12. "Department of Labor Publishes Statistics on 51 Million Women in the Work Force," *Washington Social Legislation Bulletin*, 30:5 (March 9, 1987), p. 18; "Labor Letter," *Wall Street Journal*, August 26, 1986, p. 1.

13. R. A. Hart, *Shorter Working Time: A Dilemma for Collective Bargaining* (Paris: OECD, 1984), pp. 31–53.

14. A family's sense of economic security depends upon the regular income available to meet their immediate costs of living as well as resources in reserve that may be tapped in emergencies. A two-earner family has a higher income to meet the current costs of living, but forfeits the long-run flexibility of a family with a full-time homemaker, which holds the wife's earning capacity in reserve. Gilbert, *Capitalism and Welfare State*, p. 97.

15. U.S. Bureau of the Census, *Statistical Abstract of the United States, 1987* (Washington, D.C.: U.S. Government Printing Office, 1986), p. 439.

16. "At Last, There's More in the Family," *Wall Street Journal*, August 4, 1987, p. 29.

17. U.S. Bureau of the Census, *Statistical Abstract, 1987*, p. 423; the 1986 figures are reported in "Jump in Spending By Consumers," *San Francisco Chronicle*, January 24, 1987, p. 47.

18. U.S. Bureau of the Census, *Statistical Abstract, 1986*, p. 14.

19. U.S. Bureau of the Census, *Statistical Abstract, 1987*, pp. 52–53.

20. George Gallup, Jr., "Americans Losing Confidence in Religion," *San Francisco Chronicle*, December 22, 1986, p. 10.

21. Greg Duncan et al., *Years of Poverty, Years of Plenty* (Ann Arbor, Mich.: Institute for Social Research, 1984), pp. 9–31.

22. For a detailed analysis of the trend, see Gilbert, *Capitalism and Welfare State*, pp. 47–69.

23. John Palmer and Gregory Mills, "Budget Policy," in *The Reagan Experiment*, eds. John Palmer and Isabel Sawhill (Washington, D.C.: The Urban Institute, 1982).

24. Hugh Heclo, "Reaganism and the Search for a Public Philosophy," in *Perspec-

*tives on the Reagan Years,* ed. John Palmer (Washington, D.C.: The Urban Institute, 1980), p. 43.

25. Sven Olsson, *Growth to Limits: The Case of Sweden* (Stockholm: Swedish Institute for Social Research, Reprint Series No. 176, January 1987), p. 96.

26. LeGrand, "The Market: Worker, Capital, Consumers," pp. 16–18.

27. Isidor Wallimann, "Social Insurance and the Delivery of Social Services in France," *Social Science in Medicine,* 23:12 (1980), pp. 1305–17.

28. Nathan Glazer, "Welfare and 'Welfare' in America," in *The Welfare State East and West,* eds. Richard Rose and Rei Shiratori (New York: Oxford University Press, 1986), p. 51.

29. Alvin Chenkin, "Government Support to Jewish-Sponsored Agencies in Six Major Fields of Service," paper presented at the Sidney Hollander Colloquium, April 24 and 25, 1976.

30. Lester Salamon and Alan Abramson, *The Federal Budget and the Nonprofit Sector* (Washington, D.C.: The Urban Institute, 1982). For a more detailed analysis of this development and the consequences of voluntary agencies receiving public funds see Ralph Kramer, "Voluntary Agencies and the Personal Social Services," in *The Nonprofit Sector: A Research Handbook,* ed. Walter Powell (New Haven: Yale University Press, 1987), pp. 240–57.

31. Richard Titmuss, *The Gift Relationship* (New York: Pantheon, 1971), is a classic comparison of commercial and voluntary blood bank systems. For a critique, see Harvey Sapolsky and Stan Finkelstein, "Blood Policy Revisited—A New Look at the Gift Relationship," *The Public Interest* 40 (Winter 1977), pp. 15–29.

32. Kenneth Wooden, *Weeping in the Playtime of Others* (New York: McGraw-Hill, 1976).

33. Theodore R. Marmor, Mark Schlesinger, and Richard W. Smithey, "A New Look at Nonprofits: Health Care Policy in a Competitive Age," *Yale Journal on Regulation,* 3:2 (Spring 1986), p. 334.

34. H. Birnbaum, C. Bishop, A. Lee, and G. Jensen, "Why Do Nursing Home Costs Vary? The Determinants of Nursing Home Costs," *Medical Care,* 19 (1981), p. 1097.

35. Ken Judge and Martin Knapp, "Efficiency in the Production of Welfare: The Public and Private Sectors Compared," in *The Future of Welfare,* eds. Rudolf Klein and Michael O'Higgins (Oxford: Basil Blackwell, 1985), pp. 130–49.

36. Marmor et al., "Nonprofits: Health Care Policy"; Lenard Kaye, Abraham Monk, and Howard Litwin, "Community Monitoring of Nursing Home Care: Proprietary and Nonprofit Association Perspectives," *Journal of Social Service Research,* 7:3 (Spring 1984), pp. 5–7.

37. Myron Fottler, Howard Smith, and William James, "Profits and Patient Care Quality in Nursing Homes: Are They Compatible?" *The Gerontologist,* 21:5 (October 1981), pp. 532–38.

38. Burton Weisbrod, *The Nonprofit Economy* (Cambridge, Ma.: Harvard University Press, 1988), pp. 142–59.

39. Ibid.; Kaye et al., "Monitoring Nursing Home Care."

40. Judge and Knapp, "Efficiency in the Production of Welfare," pp. 141–46.

41. Moreland Commission, "Reimbursing Operating Costs: Dollars Without Sense," Report of the New York Moreland Act Commission on Nursing Homes and Residential Facilities, March 1976.

42. Mary Mendelsohn, *Tender Loving Greed* (New York: Knopf, 1974).

43. C. R. Bergstrand, "Big Profits in Private Hospitals," *Social Policy,* 13 (Fall 1982), pp. 49–54, and J. Michael Watt, Robert Derzon, Steven Renn, Carl Schramm, James Hahn, and George Pillari, "The Comparative Economic Performance of Investor-Owned Chain and Not-For-Profit Hospitals," *The New England Journal of Medicine,* 314 (January 9, 1986), pp. 89–96. Watt et al. suggest that the investor-owned chains may employ a price strategy of setting competitive rates for the more visible "room and board" services while charging higher fees for the ancillary services that are less easy to compare among hospitals.

44. Marmor et al., "Nonprofits: Health Care Policy," pp. 334–35.

45. Regina Herzlinger and William Krasker, "Who Profits From Non-Profit?" *Harvard Business Review,* January–February, 1987.

46. "Review and Outlook: Medical Benefits," *Wall Street Journal,* June 12, 1986, p. 26.

47. See, for example, Rosabeth M. Kanter, "The Measurement of Organizational Effectiveness, Productivity, Performance, and Success: Issues and Dilemmas in Service and Nonprofit Organizations," Program on Nonprofit Organization Working Paper 8, Institute for Social and Policy Studies, Yale University, 1979; Gilbert, *Capitalism and Welfare State,* pp. 28–29.

48. This discussion is a revised and expanded version of material presented by Neil Gilbert, "The Commercialization of Social Welfare," *Journal of Applied Behavioral Science,* 21:4 (1985), pp. 371–72; and idem, *Capitalism and Welfare State,* pp. 18–20.

49. For a probing analysis of this development, see John DiIulio, Jr., "What's Wrong with Private Prisons," *The Public Interest* (Summer 1988), pp. 66–89. Also see Ed Bean, "Private Jails in Bay County, Florida, Makes Inroads for Corrections Firms, But the Jury Is Still Out," *Wall Street Journal,* August 29, 1986, p. 34; "Prisons for Profit," *Wall Street Journal,* February 5, 1987, p. 22.

50. Susan Rose-Ackerman, "Social Services and the Market," *Columbia Law Review,* 83:6 (1983), pp. 1405–38.

51. Mimi Abramovitz, "The Privatization of the Welfare State: A Review," *Social Work,* 31:4 (July–August 1986), pp. 261–62; Marmor et al., "Nonprofits: Health Care Policy."

52. Sheila Kamerman and Alfred J. Kahn, "Universalism and Income Testing in Family Policy: New perspectives on an Old Debate," *Social Work,* 32:4 (July–August 1987), p. 279.

53. Office of Management and Budget, *Budget of the United States Government, Special Analysis, FY 1988* (Washington, D.C.: U.S. Government Printing Office, 1987), p. G-35.

54. Alan Carlson, "What Happened to the 'Family Wage'? *The Public Interest,* 83 (Spring 1986), pp. 3–17; Sheldon Danziger, Irwin Garfinkel, and Robert Haveman, "Poverty, Welfare, and Earnings: A New Approach," *Challenge,* 22:4 (September–October 1979), pp. 28–34; Paul Terrell, "Taxing the Poor," *Social Service Review,* 60:2 (June 1986), pp. 272–86.

55. Alvin Schorr, *Common Decency: Domestic Policies After Reagan* (New Haven, Conn.: Yale University Press, 1986), pp. 79–113.

# 3

# *Personal Social Services: Caring for Profit*

The personal social services encompass a range of activities designed to assist those in need of care, advice, protection, and comfort. From World War II until recently, with few exceptions these services were delivered to low-income persons and addressed needs often neglected by the market economy. The delivery of services was conducted outside normal family, economic, and business channels by a variety of non-commercial entities—religious, secular nonprofit, and public—staffed by professional social service workers rather than by entrepreneurs. In some areas, such as homemaker services and counseling, a parallel commercial marketplace did exist, which served those who could afford to pay the going rate for these services. In these cases, no transfers were involved and the services were considered as normal market purchases rather than as social welfare provisions. Thus, most middle-class households had little consumer contact with the personal social services, although through voluntary associations many donated time and money to their support.

All this began to change in the mid-1960s. As previously noted (Chapter 2), the decline of family and other institutional supports made the middle class more vulnerable to an increased need for personal social services and less able to pay for whatever parallel services may exist in the private sector. At the same time, the production and delivery of personal social services were transformed by three significant developments: a shift in the balance of federal and state responsibility, the movement of profit-oriented providers into personal care activities, and the spread of tax-subsidized personal social services into the workplace.

## Changing Balance of Federal and State Responsibility

Personal social services are financed through direct public expenditures, tax expenditures in the areas of day care and employee benefits, and voluntary contributions to philanthropic causes. Direct public expenditures form the bulk of this support, which comes from the federal government and is divided among a number of programs engaged in the delivery of personal social services. These programs were initially funded through categorical grants, a method of financing that restricts the use of funds to specific activities under detailed conditions that afford a high degree of federal control over expenditures. In the early 1970s, President Nixon sought to reverse the flow of power from states and local communities to Washington, D.C., by consolidating discrete categorical programs into large block grants that gave states and localities greater authority in deciding how the funds should be used. Between 1971 and 1983, nine block grants were established containing fifty-seven categorical grant programs.[1] These grants include social services, low-income home energy assistance, community services, alcohol–drug abuse and mental health, preventative health and health services, maternal and child health, elementary and secondary education, community development, and job training. With a few exceptions, such as services financed by the Older Americans Act of 1965, the block grants encompass the main body of direct public expenditures for personal social services. Although many of these grants support different types of personal care activities, the Social Services Block Grant is the largest and most important source of financing for personal care services. The evolution of this grant illustrates some of the features of service provision that were gained and lost in the shift from federal to state responsibility.

The Social Services Block Grant emerged from the consolidation of four categorical grants for personal social services that were originally affiliated with public assistance programs. It represents the culmination of several fundamental revisions in the financing, regulation, and delivery of social services. These changes were brought about through two major legislative initiatives, which advanced the new federalism of the Nixon and Reagan administrations. First, in 1974 social service provisions initially financed through four public assistance categories (Title I, IV-A, X, and XIV of the Social Security Act) were consolidated into a single grant program under Title XX of the Social Security Act. Unlike the open-ended categorical approach to social service funding under the public assistance titles, the Title XX program introduced a formula for federal social service allotments that was strictly based on the size of state populations. While each state was thus entitled to a proportionate share of Title XX funds (which totaled $2.5 billion in 1975), the receipt of these funds was contingent upon meeting certain federal regulations and supplying local matching funds for social services that equaled 25 percent of the state's federal grant. Federal regulations governing the Title XX program included liberal eligibility criteria, program expenditure and recipient reporting requirements, broad standards for citizen participation in local planning, and a stipulation that 50 percent of the federal contribution to program funds be devoted to services for the poor.[2]

These limited regulations gave the states considerably more latitude in the planning and delivery of social services than they experienced under the previous categorical system in which benefits were restricted to the blind, disabled, elderly, and female-headed families who were on public assistance or likely to be so in the near future. Eligibility for services was extended, for example, beyond the poor and near-poor groups to include many middle-class recipients. These services were often provided without charge. Sometimes they were partially subsidized using a sliding scale of income-related fees.

As eligibility expanded so did the range of social service activities that were federally financed. Each state could offer whatever services were deemed appropriate for local needs as long as they addressed one of the five Title XX goals. But these goals were so broadly formulated that they allowed for almost any activity that social service planners might devise. In the first year, the fifty state plans specified a total of 1313 services, which were grouped into forty-one categories for purposes of tabulation and analyses by federal agencies.[3] The wide range of activities covered by these service categories is shown in Table 3.1.

*Table 3.1.* Title XX Service Categories and Delivery by Number of States, 1975

| Services | Number of States Delivering Service |
|---|---|
| Adoption Services | 40 |
| Case Management Services | 10 |
| Chore Services | 34 |
| Counseling Services | 38 |
| Day Care | |
|   Adults | 34 |
|   Children | 51 |
|   Various | 5 |
| Diagnostic and Evaluative Services | 11 |
| Educational and Training Services | 43 |
| Emergency Services | 14 |
| Employment-Related Medical Services | 28 |
| Employment Services | 37 |
| Family Planning | 49 |
| Foster Care | |
|   Adults | 23 |
|   Children | 29 |
|   Various | 16 |
| Health-Related Services | 43 |
| Home delivered and Congregate Meals | 26 |
| Homemaker Services | 46 |
| Home Management | 41 |
| Housing Improvement | 42 |
| Information and Referral | 14 |
| Legal Services | 27 |
| Placement Services | 22 |
| Protective Services | |
|   Adults | 33 |
|   Children | 35 |
|   Various | 16 |
| Recreational Services | 20 |
| Residential Care and Treatment | 22 |
| Unmarried Parents Services | 14 |
| Socialization Services | 19 |
| Special Services | |
|   Alcohol and Drug | 9 |
|   Blind | 6 |

(*continued*)

*Table 3.1.  (Continued)*

| Services | Number of States Delivering Service |
|---|---|
| Children and Youth | 6 |
| Disabled | 7 |
| Juvenile Delinquents | 9 |
| Transitional Services | 3 |
| Transportation | 47 |
| Vocational Rehabilitation | 27 |
| WIN Medical Exam | 26 |
| Other | 13 |

*Source*: U.S. Department of Health, Education and Welfare, *Social Services U.S.A.* (Washington, D.C.: U.S. Government Printing Office, 1976), p. 5.

From one perspective, the shifting balance of federal to state responsibility under the Title XX program could be seen as a propitious development.[4] The allocation of federal grants on a population basis spreads social service funds in a way that promotes a rough form of interstate equalization. While this arrangement for financing services was not especially sensitive to the greater needs of poorer states, the ''50 percent restriction'' ensured that at least half of the federal funds would be spent on poor people within each state. More importantly, the loosening of federal regulations presented states with an opportunity to design creative responses to the diverse needs for social care in their communities. At the same time, Title XX sustained a degree of federal responsibility that brought some order to the diversity of state efforts and created a broad framework within which a coherent system of personal social services might evolve.

In sum, while the reorganization of services under Title XX represented a large step in the movement toward decentralization, it retained some important elements of central control. On the face of it, this reform offered reasonable promise for the development of a nationwide social service network that would be flexible and responsive to local needs, yet centrally monitored and guided by principles of equity and concern for the disadvantaged.

The second major legislative influence on the institutional framework for social services followed the passage of the Omnibus Budget Reconciliation Act (OBRA) of 1981, which replaced the Title XX program with the Social Services Block Grant. This reform exemplified the Reagan administration's more radical approach to decentralization and the new federalism. Most of the basic federal regulations governing the framework of social services under Title XX were eliminated in the Social Services Block Grant, including the 25 percent state revenue match, the "50 percent restriction" concerning services for the poor, the eligibility criteria, and program reporting requirements. With regard to the latter, only a minimal requirement for reporting an annual preexpenditure plan was maintained.

The abandonment of federal regulatory authority gave the states considerable administrative and planning discretion over the social services. At the same time, however, federal funding for social services was reduced. Under OBRA, the $3.0 billion in the FY 1982 federal budget authority for social services was reduced to $2.4 billion, with proposed increases to $2.5 billion in FY 1983, $2.6 billion in FY 1984, and $2.7 billion in FY 1985 and each year thereafter. Although the actual budget outlays were somewhat higher than planned ($2.6 billion for FY 1983, $2.8 billion for FY 1984, and an estimated $2.8 billion for FY 1985), they were still less than the FY 1980 allocation of $2.9 billion, and significantly short of that amount when adjusted for inflation. Thus, with the implementation of the Social Services Block Grant, the states gained substantial authority to administer social service provisions, but they had to exercise this authority to accommodate a shrinking pool of federal resources. As shown in Table 3.2, between 1980 and 1986 federal outlays for all personal social services decreased by 23 percent after adjusting for inflation. To some extent, this reduction was

*Table 3.2.* Estimated Changes in Federal Outlays for Social Welfare Programs Based on Constant FY 1980 Dollars

| Social Welfare | Percentage Change 1980–1986 | Projected Percentage Change 1980–1989 |
|---|---|---|
| Education and Research | −18 | −35 |
| Health Care (All) | +20 | +25 |
| Income Assistance | +10 | + 3 |
| Employment and Training | −63 | −73 |
| Community Development | −35 | −66 |
| Personal Social Services | −23 | −37 |

*Source*: Adapted from Alan Abramson and Lester Salamon, *The Nonprofit Sector and the New Federal Budget* (Washington, D.C. :The Urban Institute, 1986), Tables 5 and 7.

offset by shuffling certain social services into the category of health care, for which expenditures increased by 20 percent during this period.

Several strategies were employed by states to compensate for the reduction in funding that accompanied the Social Services Block Grant. As just indicated, one major approach was to transfer social service costs into other federal programs, such as Low Income Home Energy Assistance and Medicaid, which were financed on an open-ended basis. In addition, an increasing proportion of social service expenditures were shouldered by state and local government. Thus, between 1981 and 1983 contributions from state and local sources rose from 49 percent to 54 percent of social service expenditures.[5] Finally, access to social services was reduced through the development of stricter eligibility criteria, the lengthening of waiting lists, and the increased use of client copayments and fees to finance part of the service costs.[6] In this case, then, the decentralization of administrative authority has been closely linked to the increasing decentralization of financing social services.

In a country as large and diverse as the United States, the impact of the block grant program obviously must vary. Social services are not on the decline everywhere. Indeed, 15 percent of the states surveyed by the General Accounting Office (GAO) in 1984 reported an increase in social service expenditures between 1981 and 1983, after controlling for inflation. Although a few states have the resources and politically liberal inclinations to expand or improve their service offerings under the Social Services Block Grant, the overall thrust of this program has undermined the development of a national personal social service system. In reducing federal financial support and abandoning federal regulatory authority for social services, the Social Services Block Grant has diminished the fiscal capacity and fragmented the administrative structure of the nationwide social service network that was starting to take shape under the Title XX program.

A national system of personal social services that is broadly equitable while responsive to diverse local needs requires a delicate balance between the degree of local autonomy and central guidance in its administrative structure. In financing such a system, a thoughtful division of responsibility between federal and state units can enhance both the sense of national purpose and the desire for local flexibility. The elimination of uniform and comprehensive reporting measures under the block grant program limits any assessment of the equitable distribution and responsiveness of social services from a national perspective. As it stands, the Social Services Block Grant provides neither the regulatory balance nor the division of financial responsibility conducive to building a coherent nationwide social service network.

## Public Finance, Private Delivery

As block grants fostered the decentralization of administrative authority for personal social services, responsibility for the delivery of these services became more dispersed. Private agencies entered what was previously, to a large extent, the realm of public activity. This occurred through the use of purchase-of-service arrangements, which authorized public agencies to contract with service providers in the private sector. Opportunities for purchase of services from private agencies were broached in the 1967 amendments to the Social Security Act and expanded significantly under Title XX, which allowed private agency donations to qualify as part of the state's local 25 percent matching share of social service grants.

Since the mid-1960s there has been an enormous growth in the systematic use of public funds to purchase services delivered by profit-oriented and nonprofit agencies in the private sector. The precise magnitude of these purchase-of-service arrangements under Title XX cannot be gleaned from existing data. However, as noted in Chapter 2, by 1980 federal funds provided about 50 percent of all the financial support that went to nonprofit social service agencies in the private sector. In addition to direct funding through purchase-of-service arrangements, these agencies also benefited from indirect public subsidies in the form of tax expenditures for charitable donations, which, as noted in Chapter 1, amounted to $14 billion in 1985. Only a portion of these funds are attributable to the support of personal social services, however; the rest goes to voluntary agencies providing health, education, cultural, research, and community services.

Although information on purchase-of-services arrangements with profit-oriented providers is fragmented, available evidence points to substantial growth of commercial interests in certain areas of personal care. This growth has occurred, in part, by classifying various types of personal care as health services, which allows for reimbursement under the open-ended financing of Medicare and Medicaid. Thus, for example, many mental health, substance abuse, disability, family planning, and illness-related services are effectively classified and reimbursed under the health care rubric (discussed in Chapter 6). Beyond the personal social services pressed into health care categories, there are several areas such as transportation, meals-on-wheels, and employment training in which profit-oriented agencies have developed a lively presence and others in which they have gained a major share of the market. Approximately 35 percent of nongovernment social service establishments operate for profit.[7]

Child welfare is one of the areas in which profit-oriented agencies maintain a substantial presence. In 1983 approximately 250,000 children were living in substitute-care arrangements. Close to 25 percent of this population (or 62,500 children) were placed in residential care, institutional treatment, and group home settings.[8] According to a national survey sponsored by the U. S. Children's Bureau in the late 1970s, among these out-of-home child placement settings, 35 percent of residential treatment, 24 percent of institutional care, and 28 percent of group home care services were purchased under contract with for-profit firms. Indeed, the overall pattern of purchase contracts for these three types of service reveals that profit-oriented agencies were used as vendors more often than were either voluntary/nonprofit agencies or public agencies.[9]

Of the other children in substitute-care arrangements, about 70 percent live with foster parents who receive financial assistance from public agencies for this service. As early as the 1860s, states contracted with foster parents for the "boarding out" of young children (as distinguished from the system of "placing out" under which the child's labor was exchanged for their board and care, usually on farms).[10] Foster parents today tend to be poorer and less educated than the general population; a number of them receive AFDC. The question is often raised: Is foster care a form of commercial activity or a voluntary altruistic service? The answer depends to a large extent on whether foster care payments offer financial gain to private service providers or barely reimburse them for a child's board and care expense. It is an issue that may be argued reasonably on each side, because both outcomes are possible. Payments vary substantially among states as well as within states according to the foster child's age and health status. Between 1982 and 1985, during which the Consumer Price Index rose 11.4 percent, the average monthly foster care reimbursement rate increased by 24 percent, climbing from $206 to $256. Payments ranged from the rock-bottom $121 a month in West Virginia to a top monthly rate of $548 in Alaska and Oregon.[11] There are also large differences among foster parents in both the generosity of care and the personal resources they bring to this service. Some estimates suggest that foster parents indeed subsidize the state's out-of-home placement service.[12] However, in states such as Oregon and California, which offer generous support payments, a foster parent on AFDC who takes in several children may derive a net income supplement from this activity. According to the American Public Welfare Association, the foster parent role should be professionalized with providers being paid for their services as a regular form of employment rather than a reimbursement of expenses for a voluntary public service activity.[13]

The commercialization of personal care activities previously performed on a voluntary basis is not without precedent. During the last decade the British have been offering limited financial remuneration— more than symbolic reward, but less than a minimum wage—to "volunteers" providing care to the elderly.[14] At a higher level of compensation, one of their foster care services for disturbed adolescent children pays a stipend equal to about $4000 a year in addition to the normal reimbursement for room and board.[15] Even parenting of adopted children, perhaps the most intimate of personal care activities, is increasingly being subsidized by state funds. In the United States, since 1976, programs of financial assistance for the adoption of hard-to-place children and for children adopted by foster parents have spread from forty-two to all fifty states and the District of Columbia. In Britain, the introduction of adoption subsidies was initially quite controversial and was seen by many as contradicting the essential nature of parental responsibility. The Children Act of 1975 allowed for the payment of adoption subsidies, but it was not until 1982 that this policy was put into effect by the British authorities.[16]

Among the personal social services perceived as operating outside the health-related categories (examined in Chapter 6), profit-oriented providers are most firmly embedded in the area of day care for children; this market is large and rapidly expanding. Before housewives entered the labor force, day-care services for most children were needed only sporadically and were provided by family and friends. Between 1960 and 1985, the rate of participation in the labor force for married women with children under six years of age rose from 19 percent to 53 percent; most of these women have full-time work. It is common knowledge that working women rate child care as one of their most worrisome concerns, creating practical problems, stress, and heavy expense. Demand for day care is augmented not only by more mothers working, but also an increasing proportion of families who have come to rely on out-of-home care services. Although in 1965 only 8.2 percent of the preschool children of working mothers attended day-care centers, in 1977 this proportion had almost doubled to 14.7 percent and climbed to 25 percent by 1985, representing 1.9 million preschool-aged children.[17]

Estimates of the number of organized-care facilities vary according to the size and operational characteristics included in the definition of day-care centers. The number of centers serving thirteen or more children and open at least twenty-five hours a week most of the year expanded fourfold from 4400 in 1960 to 18,300 in 1977, at which time profit-oriented firms had enrolled 37 percent of all children attending these facilities and accounted for 41 percent of all centers.[18] According to a less restrictive definition, the number of nongovernmental day-care facilities increased from 24,813 in 1977 to 30,762 in 1982 with profit-oriented providers accounting for about 58 percent of the centers.[19] These figures exclude numerous "mom and pop," out-of-home baby-sitting, and public school-related operations, which substantially increase the volume of service. The most liberal estimate puts the number of day-care facilities at 235,000 in 1986.[20]

Child care services are supported by a blend of public and private financing, which illustrates the way social and economic markets intermingle through several forms of public subsidy and private consumer spending. Costs range from about $2000 for the unexceptional to $9000 for high-quality care with the majority of parents paying about $3000 per year.[21] (In Sweden the network of state-financed day care costs on the average $10,000 a year per child for services provided by trained staff with a ratio of two adults for every five children under three years old in well-equipped facilities.)[22] The major source of funds comes from working mothers, who spent $11.1 billion on child care arrangements in 1984.[23] During that year, this private financing was partially subsidized by indirect public expenditures, specifically the estimated $1.8 billion in federal child care tax expenditures, plus approximately $100 million in state tax credits.[24] In addition, direct government expenditures accounted for another $1 billion, which was allocated through the Social Services Block Grant and state supplements. Direct public expenditures are likely to increase as "workfare" reform established by the Family Support Act of 1988 pays the costs of child care for welfare mothers required to participate in job training and employment programs.[25] Drawing on these various sources, a day-care center can receive payments from families, some of whom are charged the full costs of tuition but are reimbursed up to $720 (30 percent of $2400 allowable) for one child through federal tax credits; others are charged only partial tuition on an income-based sliding scale with the deficit made up through public funds from the Social Service Block Grant, and still other families receive a free fully subsidized service.

As with financing, child care services are delivered through a mix of public and private arrangements. Profit-oriented providers operating small-scale to medium-scale establishments supply a major portion of these services. While large corporate chains account for only 5 percent of the child care industry, they seem poised to gain an increasing share of this market. The largest corporate provider is Kinder-Care Inc., which was established in 1970. Between 1980 and 1987, this chain expanded from 700 to 1100 "learning centers," with projected earnings in 1987 of $44 million.[26] Other major corporate providers include Children's World and Rocking Horse Child Care Centers of America.[27]

Despite recent expansion in this area, Susan Rose-Ackerman suggests that corporate chains are unlikely to dominate the child care industry because of the fundamental economics of day-care services. Caring for young children is a labor-intensive activity, the quality of which depends more on daily interactions between workers and children than on measures that might benefit from economies of scale such as preparation of food and purchase of equipment. Nevertheless, these secondary measures play some role in consumer assessment of day care. Corporate providers could establish brand name recognition linked to a reputation for quality in regard to food, physical facilities, and the like. Also, the market for corporate providers appears on the brink of significant growth, fueled by the expansion of employer-subsidized day care. Large business firms seeking to provide these services for their employees are likely to get more attractive package deals from corporate chains than from independent day-care centers. However, direct contracting for services is not the only way to include provisions for child care in employee benefit schemes. Firms can also issue vouchers for use by employees in day-care facilities of their choice, in which case small local providers close to employees' homes might gain the market advantage.[28]

There are many unresolved problems in the delivery of child care service relating to quality and cost. Children in day-care centers are more susceptible to illnesses ranging from diarrhea and flu to hepatitis and other life-threatening diseases. Hair-raising reports of child abuse at day-care centers drive up insurance rates and heighten parental anxiety for their children's safety. Staff turnover in child care is the highest of any industry, amounting to 42 percent annually. Wages, as one might gather from the turnover rates, are remarkably low, averaging about $9000 per year. Even child care workers with professional degrees and extensive experience are poorly paid, fewer than 50 percent get health benefits, and fewer than 20 percent have a retirement plan.[29] It is an industry marked by the predominance of small-scale nonprofessional providers, which does not easily lend itself to regulation. Many small-scale centers are unlicensed, uninsured, and substandard. The growth of corporate child care providers facilitates regulation because it is simpler for government to deal with one chain that operates 1000 centers than with 1000 independent establishments. However, stringent regulations usually increase costs, while the link between regulation and quality is difficult to assess.

## The "Caring Workplace"

The provision of personal social services in the workplace opens another line of interaction between the social and economic markets of welfare capitalism. Since the 1970s, these services have become an increasingly popular component of employee fringe benefits. By 1983 the nonwage compensation for employment averaged nearly 20 percent of the annual wages in all domestic industries, rising to 24 percent in manufacturing and 34 percent in communications.[30] When paid time off is added to nonwage compensation, the average fringe benefits increased from 24.7 percent in 1965 to 37.7 percent in 1985.[31] Fringe benefits form a significant part of employee compensation, but their cash value is not treated as earned income for tax purposes. Thus, the portion of these private benefits that would be paid in taxes if they were treated as earned income is being subsidized through public tax expenditures.

In 1985, this partial subsidy for employee health-related benefits amounted to a tax expenditure of $21.2 billion (a much larger sum went to subsidize private pensions, discussed in Chapter 4). Most of these funds go to basic medical insurance and health care. However, a relatively small but growing amount supports employee assistance programs (EAPs), which deliver a variety of health-related social services, such as drug and alcohol abuse treatment, information and referral, family counseling, psychotherapy, and other activities to promote mental health. The growth rate of these programs is apparent from various surveys, which estimate that 2000 EAPs were established between 1972 and 1978, increasing to 5000 by 1980 and to 8000 by 1982.[32]

Initially EAPs were focused on the treatment of alcoholism and drug abuse. In recent years a broader service orientation has emerged.[33] The Economic Recovery Act of 1981 permitted the inclusion of subsidized day care in the employee's package of untaxed fringe benefits. Day-care benefits are gaining considerable support as employers come to realize their value as "loss leaders" in luring employees and cementing their commitments to the workplace. In 1987 about 3000 employers provided some type of child care assistance compared to 400 in 1982.[34] While a small number of employers directly sponsor centers at the site of employment, the more usual pattern of delivery involves contracting out with independent providers or directly subsidizing employees who select the provider of their choice.[35] Employer-sponsored centers at the site of employment operate in 150–550 companies, according to different estimates.[36]

Day care is an area in which public regulation can be used to stimulate private transfers from commercial firms. For example, the San Francisco City Board of Supervisors passed a law requiring developers constructing 50,000 square feet or more of downtown office space to build a child care facility on the property or to pay $1 per square foot into a child care fund. As with most subsidies from profit-making firms, the impact of this "transfer" is difficult to trace because developers are more likely to pass the costs on to firms renting the office space than to absorb it through reduction of profit. It is hard to determine the extent to which those costs are then directly passed on further down the line to employees whose children use the day-care facilities.

The emergence of the workplace as a center for the delivery of personal social services in the 1980s has drawn both praise and criticism. Some who support this trend would go beyond indirect public subsidy through tax expenditure and have federal grants for services awarded directly to private businesses. Robert Reich, one of the most influential voices for this idea, urges government and business to enter into a partnership aimed at integrating social welfare provisions and economic development. According to Reich's proposal, public funds for a range of personal social services would be allocated to businesses, eliminating the government bureaucracies that presently administer these programs.[37] Joined in this way to private enterprise, the personal social services would be seen as contributing to the formation of human capital and fostering productivity. This is certainly the strongest attraction of delivering personal social services through private channels, because it confers on welfare activities the legitimacy and value of a productive force promoting growth in the market economy.

Despite the obvious benefits, proposals to concentrate the delivery of personal social services in the "caring workplace" raise some unsettling questions.[38] As the delivery of services increases, employees are bound to become more dependent upon the workplace for meeting both economic and social care needs. The looming embrace of industrial paternalism can impart a benevolent hug or a suffocating grip on the work force. On this point, labor's experience in "company towns" during the initial stage of welfare capitalism is not entirely encouraging.[39] A degree of worker independence might be secured by schemes for employee participation in company decisions; however, experience to date with democratic management in the United States remains sketchy and inconclusive. A healthy skepticism is in order. Where democratic management has been tried, the record is not always clear about whether management was practicing employee participation or manipulation.[40]

There is also the question of what happens to those who are outside of the labor force. Who will care for the frail and seriously disabled? What agencies will address the needs of single parents who might want to stay home and care for their infants rather than have them raised in an industry-sponsored day-care center? According to Reich's proposal, some public agencies would continue to deliver services outside the workplace for special groups such as the severely handicapped. But how might these groups fare in the competition for social service resources against the organized constituencies of industrial-based programs? In a system that directs the delivery of personal social services toward the promotion of human capital, those with limited potential for productive contribution are unlikely to rate a high priority for assistance whatever the depth of their needs.

Finally, the ultimate question remains, to what extent is the "caring workplace" an oxymoron? There is a felicitous congruence of social and economic objectives when services designed to enhance employee well-being lead to improved productivity and profit. This is not always the case, though; employers may find it more beneficial to discharge high-risk workers who are identified through enrollment in drug and alcohol treatment programs, than to run the danger of their continued employment, particularly when worker responsibilities involve operating expensive machinery, dealing with sensitive materials, or protecting human lives. Historically, the relationship between management objectives and personal care has had its trying moments. At the turn of the twentieth century, numerous companies employed what were then called "welfare secretaries" to counsel, advise, and otherwise assist employees.[41] By the 1930s these industrial social workers had vanished from the scene with many of their functions being incorporated into the emerging profession of personnel management.[42] The evolution from welfare secretary to personnel management suggests that in the early days of welfare capitalism, when strains developed between concerns for employee well-being and the productivity of the work force, the latter ultimately prevailed. With the contemporary revival of social services in the workplace these strains are bound to reappear.[43]

## Shaping Demand and Supply

The growth of day-care services embodies, perhaps, the most dramatic expression of the commercialization of the social market. With the large-scale shift of housewives' labor from the home to the market economy, the daily care of children has been transformed from an interaction vested in familial benevolence to a commercial exchange. Many influences have contributed to this development; some of the most important are the women's movement, sexual liberation, market need for an expanding labor force, the extended length of education, heightened expectations, and an historically unprecedented level of divorce. Since the mid-1960s government has responded to the increasing need for day care through direct and indirect expenditures amounting to $2.8 billion in 1984 plus the subsidized portion of day-care services received as employee fringe benefits for which a dollar figure is unavailable.

To acknowledge that public subsidies did not create the need for day care is not to say that they exercise no influence on the emerging demand. Although social welfare policy initiatives rarely provide an inceptive force for social change, they may influence in varying degrees the speed and direction of change. The degree to which public subsidies shape family choices between day care and home care depends, in part, on whether this spending serves as an economic support in response to family needs or as a financial incentive to shift labor from the household to the job market. It is a question of the state assisting people to do what they must versus encouraging them to do what they might. In the case of day-care provisions, both of these forces are operating at the same time through different transfer mechanisms. About $1 billion in federal and state funds under the Social Services Block Grant, for example, are spent on day-care services that go mainly to low-income and moderate-income families. Among this group are many single-parent and poor families for whom the mother's employment is a matter of economic necessity. Public subsidies enable these families to bridge the gap between low wages and the relatively high cost of day care.

Compared to direct service expenditures, almost $2 billion in federal and state subsidies for day care are distributed to families indirectly through tax expenditures. This mechanism allows families earning more than $28,000 in adjusted gross income to claim a day-care credit of up to $960 for two or more children. The credit rises to $1440 for those with adjusted gross incomes of $10,000 or less (but to qualify for the 30 percent maximum credit they must commit $4800 or almost half their income for child care expenses). The precise impact of these subsidies is difficult to determine. Senator Edward Kennedy has suggested that the child care tax credit offers an important work incentive for women.[44] Although the degree to which the $960 maximum tax credit for middle-income and upper-income groups encourages day-care use is probably limited, the direction of influence is clearly in favor of increased demand.

But economic inducements are neither the only nor, perhaps, the strongest line of influence through which day-care credits shape demands for this service. There is a normative message about parenting conveyed by federal policy that, regardless of income, taxes parents who look after their own children at a higher rate than those who employ others to provide this care. This message says that the nonwage activities of parental care are of less personal and social value than paid employment and commercial purchase of child care service (even if the paid employment involves caring for other people's children). It is a message that ignores the socially useful work of family care at home and lends the full sanction of public policy in support of changing the delivery of child care services from a familial transfer to a commercial exchange. Under tax credits for day care, the normative influences of public policy intermingle with modest financial incentives, forming a circuit in which the provision of benefits is conducive to greater demand from the middle classes.

Another influence on the demand for personal social services, as well as other welfare benefits, involves the availability of professional assistance in the form of legal and tax advice. In the highly complex system of modern welfare capitalism, these previously nonessential advice-giving services take on a growing importance that has yet to be fully recognized.

Since 1977, when a Supreme Court ruling permitted lawyers to advertise, the development of low-cost, high-volume legal clinics and prepaid legal services has made legal assistance accessible to low-income and middle-income groups in dealing with welfare-related matters such as adoption, divorce mediation, child custody and support, social security entitlements, and landlord–tenant relations. But many people still find these services too costly, which often prevents them from exercising their full rights to social welfare benefits. In response to this situation, several observers have called for the substantial deregulation of legal practice whereby paralegals, for example, might prepare basic forms and handle elementary legal matters that do not require three years of law school training. The lower cost of these services would not only increase their availability to the poor, but also generate greater demand for other social provisions.[45]

On the supply side of personal social services, the commercialization of the social market has led to the expansion of private practice among social workers, the group most closely affiliated with a variety of personal care services. Private practice was discouraged by social work organizations in the early part of the twentieth century, when fee-for-service activities and the profit motive were seen as somewhat inimical to social work's philanthropic heritage.[46] By the mid-1960s, however, private practice began to look more inviting as the prospects for reimbursement of social work services through third-party vendor payments opened a viable market for individual practitioners. In 1964, private practice received official support from the National Association of Social Workers (NASW) in a position statement noting that "the National Association of Social Workers recognizes private practice as a legitimate area of social work, but affirms that practice in socially sponsored organizational structures must remain the primary avenue for the implementation of the goals of the profession."[47] This was a curious statement, because it endorsed private practice and urged its containment in the same breath.

An interesting sidelight on the commercialization of personal social services is revealed in social workers' beliefs concerning the therapeutic value of fee-for-service payments by clients. A study of 236 social workers in thirty-one voluntary family service agencies covering ten states reports that almost two-thirds of those surveyed "believed that clients who pay fees tend to have better treatment outcomes than clients who do not pay fees and that fees have more therapeutic value when clients view them as requiring some financial sacrifice."[48] Along the same lines, a nationwide study of family service agencies found that even after controlling for the clients' social class, social workers rated those who paid for services as having more favorable outcomes than those who were served without charge. When clients rated their own change, however, no relationship was found between payment of fees and outcome (suggesting that the effects of fees on treatment may be perceived as more beneficial by those who profit from this practice than by those who pay for it).[49] Social workers' beliefs concerning the salutary effects of client involvement in the fee-for-service transaction raise some questions about the therapeutic consequences of third-party payments under public and private insurance schemes most often used for reimbursement of private practitioners.

Despite the equivocation of NASW's 1964 endorsement and the presumed therapeutic impediment of third-party payment, the movement toward private practice has continued apace. Indeed, by the late 1980s the equivocal endorsement of the NASW had transformed into a warm embrace. The extent to which the commercial ethic has penetrated social work activities is revealed in a report on marketing in the profession's national newsletter:[50]

> A Madison Avenue concept is working its way into social workers' consciousness. Marketing, along with its business school vocabulary once seemed alien to social work and its tradition of service in public agencies. But as more social workers go into private practice, and as competition

between them and other mental health professionals heats up, marketing becomes a necessary survival tool.

While estimates vary as to the number of social workers in private practice, a 1982 survey of 56,000 NASW members indicates that 12 percent reported employment under profit-motivated auspices, mainly in private practice. That was almost a fourfold increase over the 3.3 percent reporting similar employment in a 1972 survey.[51] Findings from Massachusetts show that 45 percent of the 4400 licensed independent clinical social workers (LICSW)—the highest of four levels of licensed social workers in that state—were engaged in private practice on a full-time (19 percent) or part-time (26 percent) basis.[52] The NASW and Massachusetts surveys suggest that on the supply side of personal social services there has been an accelerated movement into private practice, a movement that has attracted the most experienced and highly qualified practitioners.

Who is served by the private practitioners? The Massachusetts survey reveals that social workers in private practice tend to serve fewer low-income and minority clients than those in agency-based practice.[53] Although one study does not make a decisive case, these findings suggest an eventual decline in the degree and quality of professional social services available to the poor and disadvantaged minorities. The lure of private practice may leave public and voluntary agencies with an increasing proportion of nonprofessionals, and inexperienced professionals to deliver services in the social market. Ultimately, this trend points toward the emergence of a two-tiered social service system under which the most qualified professionals serve the comparatively affluent in private settings. The increasing provision of social services in the workplace supplies an additional thrust to movement in this direction.

Nevertheless, the future course of personal social services remains uncertain.[54] The business sector could lose interest in social welfare activity, as it did during the 1930s, when the Great Depression caused industry to jettison social welfare provisions. Profit-oriented agencies may find it difficult to penetrate farther into the social market as third-party contracts become more demanding and focus on hard-to-serve populations. The move toward private practice by social welfare professionals may encounter stiffening resistance from psychiatrists, psychologists, and others seeking to protect their service domains in the private sector. These developments would reverse recent trends and invest the public sector with greater responsibility for the delivery of personal social services.

At the moment, however, a revival of the "liberal" welfare system characterized by a high degree of public responsibility for the production and delivery of social services does not appear imminent. The most plausible scenario depicts the delivery of social services proceeding on a course of incremental privatization. Profit-motivated providers will likely continue to penetrate the social market, and the movement toward private practice will continue to bring social work professionals into the private sector. Although government will undoubtedly remain the main source for financing personal social services, the production and delivery of these services will be increasingly delegated to the private sector through purchase-of-service arrangements and the provision of benefits in the form of vouchers redeemable on the economic market.

This course of events will promote decentralization of social service production and delivery, leading to heightened competition among public, nonprofit, and profit-oriented providers of service. In that event, those controlling governmental funds are likely to place greater demands on social service providers to justify expenditures through careful measurement of what is done and the results of these efforts. Along this line, concern has already been expressed, for example, in the 1985 Coordinated Discretionary Funds Program of the Office of Human Development Services, which called for demonstration projects "to increase productivity and efficiency in the use of purchase of service resources by use of performance contracting with individual private practitioners rather than with other public or nonprofit agencies."[55] These demonstration projects are to be evaluated through comparisons of their costs and outcomes with those of public services.

Efforts of this kind may lead to greater efficiency in the production and delivery of social services. But agencies under pressure to measure what they do tend to do only those things they can measure—particularly tasks on which they score well. The drive for efficiency can thus lead to undervaluation of the qualitative, often hard-to-measure components of personal social services.[56]

It is difficult to assess precisely the extent to which the trends toward decentralization, competition, efficiency, profit, and greater consumer choice will affect the supply and quality of personal social services. One can see clearly, however, that these developments will make the delivery system resemble that of the economic market more closely than heretofore.

# Notes

1. George Peterson et al., *The Reagan Block Grants* (Washington, D.C.: The Urban Institute, 1986), p. 6.

2. For a detailed analysis of these changes, see Neil Gilbert, "The Transformation of Social Services," *Social Service Review,* 51:4 (December 1977).

3. U.S. Department of Health, Education and Welfare, Social and Rehabilitation Service, *Social Services U.S.A., Oct.–Dec. 1975* (Washington, D.C.: U.S. Government Printing Office, 1976).

4. This discussion draws on material from Neil Gilbert, "The Reorganization of Social Services: Trends in Finance and Regulation," *Policy Notes* (Fall 1985).

5. General Accounting Office, *States Use Several Strategies to Cope with Funding Reductions under Social Services Block Grant,* Comptroller General's Report to Congress, GAO/HRD-84-68, August 9, 1984.

6. David Lindeman and Alan Pardini, "Social Services for the Elderly," in *Fiscal Austerity and Aging: Shifting Governmental Responsibility for the Elderly,* eds. Carroll Estes and Robert Newcomer (Beverly Hills, Calif.: Sage Publishing, 1983).

7. U.S. Bureau of the Census, *Statistical Abstract of the United States, 1986* (Washington, D.C.: U.S. Government Printing Office, 1985), p. 384.

8. Theodore Stein, S. V. "Foster Care for Children," in *Encyclopedia of Social Work,* 18th edition (Silver Springs, Md.: National Association of Social Workers, 1987), p. 640.

9. Catherine Born, "Proprietary Firms and Child Welfare Services: Patterns and Implications," *Child Welfare* (March–April 1983), p. 112.

10. James Leiby, *A History of Social Service and Social Work in the United States* (New York: Columbia University Press, 1978), pp. 144–45.

11. Raymond Collins, "Foster Care Rates: Trends and Implications," *Washington Social Legislation Bulletin* (August 24, 1987), pp. 61–63.

12. Alan R. Gruber, *Children in Foster Care: Destitute, Neglected . . . Betrayed* (New York: Human Sciences Press, 1978), pp. 171–72; Theodore Stein, *Social Work Practice in Child Welfare* (Englewood Cliffs, N.J.: Prentice-Hall, 1981), pp. 77–78.

13. American Public Welfare Association, *Standards for Foster Family Service Systems* (Washington, D.C.: APWA, 1975).

14. Neil Gilbert, *Capitalism and the Welfare State* (New Haven, Conn.: Yale University Press, 1983), p. 126.

15. Roger Hadley and Stephen Hatch, *Social Welfare and the Failure of the State* (London: Allen and Unwin, 1981), p. 138.

16. Malcolm Hill, "Payments for Adopted Children—Right or Wrong?" *Journal of Social Policy,* 16:4 (October 1987), pp. 461–88.

17. Susan Rose-Ackerman, "Unintended Consequences: Regulating the Quality of Subsidized Day Care," *Journal of Policy Analysis and Management,* 3:1 (1983), p. 15; "Census Bureau Reports on Child Care Arrangements, Winter 1984–85," *Washington Social Legislation Bulletin,* 30:12 (June 27, 1987), p. 46.

18. U.S. Bureau of the Census, *Statistical Abstract of the United States, 1981* (Washington, D.C.: U.S. Government Printing Office, 1981), p. 348.

19. Ibid.; and idem, *Statistical Abstract, 1986,* p. 384.

20. This figure is estimated by the National Association for the Education of Young

Children, cited in Jeanne Saddler, "Low Pay, High Turnover Plague Day-Care Industry," *Wall Street Journal*, February 2, 1987, p. 25.

21. Helen Blank and Amy Wilkins, *Child Care: Whose Priority?* (Washington, D.C.: Children's Defense Fund, 1985), p. 3. A report from the Census Bureau indicates that $38 was the median weekly expenditure for 5.3 million women who paid for child care services in 1984–1985.

22. For a discussion of the Swedish experience, see Neil Gilbert, "Sweden's Disturbing Family Trends," *Wall Street Journal*, June 24, 1987, p. 23.

23. "Census Bureau Reports on Child Care, 1984–85," p. 46.

24. The $1.8 billion federal tax expenditure includes day care for both children and the elderly, but the main body of these funds goes to child care. State tax expenditures are estimated from figures presented in Blank and Wilkins, *Child Care: Whose Priority?*, pp. 239–40.

25. For an analysis of the workfare reforms see David Kirp, "Poverty, Welfare and Workfare," *The Public Interest*, 83 (Spring 1986), pp. 34–48. Sponsored by Senator Moynihan, the Family Support Act of 1988 (P.L. 100–485) revises the Aid to Families with Dependent Children program along several lines which include: a) requiring AFDC recipients with children over three years old to enroll in the job opportunities program and b) providing child care services and Medicaid coverage for a period of 12 months after a family is no longer eligible to receive AFDC support.

26. "Day-Care Chains Gain Ground in a Mom-and-Pop Industry," *Wall Street Journal*, December 5, 1986, p. 1; *Wall Street Journal*, March, 19, 1987, p. 43.

27. For a general discussion of the "corporatization" of day care see David Stoesz, "Corporate Welfare: The Third Stage of Welfare in the United States," *Social Work*, 31:4 (July–August 1986), pp. 257–63.

28. Rose-Ackerman, "Unintended Consequences: Regulating Day Care."

29. Saddler, "Low Pay, High Turnover."

30. U.S. Bureau of the Census, *Statistical Abstract, 1986*, p. 416.

31. Cited in *Wall Street Journal*, July 31, 1987, p. 17.

32. The estimate for 1978 is reported by William Sonnenstukl and James E. O'Donnell, "EAPs: The Why's and How's of Planning Them," *Personnel Management* (November 1980), pp. 35–38; for 1980 by James T. Wrich, *The Employee Assistance Program* (Center City, Minn.: Hazelden, revised edition 1980); for 1982 by Paul Roman, "Pitfalls of 'Program' Concepts in the Development and Maintenance of Employee Assistance Programs," *Urban and Social Change Review*, 16:1 (Winter 1983), pp. 9–12.

33. Paul Kurzman, S. V. "Industrial Social Work," in *Encyclopedia of Social Work*, 18th edition (Silver Springs, Md.: National Association of Social Workers, 1987), pp. 899–910.

34. "How Government, Business Are Getting Involved," *San Francisco Chronicle*, June 19, 1986, p. 48.

35. There is also a salary reduction scheme whereby employees' salaries are reduced by the cost of day-care services, for which they receive compensation by a separate check, thereby lowering the earned income on which they pay taxes.

36. The estimate of 150 is given by Cathy Trost, "Child-Care Center at Virginia Firm Boosts Worker Morale and Loyalty," *Wall Street Journal*, February 12, 1987, p. 25; the figure of 550 is reported by Deborah Fallows, *A Mother's Work* (Boston: Houghton-Mifflin, 1985), p. 173.

37. Robert Reich, *The Next American Frontier* (New York: Time Books, 1983), p. 247.

38. See, for example, Neil Gilbert, "The Welfare State Adrift," *Social Work,* 31:4 (July–August 1986), pp. 254–55.

39. Company towns were not all as disagreeable as the impression that they generally invoke. For a balanced assessment of company towns and the initial stages of welfare capitalism, see Stuart Brandes, *American Welfare Capitalism 1880–1940* (Chicago: University of Chicago Press, 1970).

40. William Gomberg, "The Trouble with Democratic Management," *Trans-action* (July–August 1966), pp. 30–34.

41. Philip R. Popple, "Social Work Practice in Business and Industry, 1875–1930," *Social Service Review,* 55 (June 1981), p. 260.

42. Cyril Ling, *The Management of Personnel Relations: History and Origins* (Homewood, Ill.: Richard D. Irwin, 1965).

43. Gilbert, *Capitalism and Welfare State,* pp. 25–26.

44. Cited in Allan C. Carlson, "What Happened to the 'Family Wage'?" *The Public Interest,* 83 (Spring 1986), p. 13.

45. See, for example, W. Clark Durant III, "End the Cartel: Let Non-Lawyers Do Legal Work," *Wall Street Journal,* August 23, 1987, p. 16.

46. David Hardcastle, "The Profession: Professional Organizations, Licensing, and Private Practice," in *Handbook of the Social Services,* eds. Neil Gilbert and Harry Specht (Englewood Cliffs, N.J.: Prentice-Hall, 1981), pp. 683–85.

47. National Association of Social Workers, *Handbook on the Private Practice of Social Work* (Washington, D.C.: National Association of Social Workers, 1974), p. 40.

48. Mary Block and Hiasaura Rubenstein, "Paying for Service: What Do Clinical Social Workers Believe?" *Journal of Social Service Research,* 9:4 (Summer 1986), pp. 21–35.

49. D. Beck and M. Jones, *Progress on Family Problems* (New York: Family Service Association of America, 1973).

50. "Marketing: A Lifeline for Private Practice," *NASW News,* 32:9 (October 1987), p. 5.

51. "Membership Survey Shows Practice Shifts," *NASW News,* 28:10 (November 1983).

52. Thomas McGuire, Arnold Gurin, Linda Frisman, Victor Kane, and Barbara Shatkin, "Vendorship and Social Work in Massachusetts," *Social Service Review,* 58:3 (September 1984), pp. 372–83.

53. Ibid.

54. This discussion of future prospects is adopted from Neil Gilbert, "The Commercialization of Social Welfare," *Journal of Applied Behavioral Science,* 21:4 (1985), pp. 373–75.

55. *Federal Register,* 49:165 (August 23, 1984), p. 33535.

56. See, for example, Gilbert, *Capitalism and Welfare State,* pp. 28–29.

# 4

# *Income Maintenance:*
# *Indirect Methods*
# *and Private Obligations*

Welfare transfers in the form of housing, education, health care, and personal social services subsidize the consumption of resources that, for the most part, would otherwise require expenditures of personal income. Thus, all social welfare transfers contribute to income support in the sense that a dollar value may be assigned to benefits whether they are provided in cash or in kind.

While there is no comprehensive accounting for the income value of all noncash benefits, in the early 1980s the Census Bureau began to count the dollar value of several major in-kind transfers in measuring the rate of poverty. What benefits to include and the actual value of these in-kind transfers are open to interpretation. In current practice, three approaches are employed to estimate the cash value of food, housing, and medical benefits. The "market approach" equates the value of benefits to their purchase price in the private market. The "recipient" or "cash equivalent" approach equates the value of benefits to the amount of cash that would make the recipient "as well off" as the in-kind transfer, which reflects more what the beneficiary would be willing to pay for the benefit than its price in the private market. The "poverty budget share" approach limits the value of in-kind transfers to the proportions of income spent on these benefits by poor people in 1960–1961, when in-kind transfers were minimal.[1] When the cash value of in-kind transfer is added to income, estimates of poverty in 1985 drop from 14 percent to between 9.1 and 12.8 percent, depending upon which approach is used and the type of benefits included.[2]

Although the dollar value of in-kind transfers is becoming more evident, the function of income maintenance remains associated primarily with a range of direct and indirect measures that provide benefits in the form of cash. The purpose of these benefits is to compensate for the lack of income resulting from disability, retirement, death, illness, and unemployment. During the last few decades direct cash transfers have accounted for an increasing proportion of personal income. Between 1970 and 1985, for example, as the overall share of personal income derived from wage and salary disbursements declined from 66.3 percent to 59.3 percent, the proportion attributed to transfer payments increased from 10.3 percent to 14.7 percent.[3]

The major income maintenance programs providing direct cash transfers include Social Security, Supplemental Security Income (SSI), General Assistance, Aid to Families with Dependent Children (AFDC), Unemployment Compensation, Railroad Workers, Coal Miners, Public Employee Retirement and Disability schemes, and Veterans Pensions and Compensation. In 1984, federal and state expenditures on these programs totaled about $344 billion, excluding Medicare and Medicaid, which involve third-party payments for services.[4]

In critically examining this list of major income maintenance programs that provide cash transfers, one might argue that occupational retirement plans for public employees should be excluded on the grounds that because they are similar to private employer-sponsored pensions, these public plans represent more a condition of employment negotiated in the labor–wage exchange than a social transfer. Indeed, government employer-sponsored pensions fall into a gray area. Although in some respects they are similar to private plans, in other important features these public schemes resemble mandatory social security arrangements, with which they are currently in the process of being combined (a development that will be discussed later in this chapter). Also, some analysts consider food stamps and housing vouchers as, in effect, so close to direct cash transfers that they should be included among the income maintenance programs. A report by the Office of Management and Budget (OMB), for example, notes that food stamps "are so nearly the equivalent of cash that their exclusion from income subject to tax might be considered to result in a tax expenditure."[5] Although food stamps and housing vouchers are not counted as direct cash transfers in this chapter, if their dollar value were added to income maintenance expenditures, the 1984 total would increase by approximately $20 billion.

Public outlays for income maintenance are by and large a federal responsibility. States contribute significantly to unemployment compensation, general assistance, AFDC, and worker's compensation programs; however, more than 80 percent of all the direct cash transfers are financed by the federal government. Direct federal expenditures for income maintenance increased more than tenfold between 1965 and 1988, from $30.5 billion to $327 billion. The steepest rise occurred during the first half of the period when outlays climbed from 4.3 percent to 7.1 percent of the GNP. By 1975, income maintenance programs accounted for 34.3 percent of all federal outlays. During the decade from the mid-1970s to 1986 the rate of growth leveled off, and by 1988 the relative cost of income maintenance programs declined slightly to 6.9 percent of the GNP and to 31.9 percent of all federal outlays (see Table 4.1).

## Growth of Indirect Provisions

Cash outlays account for only a part of the federal contribution to income maintenance. As with health, housing, and social service transfers, indirect expenditures substantially augment direct public allocations for income maintenance.

In general, indirect measures have grown over the last decade, in both the number of tax preferences allowed and the size of the revenue losses sustained by tax spending. Tax expenditures, however, are not a recent fiscal invention. Although it is only since 1974 that systematic analyses of tax expenditure data were introduced as a regular component of the president's annual budget, the use of the tax code as a mechanism for indirect financing of various provisions goes back almost to the inception of federal income taxes in 1909. By 1913 the federal law incorporated twelve tax expenditure items. The number of tax expenditures increased to thirty-seven by 1940; during the next thirty years the number almost doubled to seventy-one items. Since

*Table 4.1.* Direct Federal Outlays for Income Maintenance, 1965–1988ᵃ

| Income Maintenance Program Categories | 1965 | 1975 | 1980 | 1986 | 1988 (est.) |
|---|---|---|---|---|---|
| Railroad and Coal Miners Retirement Disability | 668 | 4,689 | 5,083 | 5,330 | 5,396 |
| Federal Employee Retirement and Disability | 2,858 | 13,222 | 26,594 | 41,363 | 42,905 |
| Unemployment Compensation | 2,570 | 13,459 | 18,623 | 17,753 | 17,677 |
| Social Securityᵇ | 17,460 | 64,658 | 118,547 | 198,757 | 219,388 |
| Veterans Pensions and Compensation | 4,215 | 7,860 | 11,688 | 15,031 | 15,248 |
| Other Income Securityᶜ | 2,828 | 10,088 | 17,191 | 24,364 | 26,776 |
| TOTAL | 30,599 | 113,976 | 197,726 | 302,598 | 327,390 |
| Percentage of GNP | 4.3 | 7.1 | 7.2 | 7.3 | 6.9 |
| Percentage of Total Federal Outlays | 25.9 | 34.3 | 33.4 | 31.9 | 31.9 |

ᵃGiven in millions of dollars.

ᵇExcluding Medicare.

ᶜIncludes: SSI, AFDC, Refugee Assistance, Earned Income Tax Credit, and Low Income Home Energy Assistance.

*Sources*: Office of Management and Budget, *Budget of the United States Government, 1988, Historical Tables*, (Washington, D.C.: U.S. Government Printing Office, 1987), Tables 3.3, 6.1, and 11.1; U.S. Bureau of the Census, *Statistical Abstract of the United States, 1987* (Washington, D.C.: U.S. Government Printing Office, 1986), Table 698.

1970 the growth has accelerated, with tax expenditure provisions rising by another 50 percent, to a peak of 104 items in 1982. This figure will slowly to decline to an estimated ninety-four items by 1988.[6]

Between 75 and 80 percent of federal tax expenditures benefit individual taxpayers, the remainder going to corporations. Although corporations have received a smaller absolute share of the tax expenditure dollar, from 1980 to 1986 their benefits as a proportion of corporate tax revenues were considerably higher than the benefits to individuals relative to the income tax revenues collected from them. In 1983, for example, total tax expenditures for individuals equaled 72.4 percent of the federal receipts from individual income taxes, while corporate tax expenditures came to 173 percent of corporate tax revenues. The relative advantage of corporate tax expenditure, however, was eliminated in the 1986 Tax Reform Act. Estimates for 1987 and 1988 suggest that in the future tax expenditures will proportionately favor individuals over corporate taxpayers.[7]

Tax expenditures serving individuals reach a huge number of people. Of the approximately 97 million taxpayers who filed federal returns in 1983, for example, more than 22 million took advantage of the home mortgage interest deduction and almost 50 million benefited from the exclusion of private pension contributions.[8] These benefits are distributed among a broad range of income classes. Although high-income groups, as might be expected, profit more from tax expenditures than those in the lower income brackets, the distribution is only skewed to a moderate degree in favor of the wealthy; however, when these benefits are assessed in light of tax liabilities, the distribution of tax expenditures is found to be proportional to the taxes paid by various income classes.[9]

Among tax expenditures for individuals, a substantial portion of the provisions are expressly related to income maintenance. Between 1978 and 1986 these indirect supports for income maintenance increased almost fourfold from $24.8 billion to $96.3 billion. By 1988 these tax expenditures for income maintenance will decline to an estimated $79.7 billion, which still represents a 222 percent growth over the last decade (see Table 4.2). The enormous rise in tax spending for income maintenance from 1978 to 1986 was due to a combination of influences, including the development of new tax preferences and expansion of existing provisions, inflationary forces that pushed taxpayers into higher brackets, and a growth in the number of taxpayers, that enlarged the financial base for individual benefits. The anticipated decline in tax expenditures is a result of the Tax Reform Act of 1986, which cut the number of tax preferences and substantially reduced the marginal tax rates against which the revenue loss estimates of most tax expenditures are calculated.

Examining the growth of tax expenditures for income maintenance in comparison to direct federal outlays in this area reveals the importance of indirect transfers relative to direct measures and recent trends in this relationship. In 1978, tax expenditures amounted to 16.3 percent of the direct federal outlays for income maintenance, but by 1986 this proportion had nearly doubled to 31.8 percent. It is expected to drop to 24.3 percent by 1988 (see Table 4.2). As these figures illustrate, tax expenditures represent a large share of the social welfare transfers for income maintenance, one that has grown significantly since the late 1970s.

*Table 4.2.* Indirect Federal Expenditures for Income Maintenance, 1978–1988[a]

| | 1978 | 1980 | 1986 | 1988 (est.) |
|---|---|---|---|---|
| **Exclusion** | | | | |
| Railroad Retirement Benefits | 275 | 320 | 450 | 250 |
| Workmen's Compensation | 835 | 2,200 | 2,425 | 2,365 |
| Public Assistance | 350 | 390 | 580 | 360 |
| Disabled Miner's Benefits | 50 | 90 | 145 | 120 |
| Unemployment Insurance Benefits | 2,090 | 3,350 | 1,085 | — |
| Disability Pensions | 130 | 170 | 120 | 105 |
| **Net Exclusion of Pension Contributions and Earnings** | | | | |
| Employer Plans | 9,940 | 19,785 | 48,950 | 43,365 |
| Individual Retirement Accounts | — | — | 14,890 | 9,080 |
| Keoghs and Other Self-Employed | 1,650 | 1,765 | 2,135 | 1,500 |
| **Exclusion of Other Employee Benefits** | | | | |
| Group Life Insurance Premiums | 840 | 1,675 | 2,200 | 1,955 |
| Accident and Disability Insurance Premiums | 75 | 95 | 130 | 120 |
| Income of Supplementary Unemployment Benefit Trusts | 10 | 15 | 30 | 20 |
| Additional Exemption for the Blind | 25 | 30 | 35 | — |
| Additional Deduction for the Blind | — | — | — | 10 |
| Additional Exemption for Elderly | 1,350 | 2,040 | 2,750 | — |
| Additional Deduction for Elderly | — | — | — | 1,150 |
| Tax Credit for Elderly and Disabled | 170 | 130 | 105 | 85 |
| Earned Income Credit[b] | 285 | 720 | 590 | 855 |
| **Exclusion of Social Security Benefits** | | | | |
| Disability Insurance Benefits | 515 | 690 | 1,195 | 1,055 |
| OASI Benefits for Retired Workers | 4,635 | 6,890 | 13,275 | 12,200 |
| Benefits for Dependents and Survivors | 730 | 1,015 | 3,905 | 3,580 |
| Exclusion of Veterans Pensions and Compensation | 840 | 1,140 | 1,895 | 1,540 |
| **TOTAL** | 24,795 | 42,510 | 96,300 | 79,715 |
| Percentage of Total Direct Federal Outlays for Income Maintenance | 16.3 | 21.5 | 31.8 | 24.3 |

[a]Given in milions of dollars.

[b]This figure indicates the effect of the earned income tax credit on receipts, not on cash payments made when the credit exceeds a wage earner's tax liability.

*Sources*: U.S. Bureau of the Census, *Statistical Abstract of the United States, 1981* (Washington, D.C.: U.S. Government Printing Office, 1980), Table 433; and Office of Management and Budget, *Special Analyses: Budget of the United States Government, 1988* (Washington, D.C.: U.S. Government Printing Office, 1987), Table G-2; and Office of Management and Budget, *Historical Tables: Budget of the United States Government 1988*, (Washington, D.C.: U.S. Government Printing Office, 1987).

As indirect transfers for income maintenance have increased faster than direct outlays, certain categories of tax expenditures have grown more rapidly than others. Among the various categories, exclusions for private retirement plans experienced the swiftest rate of growth, soaring from $11.6 billion in 1978 to $66 billion in 1986. Between 1980 and 1986, the amount of tax expenditure in support of private pensions went from 18 percent to 33 percent of the cost of direct federal outlays for public pensions under social security. These figures reveal an important development in the changing balance between public and private provisions for income maintenance: the use of indirect public transfers to encourage the privatization of social insurance.

### Retirement Income: The Public/Private Balance

While tax expenditures for private pensions have increased more rapidly than direct federal outlays for social security, the latter have also experienced substantial growth. Indeed, the social security program has gone from providing 3 percent of all cash income for those over sixty-five in 1950 to 39 percent of all the income for this age group in 1984.[10] Such coverage, of course, entails a tremendous expenditure. By 1986 the cost of Old Age, Survivors, and Disability Insurance (OASDI) had climbed to $198.8 billion (more than $270 billion if Medicare is added), which was almost *250 times* the $784 million spent on these social security programs in 1950.

In the 1980s, the staggering costs of social security benefits coupled with the impending demands on the system from the unusually large cohort of baby boom retirees have raised serious doubts about the future viability of social security. One estimate suggests a potential deficit of $1 trillion if commitments to baby boom retirees are to be met in line with current program standards.[11] Several measures to restore the solvency of the social security trust fund were initiated under the Social Security amendments of 1983. The combined employer–employee social security tax rate was scheduled to increase from 13.3 percent to 15.3 percent by 1990, and the taxable-earnings base was to increase from $29,700 to $50,100 by 1990. The normal retirement age was increased to sixty-seven for those who become sixty-two between 2017 and 2022; finally, an income tax on social security benefits was introduced for retirees whose adjusted gross income plus half their benefits exceeds $25,000 if single and $32,000 if married. These and other cost-conscious measures apparently revived the fiscal integrity of OASDI for the near future.[12]

Beyond the next thirty years, when the baby boom generation reaches the age of retirement, the picture is unclear and generally less encouraging. What the long-range future holds is ultimately a matter of speculation. Actuarial estimates indicate that from the 1990s to the 2020s the OASDI program will experience a period of growing reserves; thereafter a period of continuing deficits is projected through 2060. Whether deficits and reserves will balance each other out during the next seventy years depends on the assumptions one uses to inform long-range forecasting.[13] While the forecasts for OASDI are variable, when the price of Medicare benefits are included, predictions about the long-term overall costs of social security are not encouraging.

Although the 1983 amendments brought social security costs and receipts into greater balance, the program has come under a cloud of uncertainty. In view of the Reagan administration's interests in reducing the role of the state, apprehensions about the future of social security quite naturally evoke thoughts about the privatization of retirement income. Three broad lines of action through which government may promote the privatization of social security involve benefit erosion, supplementation of alternative plans, and regulation. Measures that bring about benefit erosion include the failure to index pensions to the rate of inflation or to real advances in living standards, restrictions on eligibility, and increasing tax liability on benefits. When the public benefits of social insurance leave private wants unsatisfied, a "market vacuum" is generated which private enterprise abhors. Thus, one approach to privatization is simply to allow any needs for increases in retirement income to be filled over time by private schemes.[14] In contrast to the stick of necessity, the carrot of financial incentives such as tax deductions and tax credits opens another road to privatization. In this approach, individuals are encouraged to enroll voluntarily in private retirement plans, the cost of which are reduced by government supplementation. Finally, through its regulatory powers, government may promote privatization by making private insurance compulsory for individuals (as in the case of automobile insurance in some states) or by requiring employers to assume this responsibility.

Both in the United States and abroad, privatization of social security has become a topic of increasing controversy.[15] In Britain, for example,

a two-tier pension system has evolved that encourages private arrangements. The first tier requires participation in a public scheme, which
pays a benefit resembling a minimum income more than a return on
contributions. In contrast, the second-tier benefits are linked closely to
contributions. Private employers may contract their employees out of
the public second-tier pension and into a private plan as long as its
benefits are equivalent to or better than those provided under the public
scheme. This layered system was launched in 1978 as a political com-
promise endorsed by both the Conservative and Labour parties. By
1983, more than 45 percent of British workers had contracted out of the
public system and into private plans at the second tier.[16]

In the United States, among various schemes proposed to substitute
private programs for mandatory participation in social security, the
Family Security Plan set forth by the Heritage Foundation has stimulated
the most serious debate. This plan would allow workers and employers
over time to reduce their social security payments and increase tax-
exempt contributions to individual retirement accounts until private
schemes replaced the social security pension. Upon retirement, workers
inadequately covered by private arrangements would become eligible to
participate in the means-tested Supplemental Security Income program.[17]

Tax expenditures for private pensions are usually divided into three
categories: employer-sponsored plans, employee-initiated individual retirement accounts (IRAs), and Keogh plans for the self-employed. The
vast majority of workers covered by private schemes come under employer-sponsored group plans, of which there are two basic types. The
"defined-benefit plan" provides a specified pension at retirement, usually a certain percentage of the employee's salary based on years of
service. The "defined-contribution plan" provides a variable benefit
that is based on contributions, market performance, and investment
returns. During the decade from 1974 to 1984, the number of private
employer-sponsored pensions virtually doubled, from 400,000 to
795,000 with defined-contribution plans accounting for 70 percent of
the total.[18]

The Economic Tax Recovery Act of 1981 lent momentum to the
privatization of social security by extending eligibility for tax-exempt
IRAs to all wage earners. This allowed workers, even those covered by
employer-sponsored pension plans, to contribute up to $2000 in pretax
income to an IRA. At the same time, the tax-exempt contribution limit

to the Keogh retirement plan for the self-employed was raised from $7500 to $15,000. In both IRA and Keogh accounts, interest is allowed to accumulate tax free until the money is withdrawn, when it would be taxed at lower rates due to the reduction of income accompanying retirement. As private schemes were being supplemented through these tax expenditures, the introduction of cost-cutting measures such as raising the normal age of retirement, taxing social security benefits, and increasing the rates of contribution served to erode the ultimate value of public provisions.

However, the tax incentives for IRA and Keogh plans were soon to be reduced. In a sweeping overhaul of the federal tax system, the Tax Reform Act of 1986 took some air out of the sails of the privatization movement. Under this act, IRA deductions can no longer be taken if a worker or his spouse is enrolled in employer-provided retirement plans or if a couple's adjusted gross income is more than $50,000 ($35,000 for individual taxpayers). The Tax Reform Act also places tighter limits on Keogh accounts; more generally, by reducing the marginal tax rates, the act lowered the tax savings that might be achieved by IRAs, Keoghs, and private employer-sponsored pensions.

It is highly improbable that social security will be scrapped in favor of private pensions in the foreseeable future. Practically speaking, the issue of privatization is essentially one of degree. In many, if not most, developed nations, the retirement income available to elderly people involves a mix of public and private provisions. The mix, of course, varies. In Sweden where the state's commanding role in social welfare enjoys widespread public support, statutory social security benefits account for approximately 90 percent of the total spending on pensions; in Germany the figure is about 83 percent, and in England it drops to about 50 percent.[19] The remainder of spending on pensions in these countries comes from individual insurance plans and occupational retirement schemes.

A substantial number of public employees in the United States and abroad are enrolled in occupational retirement plans, which are partially financed by their employers—national and local units of government. Whereas these occupational provisions for government workers are not "private" in a literal sense, in their diversity they resemble the private exchange of fringe benefits for labor negotiated between employer and employee in the economic market more than the standardized publicly mandated transfers under universal social security programs. This diversity stems, in part, from the needs and bargaining strengths of particular occupational groups. In their general characteristics, however, government employer-sponsored pension plans resemble the social security program in several important features; to wit, they are fully indexed for inflation, involve mandatory employer and employee contributions, and often operate on a pay-as-you-go basis.[20]

The structure of government employer-sponsored schemes is in the process of significant revision. Originally, the Civil Service Retirement System (CSRS), which covers almost all federal employees, and many of the state and local government pension plans were designed to provide complete retirement income benefits that substituted for social security. In 1982 the vast majority of participants in CSRS and 57 percent of those in state and local plans were not covered by social security. Among the efforts to firm up the shaky social security system, the 1983 Social Security amendments prevented public pension schemes from opting out of social security. With public employees hired after 1985 now required to contribute to social security, new pension schemes are emerging that involve the fusion of government employer-sponsored plans and social security.[21]

In the United States, the balance between social security and private pensions is shifting. Whereas social security will continue to be the main source of retirement income for, at least, the immediate future, occupational pensions and individual plans have made rapid progress in this realm of income maintenance. Between 1962 and 1978, pension benefits grew from 9 percent to 14 percent of all cash income for persons aged sixty-five and over.[22] By 1983, 64 percent of the non-agricultural wage and salary workers aged forty-five to sixty-four were covered by occupational pension plans, and 33 percent of those in this age group had IRAs. Between 1970 and 1985 the combined assets of public and private pensions rose from $239 billion to $1.7 trillion, with the 750 percent growth rate of private funds somewhat higher than the 650 percent rate for public funds.[23] Although the overall trend has been one of significant expansion since the 1960s, more recently the growth rates for the number of private pensions show a decline from a peak annual rate of 11.5 percent in 1981 to 2.7 percent in 1984.[24]

Over the last two decades, the movement toward privatization of retirement income has been advanced by financial incentives and protective activities of the state. Social welfare transfers that derived from tax expenditures on pensions furnished the incentive, which at $66 billion in 1986 was not a trifling sum. The contingent liability assumed by the Pension Benefit Guaranty Corporation for the termination of pensions by failing companies offered private plans the financial shield of federal protection. With an expected deficit of $4.5 billion in 1987, the Pension Benefit Guaranty Corporation faces the depletion of its already inadequate reserves. During 1988, legislation was on the drawing board to strengthen that corporation's financial position by raising the premium rate charged to private pension plans.[25]

The use of indirect public expenditure to underwrite the private provision of retirement income illustrates the mechanics of one development contributing to the commercialization of social welfare. These schemes to secure support during retirement address the problems of income maintenance in old age when one has left the labor force. Income maintenance for the able-bodied younger population is an entirely different matter. In this case, the trend toward commercialization is expressed in public policies designed to reinforce the work ethic.

## Public Assistance and Private Obligations

In contrast to tax expenditures on retirement plans, which are the least visible and least controversial income maintenance transfers, direct expenditures on means-tested public assistance programs have been a highly visible source of political contention. Of the four major public assistance programs that were jointly financed by the federal and state governments—Aid to the Blind, Aid to the Permanently and Totally Disabled, Old Age Assistance, and AFDC—most disagreement has centered around AFDC.

The blind, aged, and disabled are deemed the "deserving poor." They are unable to work and cannot be held responsible for the conditions of their dependency. Under the 1972 amendments to the Social Security Act, state-administered public assistance programs for the blind, aged, and disabled were replaced by the Supplemental Security Income (SSI) program, which is financed and administered by the federal government. In part, this change reflects the fact that the federal government is rather efficient in writing checks and assuring their delivery to the appropriate addresses. It also reflects a moral consensus about the importance of these benefits and the worthiness of their recipients. This consensus reduces pressures to have the program administered by local political units that are accountable to diverse community interests.

Compared to SSI recipients, there is a cloak of moral ambiguity surrounding public regard for AFDC clients. Public sympathies run deep for the dependent children of poor single-parent families, who have become impoverished through no fault of their own. But financial support for able-bodied single parents offends the modern work ethic, particularly for parents whose children are in school most of the day. Moreover, for the large portion of these single parents whose condition of life stems from neither widowhood nor divorce, the issue of personal responsibility for the consequences of premarital relations casts a shadow on their rights to public support.

Things were not always this way under AFDC. When Aid to Dependent Children (ADC, later retitled AFDC) was established in 1935, it was conceived mainly as a protective program for widows and their children. This was a small group whom the program planners believed would shortly disappear from the public assistance rolls through absorption into the social security system under the proviso for survivors insurance. History, of course, proved the planners to be wrong. Although history affords the benefits of hindsight, from the angle of vision in 1935 it would be unseemly to fault AFDC planners for the inability to forecast the unprecedented rise in divorce and births out of wedlock that swelled the AFDC roll to its current dimensions. Indeed, in the short run, developments were not as precipitous as the trends that emerged in more recent decades. Between 1940 and 1960 the rate of birth for unmarried women was low and fairly stable, going from 3.8 percent to 5.3 percent of all births. From 1960 to 1984, however, there was a fourfold increase in these rates as they climbed from 5.3 percent to 21.0 percent of all births.[26] Over that period, teenagers accounted for almost one-half of the births to unmarried mothers.

From 1963 to 1966, AFDC rolls grew on the average of 200,000 recipients a year. Between 1966 and 1967 the growth rate accelerated to 600,000 recipients a year, and it continued climbing. In an effort to reduce the expanding relief rolls, the 1967 Social Security amendments established the Work Incentive Program (WIN). This program offered job training, work placement, and the promise of day-care services that would permit AFDC mothers the opportunity to enter the labor market. As an incentive, the first $30 of monthly earnings plus one-third of the remainder were not counted in calculating the participants' continued eligibility for relief payments. Poised behind the carrot of earnings exemptions was the stick of threatened termination of public assistance for those who refused to accept training or work without ''good cause."[27] This drive to employ welfare mothers was opposed by liberals and welfare rights activists. In practice the results of WIN were not encouraging. Of the 167,000 participants enrolled in WIN through April 1970, more than one-third had dropped out of the program and only 25,000 had gotten jobs. Those who obtained jobs were among the most qualified members of the participant pool and included a high percentage of unemployed fathers (under the AFDC Unemployed Parent option) who probably would have found employment without WIN. "Based on this conspicuously unspectacular performance," Levitan and Taggart suggest that "the wisdom of expanding WIN is questionable, and the theoretical arguments for such a move are even more dubious."[28] Similarly, after a careful assessment of the high costs of decent day-care services and work training along with the limited employment prospects of the many AFDC recipients who never graduated from high school, Steiner observes that "the more realistic approach would be to accept the need for more welfare and to reject continued fantasizing about day care and 'workfare' as miracle cures."[29]

Liberal censure of the WIN version of workfare and its generally poor showing in practice did not put this idea to rest. Two decades after the implementation of WIN, welfare reformers have kindled a startling enthusiasm for workfare programs. What is startling about this development is the breadth of its political receptivity. By the mid-1980s, with California and Massachusetts leading the way, a spate of workfare programs were generated and embraced by coalitions of liberals and conservatives.[30] These programs entail work training and job search requirements, along with the provision of day-care services and opportunities for public employment if private jobs do not pan out. In form and purpose, if not every substantive detail, they resemble the earlier WIN initiatives.

The initial evidence on workfare experiments in the mid-1980s reveals modest advances in employment and welfare savings. A comparison in five states of the behavior of experimental and control groups—AFDC recipients who were required to participate and those who were not required to participate in workfare programs—found employment gains of 3–7 percent in four of the five programs and an insignificant loss of −0.4 percent in the fifth. In all the programs, average earnings of the experimental groups were higher and average AFDC payments received were lower than those of the control groups. Although these differences were fairly consistent and in the desired directions, they were not very large. The monthly AFDC payments to the experimental groups, for example, ranged from 40 cents to $16 less than the payments to control groups. Whereas the benefits from employment gains, higher earnings, and lower welfare payments attributed to workfare schemes were modest, they were usually large enough to justify the program's costs.[31]

These positive outcomes notwithstanding, initial experiments with the 1980s version of workfare leave a number of questions unanswered. The study of five states reveals that substantial proportions (from 40 to 80 percent) of the workfare participants remained unemployed after six to fifteen months. The extent to which this type of program can ameliorate the circumstances for the socially and educationally most deficient groups of welfare recipients is highly uncertain. Whether workfare can achieve positive results in communities with very weak economic conditions is open to doubt.[32] Furthermore, where positive results are forthcoming, there is always the possibility that those already employed in low-wage jobs may be inspired to quit and go on welfare, thereby qualifying for training and other services—as demonstrated in the publicized case of a rather successful workfare graduate in Massachusetts.[33]

The most vital question, however, concerns the impact of workfare not on the AFDC mothers who enter the labor force, but on their children left to carry on in the daily absence of parental supervision. It is a question, in part, of the availability and costs of high-quality day-care services, which are in short supply and expensive to produce (as noted in Chapter 3). It is also a question of the social and psychological consequences of child care, an extremely sensitive point on which the evidence is much in dispute. Workfare programs advance nonmaternal child care arrangements as a natural, almost beneficent substitute for parental supervision, with the tacit assumption that nothing is lost in the exchange. A substantial body of research on the effects of day care supports this position with assurances such as "it typically does no harm" and "children of working mothers do as well in school as those of mothers who stay at home."[34] However, these assurances are accompanied by a host of qualifications that acknowledge the inconsistency of research findings, absence of data on long-term effects, and an inability to measure subtle characteristics. At the same time, there is a growing body of evidence that forces deliberate consideration of the possibility that full-time day care in the early years of life may increase the risk for undesirable patterns of social development.[35] There is also concern that, regardless of long-term effects, the immediate quality of daily life afforded many young children in day-care facilities rarely celebrates the joys of childhood.[36]

Despite the serious issues that remain unanswered and the limited degree of change achieved through workfare, it enjoys tremendous support, embodying what many herald as the "new public consensus" on welfare reform.[37] This consensus gave rise to the Family Support Act of 1988, which institutionalized the workfare component of AFDC, among other reforms. Political approval of this act derived less from the proven effectiveness of workfare than from a normative shift in the traditional division between household labor invested in domestic activities—such as childrearing—and paid employment in the market economy. As noted earlier (Chapter 3), the rate of employment for married women with children under six years of age more than doubled from 19 percent to 53 percent between 1960 and 1985. Half of all married mothers with infants under one year of age are employed, a 108 percent increase over the 1970 rate; projections for 1995 suggest that two out of three preschool children will have mothers in the labor force.[38]

These developments have made it awkward for even the most sympathetic welfare advocates to hold AFDC mothers exempt from the obligation to seek employment; however, a few dissenting opinions have been voiced. George Gilder, for example, argues that "by lending government authority to the idea that the mother's prime role is earning money rather than raising children, and by implying that the government is remotely competent in child-care and job creation, a national workfare scheme would subvert the foundations of both capitalism and family life."[39] Hardly known for his advocacy of welfare rights, Gilder's criticism of workfare centers on the extent to which these programs encourage a shift in the daily responsibility for childrearing from family to government. It has also been observed that the employment experiences of married mothers do not make the most convincing case for workfare. Two-paycheck families earning well above the median income typically experience difficulties in managing the daily struggles of work and childrearing. But the daily burdens of a two-wage earner family pale in comparison to those of the poor working mother in a single-parent family. Workfare has gained broad endorsement because public compassion for the unfortunate circumstances of AFDC mothers has eroded under the increasing pressures on family life that are being felt throughout the middle classes.[40]

In one sense, workfare is a program that appeared on the crest of several demographic trends: the rapid growth in size and costs of the AFDC caseload, the increasing proportions of teenagers and unwed mothers in this caseload, and the dramatic rise in the employment rates of all women with children. However, demographics tell only part of the story. Beneath these trends is a moral impetus for welfare reform that has given the movement much of its force. Where welfare was concerned, admonitions against "blaming the victim" struck a prominent chord in the zeitgeist of the 1960s. According to conventional liberal wisdom of that era, the poor were innocent casualties of capitalism. As such, they were entitled to unilateral social welfare transfers in compensation for the system's failure to provide other channels of support. Considerable emphasis came to be placed on the nature of these entitlements. And numerous studies addressed the issues: Who gets what social benefits? And are they enough?

A new set of issues about social welfare allocations came with the resurgence of popular support for capitalism in the 1980s. The focal point of concern shifted from an emphasis on recipients' social rights to their social obligations; it is to this moral reciprocity of citizenship by which "the role of the social obligations is to balance the social rights guaranteed by government" that the public attention is drawn.[41] This is quite another equation from the moral calculus of social entitlement, which weighs in variables such as "compensation" and "systemic failures." Regard for social entitlement and the reciprocity of citizenship are by no means mutually exclusive. They simply stress different moral considerations. Foremost among the social obligations of citizenship is the duty of the employable to work for their livelihood. The highly publicized "new public consensus" on welfare reform is above all a moral consensus in which the duty to earn one's way has taken precedence over parental responsibility for the daily care and supervision of children. The use of public authority to reinforce the work ethic imbues the commercialization of social welfare with a moral dimension that is deeply embedded in the American culture.

## In Support of the Working Poor

The thrust of contemporary welfare reform has aimed at making the able-bodied poor with dependent children go to work. Recent experi-

ments with unemployment insurance illustrate another approach to stim-
ulating work effort through the use of income maintenance programs.
Designed as a measure to support workers during periods of forced
idleness, unemployment benefits have been reshaped to encourage entrepreneurial activity under new schemes introduced in Britain and
France. The British Enterprise Allowance scheme pays a self-employment allowance for up to fifty-two weeks to laid-off workers who
launch their own businesses. Starting as a pilot project in 1982, this
scheme had enrolled more than 43,000 by 1984. The French *Chomeurs
Createurs* program began as an experimental project in 1979 and was
institutionalized in 1980. Under this scheme, those eligible for unemployment compensation can choose to receive their benefits in a six-
month lump sum payment as seed capital to start a business. By 1983,
more than 74,000 French citizens were participating in this program.[42]
Although unemployment insurance policies in the United States have
not incorporated these systematic efforts to promote self-employment, a
number of demonstration projects modeled on the European programs
are on the drawing boards. However, the unions are not enthusiastic
about movement in this direction, claiming that current benefits are
insufficient to meet the program's conventional objectives and should
not be tapped for other purposes.[43] In 1986, for example, only one-third
of the unemployed were receiving unemployment benefits, which in
different states replaced on the average of 28 to 45 percent of the
recipients' average weekly wages.[44]

Promoting the work ethic from the other side of the ledger, the
Earned Income Tax Credit (EITC) is a policy that combines direct and
indirect expenditures on behalf of the poor who are already employed.
Under this scheme, if a worker's tax liability is smaller than the tax
credit for which he is eligible, the difference is refunded in a cash
payment from the Internal Revenue Service. The EITC operates in some
ways as a negative income tax for the working poor with minor depen-
dents.

The negative income tax was originally conceived as a universal
program of income maintenance available to all families, but benefiting
mainly those in poverty. Attributed to both Milton Friedman and Robert
Lampman, the idea of a negative income tax gained political support in
the mid-1960s. In 1968, the New Jersey Graduated Work Incentive
Experiment was launched to study how different levels of guaranteed
payments and varying negative tax rates affected work effort over a

period of three years, using a sample of 1357 families in four sites.[45] This was the first of several federally sponsored negative income tax experiments. The Seattle–Denver Income Maintenance Experiments (SIME–DIME), initiated in 1970 with a sample of 4706 families enrolled from three to five years, was the largest and more comprehensive of the income maintenance experiments. The results of SIME–DIME were not reassuring. Findings revealed a distinct tendency toward the reduction of work effort by participating families. One estimate of the nationwide effect of this program suggests that, with a guaranteed level of support of 75 percent of the poverty line and a negative tax of 50 percent on income earned above that guaranteed level, the expected reduction in work effort would be about 6 percent for husbands, 23 percent for wives, and 7 percent for female heads of families.[46] Equally discouraging was the dramatic increase in marital dissolution among experimental families, the overall rate of which was approximately twice that of control group families.[47] Whereas many questions have been raised about the SIME–DIME findings and their long-term consequences that remain unknown, the general drift of these findings is inauspicious.[48]

At about the same time that support for the idea of a universal negative income tax was blunted by the discrepant evidence of human behavior, the EITC was introduced as a temporary measure under the Tax Reduction Act of 1975. Achieving permanent status in 1978, the EITC was initially set at 10 percent of all earnings up to $4000 (a maximum of $400), beyond which the credit decreased by 10 percent for each additional dollar earned, dropping to zero at an adjusted gross income of $8000. By 1987, the maximum credit had more than doubled to $851, or 14 percent of the first $6080 of income, and was reduced by 10 percent of earnings above $6920, providing benefits to families with income up to $15,000.[49] After 1987 these figures will be adjusted for inflation. While the maximum level of EITC benefits increased during the last ten years, the potential for refundable cash payments was further extended by the 1986 tax reforms, which raised exemptions and standard deductions thereby lowering tax liability.

The EITC is similar to negative income tax schemes originally proposed by Friedman and others in that it provides benefits through the IRS, involves extending income tax rates beyond zero to negative levels by refunding benefits in cash to those whose tax credits exceed their liabilities, and reduces benefits by a standard tax rate as income increases. It differs from the original negative income tax proposals in two important features. First, rather than being universally available, EITC benefits are extended only to those employed with dependent children. Second, instead of providing a guaranteed level of benefit that immediately declines as income increases, EITC benefits expand and contract, initially increasing with income to a maximum level beyond which they decline with additional earnings. These special features of the EITC have what might be thought of as a "pump-priming effect" on work effort, rewarding both the movement into the labor force and the initial push to raise one's level of income. In providing an incentive for low-wage workers to take a job and to seek better pay, at least up to a point, the EITC is a welfare transfer that enables the productive activities of the working poor. From another perspective, however, it may be viewed as a government subsidy in support of low-wage industry.[50]

The refundable aspect of the EITC ensures that benefits of this program will reach down to the working poor. Like the EITC, the child care tax credit is another tax-related transfer mechanism tied to work and families with children. The formula for child care tax credits is weighted to provide higher benefits to those with lower incomes; however, these benefits fail to reach workers whose incomes are so low that they incur very small, if any, tax liabilities. While it would be quite costly to make child care credits refundable, this idea for further extending benefits to the working poor has sparked political interest.[51]

Indirect expenditures that subsidize private pensions for the elderly, workfare reforms to promote employment of AFDC mothers, and refundable tax credits in support of the working poor are three arrangements that have gained an increasing role in income maintenance since the 1960s. Each of these cases lend favor to private enterprise and the work ethic. In so doing, these welfare transfers forge a link between social and economic markets that contributes to the emerging structure of modern welfare capitalism.

## Notes

1. U.S. Bureau of the Census, *Alternative Methods for Valuing Selected In-Kind Transfer Benefits and Measuring Their Effect on Poverty* Technical Paper No. 50 (Washington, D.C.: U.S. Government Printing Office, 1982).

2. U.S. Bureau of the Census, *Statistical Abstract of the United States, 1987* (Washington, D.C.: U.S. Government Printing Office, 1986), p. 446.

3. Ibid., p. 423.

4. See Table 1.1.

5. Office of Management and Budget, *Special Analysis of the Budget of the United States Government, 1982* (Washington, D.C.: U.S. Government Printing Office, 1981), p. 206.

6. Ailee Moon, "Social Welfare Financing: A Comparison of Direct and Indirect Methods," unpublished doctoral dissertation, 1989, School of Social Welfare, University of California at Berkeley, p. 90.

7. Ibid., p. 85.

8. U.S. Congress, Joint Committee on Taxation, *Estimates of Federal Tax Expenditure for Fiscal Years 1986–1990* (Washington, D.C.: U.S. Government Printing Office, 1985), pp. 23–29; U.S. Bureau of the Census, *Statistical Abstract, 1987*, p. 353.

9. John Witte, *The Politics and Development of the Federal Income Tax* (Madison: University of Wisconsin Press, 1985), pp. 299–310.

10. James Storey, "Income Security," in *The Reagan Experiment*, eds. John Palmer and Isabel Sawhill (Washington, D.C.: The Urban Institute, 1982), p. 387; U.S. Bureau of the Census, *Statistical Abstract, 1987*, pp. 344, 433.

11. Michael Boskin, *Too Many Promises: The Uncertain Future of Social Security* (New York: Dow Jones–Irwin, 1986).

12. Martha Ozawa, S.V. "Social Security," in *Encyclopedia of Social Work*, 18th edition (Silver Springs, Md.: National Association of Social Workers, 1987), pp. 644–53.

13. For an excellent, if somewhat optimistic, analysis of these assumptions see Merton Bernstein and Joan Bernstein, *Social Security: The System That Works* (New York: Basic Books, 1988), pp. 61–89. For the pessimistic view, see A. Haeworth Robertson, "The National Commission's Failure to Achieve Real Reform," *The Cato Journal*, 3:2 (Fall 1983), pp. 403–16, and Anthony Pellechio and Gordon Goodfellow, "Individual Gains and Losses from Social Security before and after the 1983 Amendments," *The Cato Journal*, 3:2 (Fall, 1983), pp. 417–42.

14. For further discussion of alternative approaches to privatization see Michael O'Higgins, "Privatization and Social Security," *Political Quarterly*, 55:2 (April 1984), pp. 129–39.

15. See, for example, Howard Glennerster, *Paying for Welfare* (Oxford: Basil Blackwell, 1985), pp. 225–30; Adam Smith Institute, *Privatising Pensions* (London: Adam Smith Institute, 1982); Stuart M. Butler, "For Services Action on Privatization," *Journal of the Institute for Socioeconomic Studies*, 10:2 (Summer 1985); Peter Ferrara, *Social Security Reform: The Family Security Plan* (Washington, D.C.: Heritage Foundation, 1982); Alvin Schorr, *Common Decency* (New Haven, Conn.: Yale University Press, 1986), pp. 50–54.

16. John Goodman, "Private Alternatives to Social Security: The Experience of Other Countries," *The Cato Journal*, 3:2 (Fall 1983), pp. 563–73.

17. Ferrara, *Social Security Reform: Family Security Plan*.

18. Emily Andrews, *The Changing Profile of Pensions in America* (Washington, D.C.: Employee Benefit Research Institute, 1985), pp. 8–27.

19. Michael O'Higgins, "Public/Private Interaction and Pension Provision," in *Public/Private Interplay in Social Protection: A Comparative Study,* eds. Martin Rein and Lee Rainwater (Armonk, N.Y.: M. E. Sharpe, 1986), pp. 99–148.

20. Andrews, *Changing Profile of Pensions,* pp. 8–27.

21. Ibid., pp. 35–40.

22. James Storey, "Income Security," p. 387.

23. U.S. Bureau of the Census, *Statistical Abstract, 1987,* pp. 353–54.

24. Andrews, *Changing Profile of Pensions,* p. 26.

25. Office of Management and Budget, *Budget of the United States, 1988* (Washington, D.C.: U.S. Government Printing Office, 1987), pp. 2–45.

26. U.S. Bureau of the Census, *Statistical Abstract, 1987,* p. 61.

27. Neil Gilbert and Harry Specht, *Dimensions of Social Welfare Policy* (Englewood Cliffs, N.J.: Prentice-Hall, 1974), pp. 34–37.

28. Sar Levitan and Robert Taggart III, *Social Experimentation and Manpower Policy: The Rhetoric and the Reality* (Baltimore: John Hopkins Press, 1971), p. 53.

29. Gilbert Steiner, *The State of Welfare* (Washington, D.C.: The Brookings Institution, 1971), p. 74.

30. See, for example, David Swoap, "Broad Support Buoys California's GAIN," *Public Welfare,* 44:1 (Winter 1986), pp. 24–32.

31. Judith Gueron, "Reforming Welfare with Work," *Public Welfare,* 45:4 (Fall 1987), pp. 13–25.

32. Ibid., pp. 24–25.

33. Mickey Kaus, "The Work Ethic State," *The New Republic,* July 7, 1986, p. 28.

34. These similar conclusions are drawn from three independent reviews of the literature: Kristen A. Moore and Sandra Hofferth, "Women and Their Children," in *The Subtle Revolution,* ed. Ralph Smith (Washington, D.C.: The Urban Institute, 1979), pp. 125–58; Barbara Heyns, "The Influence of Parents' Work on Children's School Achievement," in *Day Care: Scientific and Social Policy Issues,* eds. Edward Zigler and Edmund Gordon (Boston: Auburn House, 1982); Jacqueline Lerner and Nancy Galambos, "Child Development and Family Change: The Influences of Maternal Employment on Infants and Toddlers" in *Advances in Infancy Research,* Vol. 4, eds. Lewis Lipisitt and Carolyn Rovee-Collier (Hillsdale, N.J.: Ablex, forthcoming).

35. For a thoughtful weighing of the recent evidence, see Jay Belsky, "Infant Day Care: A Cause for Concern?" *Zero to Three,* VI:5 (September 1986); an earlier analysis leading to similar conclusions is presented in Selma Fraiberg, *Every Child's Birthright: In Defense of Mothering* (New York: Basic Books, 1977).

36. See, for example, Deborah Fallows, *A Mother's Work* (Boston: Houghton-Mifflin, 1985).

37. For the most publicized statement of this consensus, see *The New Consensus on Family and Welfare,* Working Seminar on the Family and American Welfare Policy, (Washington, D.C.: American Enterprise Institute and Milwaukee, Marquette University, 1987).

38. U.S. Congress, House of Representatives, Select Committee on Children, Youth, and Families, "Hearing Summary Child Care: Key to Employment in a Changing Economy," March 10, 1987, p. 3.

39. George Gilder, "Welfare's New Consensus," *The Public Interest* (Fall 1987), p. 21.

40. Neil Gilbert, "Caring for Children: The Unfinished Business of Welfare Reform," *Society/Transaction*, 24:3 (March–April 1987), pp. 5–11.

41. Lawrence Mead, *Beyond Entitlement: The Social Obligations of Citizenship* (New York: Basic Books, 1986), p. 246.

42. Carol Steinbach, "Eight Lessons from Europe," *The Entrepreneurial Economy*, 3:7 (January 1985), pp. 4–14.

43. Steven Galante, "One Solution for the Jobless: Make Them Business Owners," *Wall Street Journal*, November 30, 1987, p. 21.

44. Isaac Shapiro and Robert Greenstein, *Holes in the Safety Nets: National Overview* (Washington, D.C.: Center on Budget and Policy Priorities, 1988), p. 63.

45. For a history of this study and a careful analysis of its results, see Joseph Pechman and P. Michael Timpane, eds., *Work Incentives and Income Guarantees: The New Jersey Negative Income Tax Experiment* (Washington, D.C.: The Brookings Institution, 1975).

46. Michael Keeley et al., "The Labor-Supply Effects and Costs of Alternative Negative Income Tax Programs, *Journal of Human Resources*, 13:6 (Winter 1978), pp. 3–26.

47. Michael Hannan, Nancy Brandon Tuma, and Lyle Groeneveld, "Income and Marital Events: Evidence from an Income Maintenance Experiment," *American Journal of Sociology*, 82 (May 1977), pp. 1186–2110.

48. For a flavor of the critical discussion aroused by these findings, see Martin Anderson, *Welfare: The Political Economy of Welfare Reform* (Stanford, Calif.: The Hoover Institution, 1978), pp. 104–27; James Albrecht, "Negative Income Taxation and Divorce in SIME/DIME," *Journal of Socioeconomic Studies*, 4 (Autumn 1979), pp. 75–82; Robert Moffitt, "The Effect of a Negative Income Tax on Work Effort: A Summary of Experimental Results," in Paul Sommers, ed., *Welfare Reform in America: Perspectives and Prospects* (Boston: Kluwer-Nijhoff, 1982), pp. 209–229; Charles Murray, *Losing Ground: American Social Policy 1950–1980* (New York: Basic Books, 1984), pp. 147–53.

49. Office of Management and Budget, *Special Analyses: Budget of the United States Government, 1988* (Washington, D.C.: U.S. Government Printing Office, 1987), p. G-35.

50. Andrew Dobelstein, *Politics, Economics, and Public Welfare* (Englewood Cliffs, N.J.: Prentice-Hall, 1980), p. 240.

51. This approach is being advanced by the Bush administration.

# 5

## Asset Maintenance: The Special Case of Farm Welfare

American farmers have the right to all the publicly financed social welfare transfers generally available to ordinary citizens. Unlike most ordinary citizens, however, farmers have additional access to a generous range of transfers through which they are cushioned, at public expense, from a good deal of the personal risk and business viscissitudes experienced by others as a result of normal market forces. In contrast to traditional social welfare benefits, public aid to farmers bears no relation to prior financial contribution or to level of need, and has no effective upper limit. While most other social welfare programs are moving toward greater commercialization, public transfers to farmers form a major impediment to the play of market forces in the agricultural sector. It has been said, as we shall see with some justification, that in American agriculture the farmers are farming the government and harvesting the cash.

### Public Transfers to Farmers

Public transfers to farmers operate through diverse arrangements, cost large sums of money, and benefit a relatively small segment of the population. These diverse transfers fall into five general categories: price and income supports, credit and insurance subsidies, farm operation subsidies, tax expenditures, and judicial and regulatory relief.

### PRICE AND INCOME SUPPORTS

Defaultable nonrecourse crop loans are secured by crops, which are possessed by the government if farmers choose to forfeit the crops and not repay the loan (an option farmers exercise when market prices for the crops are inadequate to repay the government loan).

Deficiency payments are made to farmers when market prices fall below government-established "target prices" for a specified commodity.

Disaster payments provide direct compensation to farmers for the value of crops lost through natural disasters.

Diversion payments provide compensation to farmers for diverting acreage from crop production to conservation uses.

Public commodity operations involve public acquisition (through default or purchase), warehousing, and disposition (through resale or donation) of farm products, at home and abroad, under which net losses are transferred from the farmers to the government; government purchases are made at "target prices" rather than at market prices.

Various other public programs (such as Payment-In Kind and Grain Storage) provide special arrangements through which income is transferred to farmers or net losses are transferred to the government.

### CREDIT AND INSURANCE SUBSIDIES

Loans below the market rate and insurance on farm operations, farmland, and farm housing are either made directly or are guaranteed by government.

### FARM OPERATION SUBSIDIES

Subsidized irrigation of farmland is provided by public projects that sell water at prices below the market rate; this water is often used to grow crops, the sale of which are further subsidized with price supports.

Subsidized livestock grazing rights are conferred through below-market rental of public lands.

Subsidized electricity and phone service to rural areas are financed through credit-subsidy mechanisms.

Subsidized labor costs are realized through the use of illegal immigrant labor or special exceptions to immigration and labor law.

The government, as intermediary, absorbs any losses from subsidized domestic and international sales and donations of farm products.

Subsidies for investment in various farm operations, such as storage facilities, are available and are supplemented by payments to farmers to store government-owned crops (some of which were originally forfeited in lieu of debt repayment) in these facilities.

Farm operations also benefit from free research, education, training, and support services (as do a number of other enterprises).

TAX EXPENDITURES

Financial aid is provided through special tax treatment of farm expenditures, income, and inheritance.

JUDICIAL AND REGULATORY RELIEF

Public transfers to farmers are also promoted by special laws or interpretations of laws and procedures regarding, for example: lender rights, remedies, and liabilities in foreclosure; definitions affecting eligibility for and limits on various farm welfare entitlements; governmental assumption of unlimited open-ended (as opposed to fixed and budgeted) liabilities for farm welfare programs; agricultural import quotas and tariffs that restrict the supply and raise the prices of foreign food available to American consumers; finally, government-sponsored price-fixing for farm products (through marketing orders and agreements) whereby minimum prices are set for the sale of products to agricultural intermediaries (and indirectly for the sale of products to the consumer). Similar regulatory favors are available to other industries, but farmers are among the major beneficiaries of these arrangements.

## Farmers' Welfare: An Estimate of Costs

It is difficult to put an accurate price tag on farm welfare transfers because of the labyrinthian and fluid nature of these arrangements. A serious cost accounting must somehow cover the five categories of price and income supports, credit and insurance subsidies, farm operation subsidies, tax expenditures, and regulatory relief. However, not all of the cost figures are available in these categories, and in some cases it is not even clear how to calculate them. Moreover, figures on farm supports by state and local governments are often hard to uncover, and the interesting question of the extent to which farmers also participate in the broader system of social welfare must remain essentially unanswered, although a few clues are available. Bearing in mind these qualifications, one can draw a rough estimate of public transfers to farmers in the five categories under which these benefits are provided.

### Price and Income Supports

Most of this activity is undertaken by the Commodity Credit Corporation (CCC) under the aegis of the Department of Agriculture. The CCC operates a variety of programs to support farm prices and income, including direct payments under the loan, deficiency, disaster, and diversion programs; the commodity middleman program, through which defaulted and purchased commodities are run; the payment-in-kind program through which farmers are "paid" with salable crops for not producing additional crops; the grain storage program through which farmers are paid to store defaulted and other commodities; and other programs with the same general purpose of price and income support. There are three sets of figures relevant for estimating public costs under these programs: the total net loss for the CCC, which includes all program, interest, and operating expenses; the net program loss, which takes into account expenses only for the price and income support programs; and the documented direct government payments to farmers under all these programs. According to these measures, as shown in Table 5.1, the level of subsidy through price and income supports has increased dramatically during the last decade. The difference between net CCC loss and net program loss is a function of administrative and operational costs that have been separated out from program costs. Furthermore, the documented direct payments to farmers represent a portion of the CCC loss attributable mainly to deficiency, diversion, and disaster programs. The entire net CCC loss is the customary measure of price and income support to farmers, reflecting the total outlays made by the government under this program.

*Table 5.1.* Federal Price/Income Supports to Farmers[a]

| Type of Support | 1970 | 1975 | 1980 | 1981 | 1982 | 1983 | 1984 | 1985 | 1986 | 1987 |
|---|---|---|---|---|---|---|---|---|---|---|
| Net CCC Loss | 4.2 | .7 | 2.3 | 3.5 | 5.7 | 19.5 | 8.5 | 12.9 | 25.9 | 29.4[b] |
| Net CCC Program Loss | 3.6 | .7 | 1.5 | 2.8 | 3.6 | 17.6 | 7.1 | 10.9 | 20.0 | 27.6[b] |
| Documented Direct Payments to Farmers | 3.7 | .8 | 1.3 | 1.9 | 3.5 | 9.3 | 8.4 | 7.6 | 15.0[b] | 20.0[b] |

[a]Given in billions of dollars

[b]Estimates: Warren T. Brooks, "A Record Federal Budget for Farm Subsidies," *San Francisco Chronicle*, October 14, 1986, p. 25 and "When Will the Farm Lobby Let Up in America?", June 3, 1987, p. F6; Jeff Bailey, "Number of Imperiled Agricultural Banks Has Declined Recently Due to U.S. Aid," *Wall Street Journal*, June 15, 1987, p. 48; "Agriculture's Financial Profile: A Look Behind the Aggregates," *Farmline*, 8:1 (December–January 1987), pp. 5–9, U.S.D.A., ERS.

*Sources*: U.S. Bureau of the Census, *Statistical Abstract of the United States, 1987*, pp. 635, 630; U.S.D.A., "Commodity Credit Corporation: Report of Financial Condition and Operations," September 30, 1985; Office of Management and Budget, *Budget of the United States Government: FY 1988*, p. I-E39.

## *Credit and Insurance Subsidies*

By the end of 1986, the federal government held $252 billion in direct loans and $450 billion in guaranteed loans for all purposes. Additionally, government-sponsored but ostensibly independent enterprises (government-sponsored enterprises or GSEs) had loaned another $453 billion using federally subsidized credit. During the 1980s, the share of new direct loans provided to agriculture has ranged from one-third to over one-half of the total. New direct loan obligations amounted to $41.3 billion in 1986, with farmers accounting for 64.5 percent of the total when CCC crop loans were included, and 38 percent of the total when CCC crop loans were excluded.[1] The share of the total guaranteed loans going expressly to farmers is much smaller (about $5.8 billion or 1 percent), but this figure does not include guaranteed loans for farm housing, which are difficult to distinguish because they fall under the budget category of housing rather than agriculture.

Excluding the CCC loans that are covered in the price and income support category, much of the federal credit to farmers is supplied through the Farmers Home Administration (FmHA), which has operated partially on budget (in the category of Commerce and Housing Credit budget items) and partially off budget. Thus, in measuring an-

*Table 5.2.* FmHA Operating Outlays[a]

| Type of Outlay | 1980 | 1981 | 1982 | 1983 | 1984 | 1985 | 1986 |
|---|---|---|---|---|---|---|---|
| Off-Budget | 6.9 | 10.9 | 5.0 | 3.0 | 2.8 | 4.1 | 3.2 |
| On-Budget[b] | 2.8 | 2.4 | 2.0 | 2.0 | 1.9 | .5 | 3.2 |

[a]Given in billions of dollars.

[b]On-budget FmHA figures for 1980–1985 are estimates based on 1986 FmHA share of commerce and housing credit expenditures.

*Sources*: U.S. Bureau of the Census, *Statistical Abstract of the United States, 1986*, p. 308; Office of Management and Budget, *Budget of the U.S. Government, 1988, Supplement*, pp. 5–55.

nual federal credit outlay for farmers through FmHA, one must look at both items. In the last twelve years, off-budget costs have ranged from $2.8 billion to $10.9 billion (Table 5.2). In 1986, about 50 percent of on-budget housing credit outlay, or $3.2 billion, was funneled to farmers through the FmHA; however, these operating deficits reflect only part of the public costs. Because these credit subsidies involve below-market premiums or loan rates for high-risk transactions, there is an additional subsidy represented in the market discount of the loan (if sold) or the purchase of private guarantees or insurance (if this were to be done); this underlying transfer element of credit subsidies has not yet been fully accounted for in government figures, so the total subsidy to farmers is unknown. (Pilot projects are now under way to institute credit reform and account for this aspect of credit subsidy.) Finally, by directly funding, insuring, or guaranteeing loans, the government incurs a contingent liability for the amount of any defaults on which the assets are worth less than the loans. This contingent liability for the FmHA totals more than $27 billion on direct FmHA loans alone, and about $10 billion in FmHA loans are in fact delinquent.[2] Under the Agricultural Credit Act of 1988, the FmHA moved to relieve farmers from the burden of up to $7 billion in bad debts by restructuring and writing off loans. About 100,000 economically troubled farmers are expected to benefit from this social transfer.[3] When FmHA-guaranteed loans revert to the federal government because of default, they show up as assets rather than liabilities even though these loans are often greater than the value of the properties on which they are held.[4]

The federal government also had, as of the end of 1985, $51.5 billion outstanding in direct or guaranteed loans under the auspices of the Rural Electrification Administration (REA). The operating costs for the REA plus the rural telephone bank were about $500 million in 1986.[5] Additional subsidies are furnished by the Federal Crop Insurance Corporation (FCIC), through direct below-market provision of insurance and indemnities, partial payment of the premiums for private insurance, and government reinsurance of private providers. In 1986, the FCIC had an operating cost of about $500 million.[6] Direct federal loans are also made to foreign food purchasers under the Food for Peace Programs, in order to increase the purchasers' ability to buy American farm products. In 1986, there was $10.6 billion outstanding in these loans.[7]

The contingent liability for federally sponsored credit agencies is one of those gray areas in which the limits of public responsibility are unknown until tested. The Farm Credit Administration (FCA), for example, regulates and subsidizes the theoretically self-sufficient system of farm credit banks (Farm Credit System), initially sponsored by government and now owned by its farmer–users. Through federal land banks, federal intermediate credit banks, and banks for cooperatives, below-market rates and high-risk loans are made available to farmers for many purposes. These loans are not officially guaranteed by the government; however, there is pressure on the government to resume its more active initial role as sponsor and guarantor. The farm credit banks have more than $70 billion in loans outstanding, many of which are in questionable condition.[8] In 1987 the system was seeking a federal bailout in the form of a multibillion-dollar line of credit from the U.S. Treasury.

## Tax Expenditures

Between 1978 and 1986, annual tax expenditures of direct benefit to farm income ranged between $1.2 and $1.7 billion (see Table 5.3). These figures are expected to decline under the Tax Reform Act of

*Table 5.3.* Agricultural Tax Expenditures

| Year | 1978 | 1979 | 1980 | 1981 | 1982 | 1983 | 1984 | 1985 | 1986 |
|---|---|---|---|---|---|---|---|---|---|
| Expenditure[a] | 1.4 | 1.4 | 1.5 | 1.7 | 1.3 | 1.2 | 1.2 | 1.3 | 1.2 |

[a]Given in billions of dollars.

*Source*: U.S. Bureau of the Census, *Statistical Abstract of the United States, 1981, 1986*, p. 254; *1987*, idem, p. 310; idem, p. 297; Committee on Fiscal Affairs, OECD, *Tax Expenditures: A Review of Issues and County Practices*, 1984, pp. 80–83. In several cases these sources offer slightly different tax expenditure totals for the same year.

1986, which repealed the capital-gains benefits that farmers derived from the sale of certain products and added a new tax expenditure allowing preferential treatment on loans settled for less than the principal owed. The impact of these and other changes introduced by the 1986 tax legislation will reduce the 1988 tax expenditures in support of agriculture to an estimated $795 million.[9]

Farmers have also benefited from another type of tax relief that is not accounted for in the figures just noted. This preference involves the calculation of federal estate taxes, which, prior to 1976, was based on the fair market value of the farmland. Under this standard form of assessment, family farms with low profits and high land values would have to be sold by the heirs to pay federal estate taxes. In order to help preserve the family farm, the Tax Reform Act of 1976 permitted the special valuation of these properties for purposes of assessing federal estate taxes. Instead of resorting to the criterion of fair market value, farm property meeting certain conditions may be assessed for tax purposes by capitalizing the value of its current use up to a maximum reduction in estate tax valuation of $1 million. The estate tax reduction amounts to a unique form of hereditary privilege for farm owners.[10]

### *Farm Operation Subsidies*

There are a number of intermediary public subsidies that benefit the production, storage, and distribution of farm commodities. Between 1970 and 1984, federal agencies made storage payments to grain farmers that reached a high of $1.1 billion in 1983.[11] These payments are included in the price and income support outlays of the CCC (shown in Table 5.1). In 1984 about 25 percent of all farmland was artificially irrigated; of these farmlands, 20–25 percent were serviced by publicly built and publicly subsidized irrigation projects.[12] The amounts of these subsidies vary. According to calculations made by Phillip Leveen at the University of California at Berkeley, the price farmers pay for water from the Central Valley Project in California compensates for only 7.5 percent of actual public cost to deliver this resource.[13] More generally, analysts estimate that farmers receiving public water pay only about 20 percent of market costs, with 45 percent of water-subsidized acreage being used to grow subsidized crops. The overall cost of public water subsidies is reckoned to be about $300 million annually; this figure, however, does not include amortized investment costs.[14]

The federal government owns more than 175 million acres of grazing land, most of which is held and administered by the Department of the Interior. Almost all of this land is leased to livestock owners with approximately 20,000 permits or leases in effect and about 2.9 million cattle grazed in 1983. While the operational cost of the land in 1983 was nearly $29 million, federal income from grazing leases was only $10.2 million, an average of about $.06 per acre or $3.50 per head annually.[15] This results, at minimum, in a net public loss of about $19 million. Without knowing the quality of the grazing land, it is not possible to gauge the full value of public subsidies in this area. The minimum cost estimate would increase considerably if the fair market value of the leased land is higher than the amount that would be obtained by capitalizing the value of its current use.[16] In comparison to the average federal income of $.06 per acre, for example, highly fertile private grazing land in California may be leased for about $15.50 per acre or $31.00 per head annually.[17] Federal grazing leases and permits are generally treated as easements appurtenant to adjacent ranches. These leases are rarely put up for bid, and their rates are rarely adjusted to reflect comparable rates on private grazing land.

In addition to subsidized water and grazing rights, farm production benefits from a flow of labor that is to some extent subsidized by public funds. Whereas the use of low-paid, often illegal immigrants as farm laborers does not constitute a public subsidy in the same sense as other indirect transfers, there are public costs imposed by this practice and private benefits that accrue mainly to farmers. It is almost impossible to put a precise figure on the cost of labor subsidy to farmers. In general, the documented ratio of hired to unpaid family labor has increased substantially, from about 23.5 percent to between 40 and 50 percent in the period 1950–1983.[18] However, the percentage of illegal, undocumented, and low-paid alien labor has also risen substantially. Although there are obviously some benefits from this international flow of labor, the entry and residency of millions of illegal aliens is not without costs to the larger society. These costs include the work lost and depressed wages to U.S. citizens, increased outlays for border and immigration controls, additional expenditures on social welfare, and the less tangible cultural and political prices of uncontrolled immigration. Recent immigration reform has sought to legalize the status of several million resident illegal aliens and limit new arrivals. This reform has met with notable resistance from farmers who, at least until the law is fully implemented, are in some instances finding themselves 50 percent short on seasonal labor. In the summer of 1987, regulatory relief from the new immigration law was instituted for an indefinite period, and the stream of illegal immigrants was higher than ever.[19]

Beyond aiding production, public social welfare involvement also helps to stimulate the sale of farm goods. In 1984 and 1985, the U.S.D.A. spent about $18 billion annually on domestic food and nutrition assistance programs, such as food stamps and school lunches. By 1986, there was $10.6 billion spent on international commodity-purchase loans.[20] Much of this expenditure may be of substantial indirect benefit to farmers. While the manifest purpose of food and nutrition assistance, for example, is to help the poor and undernourished, such programs also serve to prop up consumer demand and prices insofar as the government is intervening in the market as a proxy-purchaser.

## Judicial and Regulatory Relief

Since the early 1970s, farm price and income supports were to be limited to $50,000 annually per farm family. Though not an ungenerous amount, for several reasons this limit has never been enforced in practice. First, through a liberal definition, eligible farm families may include not only owners, but also managers, lessees, and croppers. Second, where one landowner has several tenants or renters, the land operated by each is counted as a separate farm. Third, through a variety of legal mechanisms, one consanguine farm family of a couple with three children, for example, may divide itself up into several eligible farm families. Fourth, new corporate and partnership investor entrants into farming are not disqualified. Finally, one integrated farm operation may, for subsidy purposes, break itself up into several functional operations and operators. Thus, it has been quite easy for farmers and their colleagues to multiply entitlements by creating a variety of "dummy" farm operations. Between 1985 and 1986, for example, despite serious problems in the rice market in the Sacramento, California area, the number of qualified rice operators rose by 50 percent, with the new entrants each eligible for generous public subsidies and the original landowner–farmer collecting his cut in the form of lease payments from the newly subsidized farmers.[21] Similarly, when the real number of cash grain (corn and wheat) farms fell more than 12 percent between

1980 and 1986, the number of such farms for entitlement purposes rose by a remarkable 50 percent.[22]

In addition to stretching the regulatory limits of public support, farmers have been setting records in judicial relief from private lenders. In 1987 one farmer won a $60 million suit against the Wells Fargo Bank ($50 million of which was punitive damages), and another was awarded a similar amount against the Bank of America. The courts have developed a new theory of "lender liability," pioneered in farm cases and spreading to the general credit economy. According to this theory, some lenders apparently were to blame for farm failure because they aggressively sought to make farm loans, they unduly interfered in farm operations, and they failed to live up to implied promises of continued financial support.[23] Even the federal FmHA has been judicially enjoined from foreclosing on about 14,000 long-delinquent farm borrowers.

Farmers have also received specialized tax relief with regard to loan payoffs. Normally, if a creditor has a loan written down through negotiation or acquits a loan through foreclosure, the federal tax liability is based on the original debt, with tax still owed on the amount of forgiveness. While this tax policy covers most borrowers, it no longer applies to farmers who are now forgiven the tax on the forgiven loan.

### Federal Subsidies: An Appraisal

Among the various benefits reviewed earlier, there are three categories that contain reasonably firm data on transfers to farmers (noted in Tables 5.1, 5.2, and 5.3). Leaving aside the several types of farm benefits that provide indirect aid, which can be only partially quantified or otherwise elude measurement, the combined costs of price and income supports, credit subsidies, and tax expenditures yield a conservative estimate of the outright federal subsidy to farmers. Based on this conservative approach illustrated in Table 5.4, farm subsidies averaged about $20 billion annually since 1980, reaching an all-time high of $34 billion in 1986; the projections for 1987 are even higher.

Federal subsidies to farmers are among the least controversial programs delivering social welfare benefits in the United States. Indeed, until recently these subsidies were barely perceived by the public as such and hardly thought of as a form of welfare transfer. In this regard,

*Table 5.4.* Federal Subsidy to Farmers 1980–1986: A Conservative Estimate[a]

| Type of Subsidy | 1980 | 1981 | 1982 | 1983 | 1984 | 1985 | 1986 |
|---|---|---|---|---|---|---|---|
| Price/Income Supports (Net CCC Loss) | 2.3 | 3.5 | 5.7 | 19.5 | 8.5 | 12.9 | 25.9 |
| Credit and Insurance (FmHA Outlay) | 9.7 | 13.3 | 7.0 | 5.0 | 4.7 | 4.6 | 6.4 |
| Tax Expenditure | 1.5 | 1.7 | 1.3 | 1.2 | 1.2 | 1.3 | 1.2 |
| Total Subsidy | 13.5 | 18.5 | 14.0 | 25.7 | 14.4 | 18.8 | 33.5 |

[a]Given in billions of dollars.
*Sources*: See Tables 5.1, 5.2, and 5.3.

it is interesting to note that since 1980 subsidies to farmers averaged about two-thirds the cost of federal expenditures on Aid to Families with Dependent Children (AFDC), which is the most controversial large-scale social welfare program in the country. Compared to the approximately 10 million AFDC recipients, the population of farm welfare beneficiaries is smaller, wealthier, and subsidized at a much higher rate per capita.

## Beneficiaries of Farm Welfare

The farm population is officially classified as all persons living on farms in rural areas. Farms are officially defined as any place from which $1000 or more of agricultural products could have been sold during a census year, and over which control was exercised through ownership, management, lease, rental, or cropping arrangement.[24] As noted in Table 5.5, the farm population of the United States has been on the decline, falling from 15.3 percent in 1950 to 2.2 percent in 1985. By 1985, there were about 5.35 million persons in the farm population. Similarly, the number of farm operator households as a percentage of total U.S. households has dropped steeply.

Between 1960 and 1985, the percentage of the farm population's labor force employed in agriculture fell from 64.2 percent to 47.8 percent. Among the 1982 population of farm operators, 45 percent had a principal occupation other than farming, only 38 percent worked full-time on their farm, and 19 percent resided elsewhere than on their farm. Contrary to the popular image of the lifelong roots in family farming,

*Table 5.5.* Farm Population and Farm Operator Households, 1950–1985

| Population Category | 1950 | 1960 | 1970 | 1980 | 1983 | 1984 | 1985 |
|---|---|---|---|---|---|---|---|
| Number of People in Farm Population[a] | 23.0 | 15.6 | 9.7 | 6.1 | 5.8 | 5.75 | 5.35 |
| Percentage of Total U.S. Population | 15.3 | 8.7 | 4.8 | 2.7 | 2.5 | 2.4 | 2.2 |
| Number of Farm Operator Households[a] | 5.65 | 3.96 | 2.95 | 2.43 | 2.37 | 2.33 | 2.27 |
| Percentage of Total U.S. Households | 13.0 | 7.6 | 4.7 | 3.0 | 2.8 | 2.7 | 2.6 |

[a]Given in millions.

*Sources*: U.S. Bureau of the Census, *Statistical Abstract of the United States, 1986*, pp. 39, 633, 635; *Statistical Abstract of the United States, 1987*, pp. 42, 619, 621.

almost 40 percent of reporting farmers had operated their present facilities for less than ten years.[25] In 1983, less than 30 percent of the farm sector's net income was from farming.[26]

As the farm population and number of farms have diminished, the average size of farms has more than doubled, from 213 acres in 1950 to 455 acres in 1986.[27] Both the increase in real average size and decline in real number of farms, in fact, may be larger than the figures indicate if one takes into account the number of "dummy" operations created in recent years to evade the limit on farm subsidies.

Along with the shrinking population and expanding acreage, the nature of farm ownership has also changed. While the proportion of genuine tenant farmers (as opposed to farmers with full or partial ownership) has hovered around 12 percent, between 1969 and 1982 the rate of partial ownership rose from 24.6 percent to 29.3 percent of all farms (and to 64 percent of farms over 1000 acres).[28] In 1982, about 12.5 percent of farms and 29 percent of farmland was held by partnerships and corporations. However, of corporate farm operations, 88 percent of both farms and farmlands were held by family corporations.[29]

Farm values and farmer net worth rose significantly in the 1970s, peaking in the high-inflationary 1980–1982 period, and declining thereafter. Overall, between 1980 and 1985, farmers experienced about a 23.5 percent loss in average net worth and, between 1982 and 1986, a 22.5 percent loss in real estate values (see Table 5.6). Farm real estate values per acre, however, are still 200 percent higher than they were in

*Table 5.6.* Farm Values and Farmer Assets, 1970–1986

| Financial Parameters | 1970 | 1980 | 1982 | 1984 | 1985 | 1986 |
|---|---|---|---|---|---|---|
| Average Dollar Value Per Acre | 196 | 737 | 823 | 782 | 679 | 596 |
| Average Dollar Value Per Farm | 73,000 | 314,000 | 352,000 | 341,200 | 301,400 | 264,500 |
| Gross Farmer Assets[a] | 326.0 | 1108.3 | 1082.0 | 955.8 | 866.9 | — |
| Gross Farmer Liabilities[a] | 54.5 | 182.3 | 217.2 | 212.5 | 204.9 | — |
| Total Net Worth of Farmers[a] | 271.5 | 926.0 | 864.8 | 743.3 | 662.0 | — |
| Number of Farms[b] | 2.82 | 2.43 | 2.40 | 2.33 | 2.27 | 2.21 |
| Average Farmer Net Dollar Worth | 96,277 | 381,070 | 360,333 | 319,013 | 291,630 | — |

[a]Given in billions of dollars.

[b]Given in millions.

*Source*: U.S. Bureau of the Census, *Statistical Abstract of the United States, 1987*, pp. 626–27.

1970. Specifically, the average value per farm acre (including land and buildings) rose from $196 in 1970 to a high of $823 in 1982, and down to $596 in 1986. Average farmer net worth reached a high of $381,000 in 1980, falling to about $291,000 in 1985, which was still almost three times that of 1970. Median farmer net worth was more than $141,000 in 1984, and even the smallest farm operators (those with less than $2500 annual agricultural sale value) had a median net worth that year of $113,534.[30] In contrast, the 1984 median net worth of all American families was $32,667.[31] The 1983 median cash income of farm families was $21,534, and that of nonfarm families was $25,486.[32] However, because farm housing, housing maintenance, taxes, and some food involve business-connected expenses, the real disposable income of farmers is somewhat higher than the median income figure would imply.

Another perspective on wealth is obtained by dividing farms into four groups: rural residences, small family farms, mid-sized family farms, and large farms. About half of all farms are considered rural residences, those with an annual sale of less than $10,000 worth of farm products.

Small family farms, with average sales of $10,000 to $39,999 worth of products, account for 23 percent of all farms. An additional one-quarter of all farms are mid-sized operations selling products worth $40,000 to $200,000, and the remaining 5 percent are large farms, producing almost half the nation's food and selling more than $200,000 worth of farm products annually. In 1982, rural residences averaged assets of more than $133,000, small family farms more than $313,000, mid-sized operations approximately $791,000, and large farms more than $2.3 million.[33]

In the allocation of farm welfare transfers, public outlays are not evenly divided among all who work the land. Indeed, only about 50 percent of farmers are eligible to participate in the major price and income support programs, and of those eligible about 70 percent actually participate, which amounts to 35 percent of all farmers. Producers of vegetables, fruits, tree nuts, horticultural products, and nondairy livestock are ineligible for direct price and income support payments. But many of these farmers participate in government-sponsored price-setting through marketing agreements and orders. Under these arrangements, about $6.4 billion worth of their products were price-fixed in 1985.[34]

Based on the previous estimate of the overall federal subsidy, the average cost per farm household was $15,158. Taking only those subsidies that involved a direct cash payment, the average check received from the government amounted to $6787. Eliminating the approximately 50 percent of farmers who are ineligible for the direct income supports, the average direct cash outlay per eligible farm doubles to $13,574. Furthermore, because not all eligible farmers choose to participate, the actual direct cash average per participant is even higher. In 1986, for example, about 70 percent of eligible farms received these supports, amounting to more than $19,000 per recipient, with some estimates as high as $24,000 per recipient.[35] In general, the vast majority of direct cash payments go to the mid-sized and large farms.[36]

Though not fabulously wealthy, the average farmer's net worth is many times higher and the median net worth about twice as high as the average and median net worth of all citizens. While their assets are greater, the average farmer income is about the same as the average American income. In 1986, farmers eligible for price and income supports received an average direct cash payment from government that about equaled the median income of 10.2 million female-headed fami-

*Table 5.7.* Per-Capita Subsidies and Cash to Farmers, 1980–1986

| Recipient Parameter | 1980 | 1981 | 1982 | 1983 | 1984 | 1985 | 1986 |
|---|---|---|---|---|---|---|---|
| Number of Farmer Households[a] | 2.43 | 2.43 | 2.40 | 2.37 | 2.33 | 2.27 | 2.21 |
| Total Federal Subsidy[b] | 13.5 | 18.5 | 14.0 | 25.7 | 14.4 | 18.8 | 33.5 |
| Average Subsidy per Household[c] | 5,556 | 7,613 | 5,833 | 10,844 | 6,180 | 8,282 | 15,158 |
| Documented Direct Cash Payments[b] | 1.3 | 1.9 | 3.5 | 9.3 | 8.4 | 7.6 | 15.0 |
| Average Direct Cash per Household[c] | 535 | 782 | 1,458 | 3,924 | 3,605 | 3,348 | 6,787 |
| Average Direct Cash per Eligible Farmer[c] | 1,070 | 1,564 | 2,916 | 7,848 | 7,210 | 6,696 | 13,574 |

[a]Given in millions.

[b]Given in billions of dollars.

[c]Given in dollars.

*Source*: See Tables 5.1, 5.4, and 5.5.

lies. Much of farm aid is sentimentally predicated on saving the traditional family farm; however, 40 percent of the farmers have operated these enterprises for less than ten years, and many ostensible family farms are in reality "dummy" corporations run by financial operators. If the average means test for public assistance recipients were applied to the allocation of farm subsidies, it would quickly become apparent that, by American standards, personal need has had almost no bearing on public transfers to the farmer.

## Asset Maintenance: Why Special Protection for Farmers?

The array of public transfers available to farm households form a unique category of social welfare, the function of which is best characterized as asset maintenance. Although the government cannot entirely control the value of farm assets, through a steady stream of cash, in-kind subsidies, and market interventions it has provided farmers the wherewithal to continue operations that might otherwise collapse and to expand their real estate holdings. Because the price of farmland is based largely on the future income one expects it to generate, huge federal subsidies not only undergird the immediate farm earnings but also sustain the market value of the farmers' real estate holdings, which averaged more than $260,000 in 1986.

Farm operators are in many ways similar to small business entrepreneurs except that the latter are not cushioned as extensively by government subsidies and go out of business as frequently as the market and their skills determine. When land values and commodity prices plunged in the early 1980s, considerable media attention was devoted to the growing plight of farmers and the farm "crisis." Between 1982 and 1985, more than 120,000 families in the midwestern grain belt lost their farms to foreclosure.[37] And from 1984 to 1985, the rate of business failures in agriculture increased by 35.6 percent.[38] Although these figures represent serious hardships for many people (especially those who expanded real estate holdings in the rising market of the 1970s), most farmers remained solvent and relatively prosperous during that period. Indeed, from 1983 to 1986, the real per-capita income in the grain belt states on the average rose 7 percent faster than the national growth in per-capita income.[39] Furthermore, whereas the 120,000 farm foreclosures in the grain belt states between 1982 and 1985 represent a cumulative failure of almost 5 percent of all farms, the cumulative failure rate for all the commercial and industrial concerns in the nation also amounted to about 5 percent during this period.[40]

Just as the adversity that farmers experienced in the 1980s attracted more public attention and sympathy than similar difficulties normally experienced by businesses in other sectors of the economy, the generous package of public benefits and special protection afforded farmers places this group in an unusually favorable social position. The reasons for this state of affairs involve a complex blend of psychological, political, and economic considerations. Psychologically, farmers and the rural way of life have a sentimental and symbolic value that seem to increase with the social costs of industrialization. Assembly line workers do not evoke as sharp an image of virtue and determination as farmers. It is an image cultivated by remarks such as Daniel Webster's, that "farmers are the founders of human civilization." Thomas Jefferson praised those who work the earth "as the chosen people of God, if ever He had a chosen people, whose breasts He has made His peculiar deposit for substantial and genuine virtue." In more recent times, memories of farmer suffering in the Great Depression lend an air of vulnerability to the rugged individualism of farm life.

However, sentimental visions of pastoral life alone are not sufficient to generate billions of dollars in public subsidies. Relative to their numbers, farmers have an inordinate degree of political power, particularly in the Senate, where senators from a sparsely populated, mostly rural grain belt state exercise the same two votes as their senatorial counterparts from a densely populated urban industrial state. Drawing on this political strength, farm interest groups have been remarkably successful in creating a labyrinthian network of public transfers that is nearly incomprehensible to outsiders. Until recently, these transfers have gone almost unnoticed by the general public and have thus exacted a very low political toll.

Diverse economic considerations also encourage special protection for farmers. Farm subsidies appear to keep food prices relatively low. The federal government, as financial guarantor of many farm loans, has an immediate vested interest in preventing farm failures, as do other large financial institutions with significant farm credits.

From an economic perspective, one could develop a legitimate justification for some measure of producer asset maintenance if a vitally important scarce resource were at risk; however, the United States and the world are awash in food.[41] In the United States there is literally no available storage space for all the surplus food, despite government storage subsidies. The publicized cases of starvation in some parts of the world are less a problem of food supply than of politics, purchasing power, and distribution. Food oversupply is the result of technological advances leading to vastly increased productivity and political changes that have prodded many nations into increased agricultural development aimed at self-sufficiency.

Oversupply is also caused by government farm subsidies that act as a disincentive to reduce food production capacity in the presence of national and international surpluses. Agricultural subsidy is a worldwide phenomenon.[42] Western Europe, Japan, and the United States now spend $100 billion to $150 billion annually on farm subsidies. In the United States, sugar prices are three to four times the world market prices. In West Germany the government pays farmers four to five times the market price of butter before reselling it at a loss in Eastern Europe. Very few nations are willing to forfeit the agricultural infrastructure requisite to basic food self-sufficiency or to feeding themselves in an emergency. Most producer nations are as yet unwilling to pull the government plug on farm subsidies, despite costly surpluses, because they hold out hopes of eventually supplying food to others. From this perspective, farm subsidies are viewed as a national investment that both ensures food independence and assists the agricultural sector to capture a share of the world market. Having evolved an international market in which competition is underwritten by huge government subsidies, the producer nations find themselves caught in a bind. Independent action by a single nation to eliminate subsidies would probably reduce the competitive edge and jeopardize the general health of its agricultural sector. Coordinated action among nations is difficult to achieve under the best of circumstances, let alone when it promises to elicit intense opposition from politically powerful agricultural interests.

These various political and economic pressures have forged an elaborate program of social protection for farmers—one that bears little resemblance to traditional social welfare programs. In form and substance, public aid to farmers represents a special case of welfare transfers. Unlike the conditions associated with income maintenance under public assistance, there is no means test, no asset reduction, no push toward economic self-sufficiency, and no stigma. Unlike contributory social insurance, there is no prior financial contribution, no actuarial accounting, and no effective benefit limit. Unlike unemployment insurance, benefits are large, of unlimited duration, and not tied to job-seeking activities (indeed, farmers are often paid for not producing certain crops). Unlike charity, benefits are an entitlement rather than a largesse. Beyond the normal public mechanisms for social protection, there is a vast federal bureaucracy devoted to farmer interests. Furthermore, in contrast to the prevailing thrust of government initiatives, which seek to introduce the "invisible hand" of the market economy into the workings of traditional social welfare programs, welfare transfers in agriculture promote an artificial market endowed by the "bountiful hand" of the political economy.

## Notes

1. Office of Management and Budget (OMB), *Budget of the United States Government, 1988, Historical Tables* (Washington, D.C.: U.S. Government Printing Office, 1987), Table 14.2.

2. U.S. Department of Agriculture (U.S.D.A.), *Agricultural Statistics 1986* (Washington, D.C.: U.S. Government Printing Office, 1987), pp. 434–35; "New U.S. Push on Collecting Loans and Taxes," *San Francisco Chronicle,* July 23, 1987, p. 12.

3. Keith Schneider, "Agency Plans Aid on $7 Billion Debt Owed by Farmers," *The New York Times,* March 2, 1988, pp. 1, 13.

4. John E. Butarezzi, "U.S. Should Sell Loans to Meet Deficit Target," *Wall Street Journal,* July 22, 1987, p. 22.

5. OMB, *Budget of the United States Government, 1988, Supplement* (Washington, D.C.: U.S. Government Printing Office, 1987), p. 5-55.

6. Ibid.

7. Ibid., p. 5-26

8. U.S. Bureau of the Census, *Statistical Abstract of the United States, 1986* (Washington, D.C.: U.S. Government Printing Office, 1985), p. 500.

9. OMB, *Budget of U.S. Government, 1988, Suppl.,* p. 5-59.

10. Boyd Dyer, "Estate Tax Savings and the Family Farm: A Critical Analysis of Section 2032A of the Internal Revenue Code," *University of California, Davis Law Review,* May 1978, pp. 81–113. As Dyer explains, the "fair market value" is the price a buyer and seller would agree on when neither is under any compulsion to buy or sell and both have reasonable knowledge of relevant facts. The "value of current use" is determined by dividing the gross cash rental of comparable farmland after state and local taxes by the average interest rate for all new Federal Land Bank loans.

11. U.S. Bureau of the Census, *Statistical Abstract, 1986,* p. 650.

12. Ibid., p. 625.

13. Dr. Phillip Leveen, cited in "Hearing on Farmers' Water Needs," *San Francisco Chronicle,* August 27, 1987, p. 16.

14. "Hot Debate over Subsidizing Water to Grow Surplus Crops," *San Francisco Chronicle,* May 13, 1987, p. 7.

15. U.S. Bureau of the Census, *Statistical Abstract, 1986,* pp. 327–28.

16. See note 10 for definitions of fair market value and value of current use.

17. Conversation with owners of ranch near Mineral, Calif.

18. U.S. Bureau of the Census, *Statistical Abstract, 1986,* pp. 633, 654.

19. Diana Solis, "Illegal Immigration Seems on Rebound, Fueling Doubt about New Law's Impact," *Wall Street Journal,* July 7, 1987, p. 2; Susan Krohn and Sean P. Means, "Panicked Farmers Say Immigration Law Is Costing Them Their Crops," *San Francisco Chronicle,* June 14, 1987, p. B5; "The Immigration Law's Harvest," *Wall Street Journal,* June 17, 1987, p. 24.

20. U.S. Bureau of the Census, *Statistical Abstract, 1986,* p. 306; OMB, *Budget of U.S. Government, 1988, Suppl.,* p. 5-54.

21. Mitzi Ayala, "Farm Subsidies Yield Costly Harvest," *Wall Street Journal,* June 4, 1987, p. 22.

22. Warren T. Brookes, "A Record Federal Budget for Farm Subsidies," *San Francisco Chronicle,* October 14, 1986, p. 25.

23. Richard B. Schmitt, "Farmers, Attacking Lending Practices, Are Taking Banks to Court and Winning," *Wall Street Journal,* July 6, 1987, p. 5.

24. U.S. Bureau of the Census, *Statistical Abstract, 1986,* pp. 631–32.

25. U.S. Bureau of the Census, *Statistical Abstract of the United States, 1987* (Washington, D.C.: U.S. Government Printing Office, 1986), pp. 620, 638.

26. Farm Credit Administration, *Agricultural and Credit Outlook '85*, p. 13.

27. U.S. Bureau of the Census, *Statistical Abstract, 1986*, p. 635; idem, *Statistical Abstract, 1987*, p. 621.

28. U.S. Bureau of the Census, *Statistical Abstract, 1986*, p. 635.

29. Ibid., p. 638.

30. Ibid., p. 643.

31. U.S. Bureau of the Census, *Statistical Abstract, 1987*, p. 449.

32. Ibid., p. 447.

33. Elmer Learn, Philip Martin, and Alex McCalla, "American Farm Subsidies: A Bumper Crop," *The Public Interest*, Summer 1986, pp. 67–68.

34. U.S.D.A., *Agricultural Statistics 1986*, p. 463.

35. Eric Van Chantfort, "Who Gets Those Farm Program Payments," *Farmline*, 8:1 (December–January 1987), pp. 3–5.

36. Learn et al., "Farm Subsidies: Bumper Crop," p. 69.

37. Paul Seindet and Joanne Mermelstein, "Helping the New Rural Poor," *Public Welfare*, 45:3 (Summer 1987), p. 15.

38. During the same period, the rate of failure in the services industry increased by 30 percent, with no mention of a pending crisis. U.S. Bureau of the Census, *Statistical Abstract, 1987*, p. 510.

39. Warren T. Brookes, "Death-Knell for Gephardt Farm Belt?" *San Francisco Chronicle*, May 6, 1987, p. 6.

40. U.S. Bureau of the Census, *Statistical Abstract, 1987*, p. 509.

41. Eric Van Chantfort, "The Farm Bill vs. the Surpluses," *Farmline*, 7:2 (February 1986), pp. 4–6.

42. For a comparative analysis of government subsidies, see Doug Martinez, "Measuring Governments' Role in Agriculture around the World," *Farmline*, 7:5 (May 1987), p. 4.

# 6

# *Health Care: Cost Containment and the Service Ethos*

At the end of the 1980s, the fundamental issues in health care relate to cost containment, quality, and access. With increasing pressures for universal health care entitlement, unprecedented increases in health care expenditures, and a continually growing need (e.g., in response to sociomedical problems such as an expanding aging population and the emergence of AIDS), cost containment stands as the overriding priority. The key question to be resolved is how the health care cost burden can be lightened or redistributed, while maintaining quality and extending access.

The growing cost of health care since 1960 is reflected in several measures. Between 1960 and 1985, the health expenditure share of GNP rose from 5.3 percent to 10.7 percent and per-capita health expenditures from $146 to $1721. Average annual expenditure increases have ranged from 8.9 to 15.7 percent, with the medical care price index of recent years rising almost three times as fast as the consumer price index (CPI). Despite a huge real increase in the supply of key health care personnel and facilities, the average hospital cost per patient day has grown by about 400 percent since 1970, as has the average cost per patient stay.[1]

While health care expenditures continue to rise, there are some indications that the rate of growth is slowing down. The 8.9 percent expenditure increase in 1985, for example, represents the smallest gain in spending during the last decade. This slowdown is attributable to a reduced rate of inflation coupled with cost containment measures in the delivery and financing of care, such as the increased use of health maintenance organizations (HMOs) and the replacement of a cost-based reimbursement system of payments with diagnostic-related group rates.[2] In light of these and other cost containment efforts, growth in health care spending is expected to level off at an average annual rate of 8.7 percent through 1990. Overall, projections suggest that health care expenditures will rise slowly to 11.3 percent of the GNP by 1990.[3]

As health care costs have increased, so have public expenditures in this area. Between 1970 and 1984, the overall percentage of personal health care expenses paid directly by individuals dropped from about 40 percent to 28 percent, with a concomitant rise in third-party payers. The public share of all health care payments almost doubled from about 21 percent in 1960 to 41 percent in 1985, with the federal portion amounting to more than 70 percent of direct public expenditures.[4] Although the public share of medical spending in the United States has experienced significant growth during the last several decades, it still remains far below that of other major industrial nations. For example, publicly financed outlays in Sweden, Denmark, Italy, and England accounted for approximately 80–90 percent of their total medical care spending in 1984.[5]

## Health Care Transfers and Coverage

From 1970 to 1985, direct public expenditures for health climbed from $28 billion to $175 billion. During that period, the federal share of these expenditures increased from 64 percent to 71 percent. Most of the nonfederal public expenditures involve state contributions to Medicaid and funding of state and local hospitals. On the federal side, about 60 percent of spending is devoted to Medicare payments, another 18 percent to the federal portion of Medicaid funding, 10 percent to public health activities, and 7 percent for the care of veterans. The remaining 5 percent is divided among medical research, hospital and medical costs for the Defense Department, child health programs, and other activities.[6]

The figures for direct expenditures illustrate only part of the public contribution to health care financing. A substantial public transfer, amounting to almost $28 billion in 1985, is provided through tax expenditures for health-related purposes.[7] Most of this indirect financing comes from the exclusion of payments for employee health insurance. The estimate of health care tax expenditures does not count what some would consider the tax preference for Medicare benefits. When tax expenditures are included, the public share of national health spending increases from 41 percent to 48 percent in 1985. This is a large increase, but it still leaves the public/private ratio of expenditures for health in the United States far below that of other industrial countries. There are, however, other ways to consider indirect expenditures. Poullier notes, for example, the suggestion to treat tax-supported "private" insurance as quasi-public, in which case public contributions in the United States would have increased to 72.6 percent in 1983.[8]

Beyond the financial provision of tax expenditures, another indirect approach to public support of health care financing involves the use of government's regulatory powers to require businesses to provide employee health insurance benefits. The Massachusetts Health Security Act of 1988, for example, is one of the first such measures that mandates businesses with more than six employees either to give their staff health insurance or to contribute to a state account that would be used to purchase the insurance. In an era of fierce public opposition to tax increases, the use of "mandated benefits" is seen by some as a politically viable course to induce social transfers without lending the appearance of fiscal profligacy. Others suggest that while mandated health benefits may avoid the need, for example, to tax private enterprise directly and use the revenues for publicly sponsored health insurance, they operate in effect as an implicit tax on business firms.[9] Although mandated benefits could expand health insurance coverage for employees, those outside the labor force would remain dependent mostly on public programs.

Health insurance coverage has advanced substantially since 1960. At that time, before the passage of Medicare and Medicaid, 69 percent of the population were covered for hospital expenses, 47 percent for physicians' expenses, and less than 6 percent had dental insurance. By 1983, 196.2 million Americans, or 85 percent of the population, were covered by some form of health insurance. Among the insured, 74.7 percent had private coverage, four-fifths of which stemmed from employment benefits. Looking at the family unit, about 34 percent of American households were covered by public insurance programs, 24.5 percent by Medicare and 9.5 percent by Medicaid. Under Medicare alone, reimbursements per patient were up about 250 percent between 1975 and 1983, and the number of persons served among those covered was up about 19 percent. Dental care coverage by private insurers rose to 46 percent of the population.[10]

Health insurance coverage is a strong indicator of access to care. Findings from the 1977 National Medical Care Expenditure Survey reveal that the insured visited physicians 54 percent more often and received 90 percent more hospital care than the uninsured. Examining access from a different perspective, another national poll shows 7 percent of all families and 13 percent of families without insurance reporting that they did not receive all the medical care that they believed they needed. But nearly all those surveyed indicated they had a regular source of medical care.[11]

It is difficult to judge the extent to which the increased costs and coverage of benefits have influenced health conditions. However, as noted in Table 6.1, following the extension of benefits since 1960, there have been significant improvements in the quality of health in several important areas. But despite these improvements, in the 1980s the United States ranked among the bottom third of twenty-three major industrial nations on measures of infant mortality and childhood immunization against diphtheria, tetanus, and whooping cough, and in the bottom half for life expectancy at birth.[12] This low standing is particularly insupportable in view of the position of the United States as first among these nations in health expenditures per capita and as a percentage of the GNP.[13]

Thus, despite vastly increased spending, wider and better coverage, and real improvements in health, serious health care service and insurance gaps either remain or can be anticipated. Foremost among these is the gap encountered by elderly persons who require expensive long-term intermediate or intensive care. When their Medicare and private benefits run out, many of these elderly are not impoverished enough to be eligible for Medicaid or free care, leaving them with heavy costs and no coverage. They must deplete (spend down) their life's savings in order to qualify for public aid. Indeed, findings from six major studies

*Table 6.1.* Selected Measures of National Health

| Health Parameters | 1960 | 1970 | 1983 |
|---|---|---|---|
| Percentage of Low-Birthweight Babies | 7.7 | 7.9 | 6.8 |
| Life Expectancy at Birth | 69.7 | 70.8 | 74.6 |
| Deaths per 1000 Population | 9.6 | 9.5 | 8.6 |
| Infant Deaths per 1000 Live Births | 26.0 | 20.0 | 11.2 |
| Maternal Deaths per 1000 Live Births | 37.1 | 21.5 | 8.0 |

*Source*: U.S. Bureau of the Census, *Statistical Abstract of the United States, 1987*, pp. 62, 69, 74, 75.

reveal that about 29 percent of the elderly entering nursing homes as non-Medicaid patients converted to Medicaid at some point in their stay. Analyses of the time it takes to spend down assets suggest that more than one-half of Medicaid conversions occur within the first year of entering a nursing home.[14] Next, there is the problem of health care for the 15 percent of Americans without or only partially covered by either public or private insurance. Many of these persons are low-income workers, technically not poor enough to qualify for Medicaid under varying local standards; others live in localities that offer few or no Medicaid benefits. Finally, looming ahead is a crisis of AIDS health care, with an epidemic of long duration imminent and no way to reduce the costs of this disease in sight.

The need to expand coverage while holding down costs weighs upon a health care system in which the finance and delivery of provision are in the midst of basic changes. Once paid for mainly from private sources, it is a system of care now financed almost evenly by public and private expenditures, with the public share growing. The method of reimbursement by public and private third-party payers increasingly favors the use of set rates for medical procedures over the previous practice of cost-based payments. Accompanying these developments, the delivery of health care is marked by a growing corporate presence and the consolidation of insurance and service delivery plans.

## The Growing Corporate Presence

American health care has always been segmentally commercialized in the sense that many of its participants made "profits," notably high-income physicians, drug and equipment companies, and entrepreneurial nursing home operators. At the same time, the supposedly noncommercial service ethos symbolized by the doctor's Hippocratic oath, the consolidation of medical authority, and professional resistance to corporate involvement in medical practice served to mask and contain the commercial ethos and methods in much of American health care.[15] The new commercial ingredient then is not profit per se but the emergence of a highly competitive marketplace accompanied by the hitherto-restrained business ethos and corporate modes of organization.

These developments have been fueled in part by public spending, particularly under Medicare and Medicaid. As Starr points out, the initial financial impetus to the growth of proprietary chains was supplied by the expansion of private insurance and Medicare.[16] Indeed, several years after coverage by Medicare and Medicaid became available, the market share of profit-oriented health care providers increased from 60 percent to 72 percent for nursing homes, from 4 percent to 21 percent for dialysis centers, and from 7 percent to 25 percent for home health agencies.[17]

There was money to be made here. Of the largest public companies in the forty-two major industrial sectors, health care ranked fourth in profitability for the five-year period 1980–1984, with an average return on equity of 19.9 percent and a net profit margin of 7.6 percent (see Table 6.2). Although there was a venture capital seed money lull in the early 1980s, by 1986 more health care seed money than ever was available, up 20–25 percent over 1984 and amounting to $250 million.[18] The nexus of corporate involvement resides in private hospitals and nursing homes.

Proprietary control of hospitals has increased in the last fifteen years, but not as dramatically as conventional wisdom would lead one to imagine. In fact, it is far lower than the 60 percent proprietary control in the early part of this century.[19] Between 1971 and 1983, the proprietary share of hospital control rose from about 13.6 percent to 14.5 percent. For nonfederal short-term general and special hospitals, the percentage of institutions under proprietary controls actually fell from 16 percent to 13 percent between 1960 and 1983, although the percentage of bed control rose from 6 percent to 9 percent. In 1983, while control by profit-oriented entities of all hospitals was 14.5 percent, their share of psychiatric hospitals was 29 percent.[20]

Although propriety involvement has not increased much in overall magnitude, the structure of proprietary control over hospitals has

*Table 6.2.* Profitability and Growth of the Largest Public Companies in Health Care Compared to Other Major Industrial Sectors, 1980–1984

| Economic Parameters | All-Industry Median[a] | Health Care |
|---|---|---|
| *Profitability* | | |
| Five-Year Rank | — | 4 |
| Average Return on Equity (%) | 15.1 | 19.9 |
| 1984 Return on Equity (%) | 13.4 | 15.6 |
| 1984 Net Profit Margin (%) | 3.7 | 7.6 |
| 1984 Debt–Equity Ratio (%) | 40.0 | 30.0 |
| | | |
| *Growth, Sales* | | |
| Five-Year Rank | — | 20 |
| Five-Year Average Increase (%) | 10.2 | 10.5 |
| 1984 Increase (%) | 11.5 | 7.4 |
| | | |
| *Growth, Earnings* | | |
| Five-Year Rank | — | 6 |
| Five-Year Average (%) | 0.6 | 10.3 |
| 1984 Increase (%) | 15.8 | 8.6 |

[a]Forty-two industries.

*Source*: U.S. Bureau of the Census, *Statistical Abstract of the United States, 1986*, p. 536.

changed significantly. This change involves the consolidation of locally governed freestanding hospitals into multihospital systems managed by large corporations. These corporations controlled about 30 percent of the nation's community hospital beds in 1980. Nonprofit organizations accounted for more than 50 percent of the beds in multihospital systems, and another 35 percent of these beds were controlled by proprietary chains. Between the late 1960s and the early 1980s, the proprietary chains grew at a tremendous rate—faster even than the computer industry. The major profit-oriented corporations controlling hospitals include American Medical International (AMI), Hospital Corporation of America (HCA), Humana, and National Medical Enterprises (NME); these chains were all formed in the wake of Medicaid in the late 1960s, except for AMI, which developed in 1976. The largest of these chains, HCA, exemplifies the remarkable pattern of growth in this area, with the number of hospitals owned or managed increasing from 23 in 1970, to more than 300 in 1981, to 380 in 1987.[21]

By the late 1980s, several of the giant hospital corporations were forced to cut back operations. Unsuccessful attempts to diversify into health insurance and a reduction in hospital profit margins led HCA to sell off 104 facilities in 1987, NME divested itself of eight acute-care facilities in 1986, and AMI reported its first full-year loss in 1986.[22] Despite this unfavorable change in fortunes, proprietary corporations continue to attract interest, particularly among nonprofit hospitals seeking to unite with profit-oriented partners in joint ventures. A 1985 survey of 700 nonprofit hospitals found that one-third were already involved in such ventures, with many more giving it serious consideration.[23]

Along with hospitals, the corporate presence in health care is strongly represented in the nursing home industry. By 1985, nursing home care was a $35.2 billion industry, having risen from 6.3 percent to 8.3 percent of national health care expenditures since 1970. The number of facilities rose about 18 percent in the period between 1971 and 1982 to almost 26,000, with the number of beds increasing 33 percent to 1.6 million.[24] The yearly cost of nursing home service averages $22,000 and is expected to increase.[25]

Entrepreneurship has always predominated in nursing home care, with for-profit ownership accounting for 81.8 percent of institutions by 1982.[26] The trend toward large-scale corporate-chain ownership continues to accelerate, with some observers predicting almost total corporate control by a few entities in the not-too-distant future.[27] The largest corporate provider is Beverly Enterprises; its control of 38,488 beds in 1981 grew to 88,198 in 1984 and to about 100,000 in 1986. By 1987, in a cautious mood, the company declared its intent to cut back on the annual bed acquisition from 13,500 to 3000–5000 beds.[28]

At present, only about one-half of nursing home costs are paid for with public health care funds. The remainder is usually paid out of the regular income and assets of the elderly (including their public income supports) and of their children, since long-term nursing home care is almost totally uninsured by the private market. Of the public health care funds for nursing homes, about 55 percent is federal, with the rest provided by the states under the Medicaid matching program.[29] The elderly insured under Medicare cannot qualify for Medicaid until they exhaust all of their assets, at which time they become eligible for aid as medically indigent (a process of impoverishment known in the nursing home trade as "spend down"). There is a strong political pressure to expand the nursing home coverage of insured seniors under Medicare.

At least four major proposals have been under consideration by Congress since 1986, which include some type of federal insurance for long-term care of the elderly.[30] A little progress in this direction was registered under the Medicare Catastrophic Coverage Act of 1988, which extended hospital benefits, added payment for 38 days of continuous home care per year, and increased the period of coverage in a skilled nursing home facility from 100 to 150 days.[31] If some additional form of expanded federal coverage is passed, as expected, the influx of public dollars would be a boon for an already thriving nursing home industry, which can easily change its focus to incorporate whatever specified services might be reimbursed by Medicare.

## Joining Insurance and Delivery

As previously indicated, the public share of health insurance has increased relative to private insurance, with the public sector now insuring 34 percent of American households and paying 48 percent of all health care costs, through direct and indirect expenditures. Nevertheless, profit-oriented health insurance continues to grow, by both incursion into the nonprofit insurers market and subcontractual arrangements that "capture" public insurance.

In line with health care trends, profit-oriented health insurers are transforming themselves from traditional fee-for-service to prepaid managed-care insurers, an insurance device that was pioneered in the 1940s by the still-thriving nonprofit Kaiser-Permanente. Until recently, this device was employed almost totally by nonprofit entities. Prepaid managed care is generically referred to as Health Maintenance Organizations (HMOs), of which there are two basic types (with variations therein). First, "group care" offers full-service care under one roof wherein physicians function as employees, facilities are owned by one organization, and patients have limited choice within the system. Second, "independent provider associations" (IPAs) give full service under coordinated separate roofs; here physicians (though under partial contract) maintain an entrepreneurial status, and facilities are used on a contractual basis. While group-type organizations still predominate, they are giving way rapidly to IPAs, which have a broad appeal to both physicians and patients. The IPA allows physicians to maintain their entrepreneurial status, albeit in a new format, and permits patients some

*Table 6.3.* The Growth of HMOs

| HMO Characteristics | 1976 | 1980 | 1983 | 1985 | Percentage Increase, 1976–1985 |
|---|---|---|---|---|---|
| Total Number of HMOs | 175 | 236 | 280 | 393 | 125 |
| Number of Group | 134 | 139 | 181 | 212 | 58 |
| Number of IPA | 41 | 97 | 99 | 181 | 341 |
| Enrollment[a] | | | | | |
| Group | 5.6 | 7.4 | 10.6 | 14.3 | 155 |
| IPA | .4 | 1.7 | 1.9 | 4.7 | 1075 |
| Total | 6.0 | 9.1 | 12.5 | 19.0 | 217 |

[a]Given in millions.

*Source*: U.S. Bureau of the Census, *Statistical Abstract of the United States, 1987*, p. 90.

degree of choice, which is absent in group HMOs. Prepaid managed care of all types has grown enormously during the last decade, with the number of entities having more than doubled, and the number of enrollees increased about threefold (as shown in Table 6.3). By 1990, HMO membership of 30 million patients and revenues of $25 billion are anticipated.[32]

An entirely new development is the organization and sponsorship by traditional insurance corporations of HMOs on a regional or national level; for example, Partners National Advantage, a nationwide affiliation of IPAs designed to appeal to large national employers with several locations, is sponsored by Aetna Life Insurance Company and Voluntary Hospitals of America. By 1983, about 21 percent of all HMOs were proprietary, among which HealthAmerica, started in 1980, is the largest with its 400,000 patients.[33]

In several schemes implemented by the Reagan administration, avenues are being opened through which profit-oriented insurers—in competition with private nonprofit insurers—may eventually capture the public insurance market, previously the sole preserve of fee-for-service providers and the government payers. First, under a demonstration program, employers and unions—which now often administer supplemental private health benefits to retirees—can contract with the government to assume full administrative responsibility for their retirees' Medicare benefits, and subsequently subcontract with private providers who will compete for these large contracts in the open market. The hope in this arrangement is that increased competitiveness, benefit amalgamation, and overall efficiency will result in better health care at lower costs. Second, the government is starting to contract directly with HMOs (both nonprofit and for-profit) to provide prepaid benefits to Medicare enrollees who are agreeable; currently, about 900,000 persons are enrolled in about 150 such plans involving a public outlay of more than $1 billion. Under this scheme, the government pays subcontracting HMOs 95 percent of the amount that it would expect to pay out in benefits under the Medicare system. In the interest of quality and risk control, HMOs participating in this plan are required to have at least 50 percent non-Medicare enrollment (an example of "proxy shopping" discussed in Chapter 2).

The initial results have been mixed. Patient complaints are typical of those of all HMO enrollees, but the poorer health and higher visibility of the elderly mean that errors and poor service have severe consequences. It may also turn out to be quite difficult to make a profit on prepaid senior health care, given the risk pool. One of the most costly experiences to date has been that of International Medical Centers Inc. (IMC), the nation's largest HMO enroller of Medicare patients, with 70 percent of its 179,000 members and 83 percent of its 1985 revenues of $368 million accounted for by Medicare. The IMC operation was illegally undercapitalized and mismanaged. In 1987, the Health Care Financing Administration canceled its Medicare–HMO contract with IMC, shortly after the company's president was indicted by a federal grand jury on five counts of illegal conduct. Another costly experience with the Medicare–HMO enrollment scheme was that of ChoiceCare, which did not renew its Medicare contract, claiming that it was impossible to make a profit at existing reimbursement levels without seriously cutting the quality of care. Other HMO providers apparently have sought to reduce their costs by limiting certain types of services. Administrators of the Medicare–HMO plan at nonprofit San Francisco Children's Hospital, for example, openly advised their physicians against "overtreating" the elderly enrollees with heroic lifesaving or elective surgery.[34]

A similar demonstration program with prepaid care is also under way with Medicaid, wherein private HMO insurers may capture the funds and patients previously funneled into the public hospital care system for indigents. Enrollment of Medicaid recipients in HMOs and other prepaid health plans soared from 280,000 in 1981 to 840,000 in 1986, at which time twenty-five states offered prepaid schemes for those eligible.[35] Prior to these arrangements the public system was grossly inefficient and ineffective, insofar as indigents were forced to rely on sporadic expensive hospital care or no care at all when what was often needed were routine visits to family physicians and access to specialists. As with Medicare, the results of HMO–Medicaid demonstrations are mixed. In Jackson County, Missouri, the program reduced the number of costly and unnecessary Medicaid inpatient days by 46 percent, improving the access of poor patients to the type of routine nonhospital care available to other Americans. In Monroe County, New York, eight of the eleven affiliated providers withdrew from the program two years after it began, having sustained a combined estimated loss of $2.8 million in the second year.[36]

The problems with Medicare and Medicaid HMOs reflect larger issues regarding the organization of health care in an era of struggles over cost containment. The intermingling of public and private roles in the finance and production of health care is an arrangement under which public responsibilities for controlling costs and assuring quality have been difficult to exercise. In the 1980s, several measures have been introduced to economize on public spending, which sharpen public and private roles in the cost–quality trade-off.

## Cost Control and Quality: Shifting the Burden

Under Medicare and Medicaid, the fee-for-service model of public insurance has been characterized as "contracting without a contract."[37] Quality, quantity, and price of health care services were left, with minor exceptions, to the determination of private providers and patients. Doctors could offer services of the highest quality and charge accordingly. As would be expected, expenditures spiraled upward.

By the early 1980s, efforts were launched to economize on public medical care spending. These efforts involved the use of various mechanisms such as bidding, vouchers, and administrative price-setting. Bidding allows third-party public payers to create a competitive arena in which the winning bid theoretically represents the lowest price for producing health services. Because the third-party payers do not themselves consume the service, this transaction cannot rely on the use of consumer choice as a mechanism of quality control. To ensure that the lowest bidder does not simply deliver the most inferior level of care, it is necessary to specify in advance an acceptable quality of medical service that must be produced for the contract. Here, of course, lies the rub. Not only is it technically difficult to specify quality for many medical services, but where such measures may exist it is also politically awkward to specify anything less than the highest quality. By modifying the model of the single successful bidder and allowing several successful participants in a bidding arrangement with no guaranteed quantity for each, a degree of quality control can be introduced through the process of consumer choice. Bidding experiments in California and Arizona have been implemented under waivers of the federal Medicaid rules. Hospitals were invited to submit advance bids fixing their service rates prospectively. In both states, officials encountered difficulties in arriving at acceptable prices through pure bidding procedures and in the end had to rely heavily upon negotiations, which moved the process toward one of political price-setting.[38]

Widespread administrative pricing of medical services by government was introduced in 1983 when Medicare established a prospective-payment system based on diagnosis-related groups (DRGs). Under the DRGs, patients are diagnosed and hospitals receive a fixed fee for each case based on the average costs of treating their condition. Extra payments are provided for "outlier" cases in which complications arise that turn out excessively expensive to treat. Critics charge that the DRGs have led to "quicker and sicker" hospital discharge of Medicare beneficiaries.[39] While the DRGs undoubtedly have had some influence on reducing hospital utilization rates, they arrived at a time when both admissions and average length of hospital stays were on the decline for the entire population.[40] Other changes in health practices such as the growth of outpatient surgery and home health care also helped to lower hospital utilization rates. Moreover, whether "quicker and sicker" discharge is actually harmful to patients remains to be shown. After patients are treated, spending part of their recovery time at home or in health care settings other than the hospital often entails few risks.

As a method of payment, DRGs may encourage practices that eventually undermine cost containment objectives and access to service for certain groups. As Starr suggests, it is a payment system that tempts hospitals to adopt the strategy of "DRG creep"—the manipulation of diagnostic coding in order to place patients into high-yield categories. With DRG payment schedules for surgical cases more profitable than for other conditions, the system generates a bias in favor of costly invasive treatment. The system also creates an incentive to shun cases that are likely to suffer complications because a patient's health status is generally weak, which militates against service to the very old and the poor.[41]

In contrast to bidding schemes and administrative pricing through DRGs, which focus on arrangements between public third-party payers and private producers of health care, the health care voucher is a patient-oriented scheme, which deploys public spending in a way that enhances consumer power. Rather than fee-for-service benefits, for example, Medicare recipients can be given government-financed vouchers with which to purchase private insurance under prepaid HMO-type plans. This arrangement transfers the administration of health insurance plans from the federal Health Care Financing Administration to private firms, allowing consumers to select among the private plans. As previously noted, initial experiences with HMO–Medicaid demonstrations have shown mixed results.

Bidding, administrative pricing, and vouchers each in their own way attempt to set public parameters for cost containment while leaving determinations about the quality of health care to others. Under the previous fee-for-service insurance schemes, costly procedures were routinely employed because the physician's service ethos recommended providing the best care that money could buy. Hospitals could cross-subsidize unprofitable services and destitute patients by charging higher fees for more remunerative types of services and patients. Overall, the fee-for-service principle engendered a felicitous congruence between the service ethos and the financial interests of health care providers. With benefit payments fixed, the private provider is under increasing pressures to make the necessary cost, quality, and access trade-offs that now come to divide the service ethos and medical business interests.

What is emerging in health care is a field in which both finance and production of services have taken on distinctly commercial attributes. On the finance side, public insurance for health care has moved in this direction through the introduction of market-oriented reimbursement mechanisms and efforts to increase private payments. As just described, bidding and vouchers are market-oriented mechanisms that allow third-party payers to promote greater competition among providers and more attentive consumer choice in the delivery of health care. At the same time that these mechanisms are being adopted to temper the cost of public financing, serious consideration is being given to various ways of using government's regulatory powers to increase private responsibility for providing health insurance benefits. As previously noted, a model for this approach is illustrated in the mandated employee benefits under the Massachusetts Health Security Act of 1988.

On the production side of health care provisions, the commercial orientation is powerfully impelled by the growth of corporate providers. The corporate ethos, according to Starr, permeates not only profit-making medical care organizations, but voluntary hospitals and government health care agencies as well. "Those who talked about 'health care planning' in the 1970s now talk about 'health care marketing,' " he observes, as "the 'health center' of one era is the 'profit center' of the next."[42] In addition to changing the organizational culture of health care, the rise of corporate medicine is likely to result in a significant loss of autonomy for physicians. Interestingly, this development may have a somewhat different effect on nurses. With the reorganization of medical care and increasing concerns for service efficiency, new opportunities have developed for nurses and other paramedical professionals. Approximately 35,000 nurses now run companies or offer independent services in, for example, home health care, individual health counseling, public health education, prenatal care, and geriatric care. They are even doing routine physical exams and basic nonemergency medical care. Contracting with employers and health care providers, nurses may soon be directly reimbursable by insurers without the traditional intermediaries.[43]

Finally, the production of health care has increasingly been linked to the administration of insurance schemes. Drawn together under corporate auspices, the consolidation of insurance and service delivery within prepaid plans such as HMOs endows the health care system with a high level of integrated control. What was once a loosely connected system of independent physicians and autonomous hospitals generously supported by third-party payers, has become a more cost-conscious, commercially oriented, and tightly integrated service industry. The erosion of physicians' control over health care decisions is accompanied by the incremental decline in a service ethos that promoted access and quality of care. Not without shortcomings, this service ethos served important functions. As the commercialization of health care progresses, it is unclear where the responsibility for these functions will reside and how firmly they will be maintained under cost control pressures.

In effecting social transfers for health care, the state may exercise various options. Regulatory powers of government can be used to set prices or shift the burden of insurance costs to private employers through mandated benefits. Direct expenditures may be channeled through bidding and voucher mechanisms, which foster competition and choice. Indirect expenditures may be extended along several lines—as proposed by the 1986 Bowen Report on Catastrophic Health Insurance—in the form of tax-favored Individual Medical Accounts, revised IRA provisions that allow tax-free withdrawals for certain medical expenses, and refundable tax credits for long-term care insurance premiums.[44] There are merits and liabilities to each approach. The challenge remains to fashion a mix of health care transfers that achieves an agreeable balance among pressing concerns about cost, quality, and access.

# Notes

1. U.S. Bureau of the Census, *Statistical Abstract of the United States, 1986* (Washington, D.C.: U.S. Government Printing Office, 1985), pp. 96–97, 109; idem, *Statistical Abstract of the United States, 1987* (Washington, D.C.: U.S. Government Printing Office, 1986), p. 84.

2. Katherine Levit et al., "National Health Expenditures, 1984," *Health Care Financing Review*, 7:1 (Fall 1985), pp. 1–35.

3. Ross Arnett et al., "Projections of Health Care Spending to 1990," *Health Care Financing Review*, 7:3 (Spring 1986), pp. 1–36.

4. U.S. Bureau of the Census, *Statistical Abstract, 1986*, p. 96; idem, *1987*, p. 84.

5. Jean-Pierre Poullier, "From Risk Aversion to Risk Rating: Trends in OECD Health Care Systems," *International Journal of Health Planning and Management* (forthcoming).

6. U.S. Bureau of the Census, *Statistical Abstract, 1987*, pp. 85, 343.

7. Ibid., p. 297.

8. Poullier, "From Risk Aversion Risk Rating: Trends," pp. 18–19.

9. Melvyn Krauss, "Taxes By Any Other Name . . . ," *The New York Times*, August 9, 1988, p. 23.

10. U.S. Bureau of the Census, *Statistical Abstract, 1986*, pp. 101, 102, 373.

11. Paul Starr, "Health Care for the Poor: The Past Twenty Years," in *Fighting Poverty*, eds. Sheldon Danziger and Daniel Weinberg (Cambridge, Mass.: Harvard University Press, 1986), p. 118.

12. Poullier, "From Risk Aversion Risk Rating: Trends," p. 19; Organisation for Economic Cooperation and Development, *Living Conditions in OECD Countries* (Paris: OECD, 1986), p. 30.

13. Poullier, "From Risk Aversion Risk Rating: Trends," p. 6.

14. Miriam Arnold, "Covering the Uncovered: Issues and Challenges in Financing and Organizing Long-Term Care for the Elderly in the United States," unpublished doctoral dissertation, 1988, University of California at Berkeley, pp. 79–84.

15. Paul Starr, *The Social Transformation of American Medicine* (New York: Basic Books, 1982), pp. 199–232.

16. Ibid., p. 435.

17. Theodore Marmor, Mark Schlesinger and Richard Smithey, "A New Look at Nonprofits: Health Care Policy in a Competitive Age," *Yale Journal on Regulation*, 3:2 (Spring 1986), pp. 326–27.

18. Udayan Gupta, "Venture Capitalists Cautiously Returning to Investments in Health Care Companies," *Wall Street Journal*, October 29, 1986, p. 29.

19. Carson Bays, "Why Most Private Hospitals Are Nonprofit," *Journal of Policy Analysis and Management*, 2:3 (Spring 1983), pp. 366–85. These were mostly small hospitals owned by doctors.

20. U.S. Bureau of the Census, *Statistical Abstract, 1986*, pp. 106–107.

21. Starr, *Social Transformation*, p. 430. The 1987 figure for HCA-owned hospitals is cited in Calvin Sims, "Hospital Chain Sells 104 Units," *The New York Times*, June 1, 1987, p. D1.

22. Rhonda Rundle, "American Medical International to Cut Staff, Close Insurer in Reorganization," *Wall Street Journal*, August 25, 1986, p. 11; "Hospital Chain Sells 104 Units."

23. Survey by the firm Ernst and Whinney, cited in Udayan Gupta, "Hospitals Enlist Profit-Minded Parties for Ventures to Generate New Business," *Wall Street Journal*, January 23, 1987, p. 23.

24. U.S. Bureau of the Census, *Statistical Abstract, 1987*, pp. 85, 93.

25. U.S. Congress, House of Representatives, Select Committee on Aging, *Long-Term Care and Personal Impoverishment: Seven in Ten Elderly Living Alone Are at Risk*, (Washington, D.C.: Select Committee on Aging, October 1987).

26. U.S. Bureau of the Census, *Statistical Abstract, 1987*, p. 93.

27. W. Spicer, "The Bloom in Building," *Contemporary Administrator*, February 1982, pp. 13–14.

28. David Stoesz, "Corporate Welfare: The Third Stage of Welfare in the United States," *Social Work*, July–August 1986, p. 246; see also *Wall Street Journal*, December 31, 1986, p. 6.

29. U.S. Bureau of the Census, *Statistical Abstract, 1986*, pp. 98–99.

30. For discussion of these proposals see Miriam Arnold, "Covering Uncovered: Issues Financing Elderly in U.S."

31. For a more detailed discussion of this legislation, see Edward Lawler, "Medicare's Almost Catastrophic Protection," *The Public Policy and Aging Report*, 2:4 (July–August 1988), pp. 1–4.

32. National Industry Council for HMO Development, *Ten Year Report 1973–1983* (Washington, D.C., 1983), cited by Stoesz, "Corporate Welfare: Third Stage." One estimate indicates that the number of HMO enrollees had already increased to 28 million by early 1987. See Rhonda Rundle, "Medical Debate," *Wall Street Journal*, October 6, 1987, p. 1.

33. Stoesz, "Corporate Welfare: Third Stage," p. 247.

34. For reports on recent experiences and problems with HMOs, see Martha Brannigan, "A Fast-Growing HMO Shows It's Tough to Make a Profit Caring for the Elderly," *Wall Street Journal,* August 22, 1986, p. 41; Rhonda L. Rundle, "Several Employees and Unions Propose to Administer Retirees Medicare Plans," *Wall Street Journal,* August 18, 1986, p. 44; Ruth R. Pitlick, "Medicare HMOs: Not in Perfect Health," *Wall Street Journal,* June 17, 1987, p. 24; Elaine Herscher, "A Furor Over Corner-Cutting by Medicare HMOs," *San Francisco Chronicle,* June 20, 1987, p. 4; Michael Herschorn, "Medical Discord: Some Doctors Assail Quality of Treatment Provided by HMOs," *Wall Street Journal,* September 16, 1986, p. 1.

35. Deborah Freund and Edward Nuschlar, "Overview of Medicaid Legislation and Case-Management Initiatives," *Health Care Financing Review,* Annual Supplement 1986.

36. Peter Volgyes, "State-Managed Health Care: Financial Implications for Provider Organizations," *New England Journal of Human Services,* 7:4 (1987), pp. 17–20, and Clare Ansberry, "After Five Years, Experimental Health Project for Medicaid Shows Mixed Results," *Wall Street Journal,* June 1, 1987, p. 48.

37. Randall Bovbjerg, Philip Held, and Mark Pauly, "Privatization and Bidding in the Health-Care Sector," *Journal of Policy Analysis and Management,* 6:4 (Summer 1987), p. 653.

38. Ibid., pp. 653–57.

39. U.S. Congress, House of Representatives, Select Committee on Aging, *Out "Sooner and Sicker": Myth or Medicare Crisis?,* Comm. Publ. No. 99–591 (Washington, D.C.: U.S. Government Printing Office, 1986).

40. U.S. Bureau of the Census, *Statistical Abstract, 1987,* p. 96.

41. Starr, "Health Care for Poor: Past Twenty Years," pp. 121–23.

42. Starr, *Social Transformation,* p. 448.

43. Gregg Levoy, "Nurse Power," *Image Magazine,* June 21, 1987, pp. 5–6.

44. Jules Berman, "The Bowen Report on Catastrophic Health Insurance," *Washington Social Legislation Bulletin,* 30:1 (January 12, 1987), pp. 1–4.

# 7

# *Housing:*
# *A Joint Venture*

Despite recurrent headlines about the homeless, housing in the United States is not in a state of crisis. Homelessness is a problem the dimensions of which have been frequently overdrawn. To sharpen public awareness of and garner political support for their cause, advocacy groups in their estimates of the number of homeless tend to exaggerate the size of this problem by substantial proportions. One such estimate by the Community for Creative Non-Violence in 1982 claims that there are 2.2 million homeless (or about 1 percent of the population), but fails to specify an empirical basis for this figure. That highly publicized figure is more than ten times the 192,000 estimate extrapolated from empirical findings of street and shelter population counts in three cities and about four times the 586,000 figure calculated from the highest local estimates published between 1981 and 1983.[1] In 1985 and 1986, Peter Rossi and his associates conducted rigorous scientific surveys of street and shelter populations in Chicago; their data revealed an estimated homeless population of 2772, which was about one-eighth of the 20,000–25,000 estimate advanced by the Chicago Coalition for the Homeless.[2]

Beyond the question of size, homelessness is a problem in many cases mislabeled. It has more to do with a complex of social ills—

mainly alcoholism, drug abuse, and mental disabilities—than with a critical deficiency in living quarters. Since the mid-1960s, the deinstitutionalization movement has afforded greater freedom to mentally disabled groups along with lower levels of public care and supervision. As a result of this movement, the resident populations in state hospitals declined dramatically from 475,000 in 1965 to 137,000 in 1980, and the numbers are still falling.[3] A large number of these patients ended up in nursing homes and in board-and-care facilities. Many others drifted away from supervised arrangements and live on the streets. For example, the Keener Building on Ward's Island in New York City, once a psychiatric hospital, is now a men's shelter providing refuge to some of the same people who previously received daily care and professional treatment at this facility.[4]

Various estimates suggest that the mentally ill constitute between 33 and 75 percent of homeless persons, depending on whether the count focuses mainly on those living in shelters or those living on the streets and in the parks.[5] Large proportions of the homeless are also substance abusers. Based on a sample of nearly 30,000 people seen in the National Health Care for the Homeless Program in sixteen cities, Wright estimates that 40 percent of the homeless are alcohol abusers, 10 percent abuse other drugs, and 33 percent are mentally ill.[6] The Chicago surveys found that about 60 percent of the homeless people suffered from alcoholism, mental illness, or both.[7] A study in Ohio reports finding 30 percent with psychiatric symptoms, 54 percent with a behavior problem, and 21 percent with a drinking problem.[8]

It is true that a shortage of inexpensive housing exists, particularly in thriving metropolitan areas such as New York, Boston, and San Francisco, but the majority of homeless people have severe problems that go well beyond the lack of shelter. In a tight housing market it is very often, as Thomas Main observes,

> the weakest families that are unable to cope with the situation and end up homeless. And 'weakness' here should not be taken to mean simply those families that are poor in a strictly economic sense. The greatest obstacle to surviving in a tight housing market may not be so much economic poverty as functional problems which make it difficult to make the relevant alternatives to homelessness—such as doubling up—work.[9]

Many, if not most, of the homeless are people suffering from psychosocial dysfunctions of long duration. Even with adequate cash and easily accessible housing, they would remain incapable of healthy functioning on their own. They require care and supervision as well as shelter. The needs of this group are critical and deserve serious attention. But their plight has relatively little to do with the performance of the regular housing market.

## Housing Performance: Standards and Affordability

Conventional measures of decent housing have been continually elevated over the years. With overcrowding and inadequate plumbing nearly eliminated, advocates of housing reform have shifted their focus of concern to the emerging problem of "affordability"; this problem is said to exist when more than 25–30 percent of the income of a household goes to rent.

However, it is not at all clear at what level the proportion of household income allotted to shelter can be judged as too high. Many variables influence this calculation. The cash value of in-kind social welfare benefits has increased substantially since the 1960s.[10] Families receiving these benefits may devote a higher proportion of their cash income to housing without appreciably changing earlier patterns of household consumption. Even if the pattern of household consumption changes, whether such change is symptomatic of a problem remains an open question. Families that allocate a greater proportion of their income to housing may be expressing a preference for higher quality dwellings and a willingness to spend relatively less on, for example, recreation or education. Those who buy new housing tend to obtain units with more amenities. From 1970 to 1984, the proportion of new privately owned houses with more than one bathroom increased from 68 percent to 86 percent, and the units with central air-conditioning more than doubled from 34 percent to 71 percent (as shown in Table 7.1). The affordability concept, as Salins points out, is difficult to interpret in the context of well-housed middle-income families who deliberately choose to assign a high proportion of their income to shelter.[11]

The problem of "affordability" is coupled with the sharp climb in the nominal costs of housing. During the decade from 1970 to 1980, the median price of a new single-family house increased almost threefold. Mortgage rates also rose substantially during this period. Combining mortgage rates and price, the monthly mortgage payments on a new

*Table 7.1.* Selected Characteristics of New Privately Owned One-Family Houses, 1970–1985

| Characteristics | 1970 | 1980 | 1985 |
|---|---|---|---|
| Total Number Constructed | 793,000 | 957,000 | 1,072,000 |
| Average Area (Sq. Ft.) | 1,500 | 1,740 | 1,785 |
| Median Area (Sq. Ft.) | 1,385 | 1,595 | 1,605 |
| Number of Bathrooms (%) | | | |
| 1 or less | 32 | 18 | 13 |
| $1\frac{1}{2}$–2 | 52 | 58 | 58 |
| $2\frac{1}{2}$ or more | 16 | 25 | 29 |
| Central Air-Conditioning | 34 | 63 | 70 |
| Median Sale Price | $23,400 | $64,000 | $84,300 |

*Source*: U.S. Bureau of the Census, *Statistical Abstract of the United States, 1987* (Washington, D.C.: U.S. Government Printing Office, 1986), pp. 706, 707.

house quadrupled. This increase was twice as high as the rise in family income. The actual cost of new housing, however, was not as burdensome as it appears. On the one hand, housing has become more expensive largely because, as Carroll observes, "quality and building codes have been upgraded; enforcement toughened; underground utilities mandated; zoning made more stringent."[12] Indeed, several estimates indicate that if the increase in quality of housing is held constant, the rise in cost over the last ten to fifteen years almost vanishes.[13] On the other hand, as a result of inflation, the value of housing appreciated more in most years than the interest paid on mortgages. These interest payments thus became a form of savings, which possessed the added attraction of being tax deductible. For many families, Jencks observes, "the cost of home ownership, even after allowing for maintenance and depreciation, was probably negative during the 1970s."[14] Housing was a good investment, a point not lost on the general public. Between 1970 and 1983 the rate of home ownership rose from 62.9 percent to 64.7 percent of all American households. This was slightly larger than during the 1960s, when ownership advanced from 61.9 percent to 62.9 percent. Apparently, as the problem of "affordability" increased so did the rate of home ownership.

Whereas the overall rate of home ownership is still very high and financing alternatives are multiplying, during the last decade the cost of housing has climbed beyond the means of many first-time and younger home buyers. In 1970, the median family income was almost 150 percent of the income level required to qualify for a mortgage on a median-priced single family home that year; by 1983, the median family income was less than 85 percent of the qualifying figure. However, by 1986 the median income relative to housing costs had moved up to slightly more than 100 percent of the amount needed for the purchase of a median-priced home. Often it is the high down payment that is more of a problem for cash-strapped young home buyers than the carrying costs. From 1979 to 1983, home ownership among households in the age cohort under twenty-nine years old declined by 17 percent, even as more two-income households were being formed.[15] Home ownership, like marriage, household formation, and childbearing, is not fading away, but occurring at a later stage in life and with the support of two incomes rather than one.

To suggest that the affordability of housing in the 1980s is rather less compelling a problem than some would have it, is not to say the market is without flaws, which create real hardships for different groups. Figures on national trends can obscure local facts. And the housing market is essentially a local operation. Many people cannot or will not make housing decisions apart from other considerations such as job availability, educational opportunity, local ties, and life-style. Thus, while housing may cost on the average only 18 percent of the family income in St. Louis, Missouri, those who live, work, and enjoy the amenities in New York City or San Francisco, where housing costs average well above 30 percent of family income, are rarely drawn to St. Louis by the promise of a lower mortgage.

The affordability of housing is a serious issue for low-income renters. In contrast to the rate of home ownership, which has grown slightly since 1970, the income disparities between owners and renters have increased significantly. The renter–owner income ratio declined from 70 percent in 1970 to 51 percent in 1983.[16] The impact of this comparative decline in renter income has been cushioned somewhat by relatively smaller increases in rental costs.[17] Nevertheless, as renters in general have become poorer, finding decent shelter for those at the bottom of this group poses a major challenge. In 1981 about 37 percent of renter households fell into the "very low income" category used to define eligibility for participation in federal housing allowance programs. Furthermore, one estimate suggests a huge gap between low-income families and the number of low-income units available to house them, spreading from 3.7 million units in 1993 to 7.8 million units by

2003.[18] These figures reflect not so much a scarcity in housing units as a shortage in units renting at a price low-income families can afford. In the third quarter of 1987, for example, almost 3 million year-round rental housing units were vacant, amounting to the highest vacancy rate in over two decades.[19]

Despite regional variations—the delay in home ownership for young households and the long-standing problem of excessive rent burdens for the very poor—by any objective standard of historical or international comparison, most Americans have access to large, high-quality dwelling units at reasonable cost. Only 1 percent of owner-occupied units and 3 percent of rental units lack complete plumbing. More than 90 percent of all units have a telephone, and almost 60 percent have some air-conditioning. Approximately 17 percent of American households live in dwelling units constructed within the last fifteen years. While rental and older units are usually smaller and of lower quality, they generally cost less and contain fewer persons per unit. Overall, the number of persons per unit and indoor dwelling density have declined markedly in recent decades. Between 1960 and 1983, the number of persons per dwelling unit fell almost 20 percent (to 2.5 persons) in owner-occupied housing and about 23 percent (to 2 persons) in rental units (see Table 7.2). To appreciate fully the improvements in American housing, it is illustrative to recall that in 1950, 45 percent of the homes were heated with wood or coal—a figure down to only 5 percent in the 1980s.[20]

The size and quality of dwelling units compare well not only to past circumstances, but also to current conditions in other major developed

*Table 7.2.* Housing Amenities, 1960–1983

|  | 1960 | 1970 | 1980 | 1983 |
|---|---|---|---|---|
| Median Number of Rooms | 4.9 | 5.0 | 5.1 | 5.1 |
| Average Area (Sq. Ft.) per Household | — | — | 1745 | 1672 |
| Median Area (Sq. Ft.) per Household | — | — | 1488 | 1434 |
| Number of Persons per Unit |  |  |  |  |
| Owner-Occupied | 3.1 | 3.0 | 2.6 | 2.5 |
| Renter-Occupied | 2.6 | 2.3 | 2.0 | 2.0 |
| Units with All Plumbing (%) | 86.8 | 93.5 | 97.3 | 97.6 |
| Units with Telephone (%) | 78.5 | 87.0 | 93.0 | 90.4 |
| Units with Some Air-Conditioning (%) | 12.4 | 36.7 | 55.0 | 59.1 |

*Source*: U.S. Bureau of the Census, *Statistical Abstract of the United States, 1987* (Washington, D.C.: U.S. Government Printing Office, 1986), pp. 710–14.

*Table 7.3.* International Comparison of Housing Density and Basic Amenities

| Characteristics | United States 1980 | France 1978 | Germany 1978 | Japan 1978 | Sweden 1980 | United Kingdom 1980 |
|---|---|---|---|---|---|---|
| Average Number of Persons Per Room | 0.5 | 0.8 | 0.6 | 0.8 | 0.6 | 0.6 |
| % Population in Dwellings with under One Person per Room (%) | 96 | 48 | 85 | 56 | 80 | 90 |
| Population in Private Households with Flush Toilet inside Dwelling (%) | 97 | 83 | 93 | 46 | 96 | 94 |
| % Population in Private Households with Fixed Bath or Shower Inside Dwelling (%) | 97 | 83 | 89 | 83 | 93 | 96 |

*Source*: Organisation for Economic Co-operation and Development, *Living Conditions in OECD Countries* (Paris: OECD, 1986), pp. 133, 134, and 139.

countries. In 1980, indoor dwelling density of American housing—at an average of 0.5 persons per room—was the lowest among industrialized nations; furthermore, American housing rates highest in comparison with other nations on the percentage of the population in private households with basic amenities, such as flush toilets and fixed baths or showers, inside the dwelling unit (Table 7.3). While there are pockets of low-quality dwelling units, scarcity, and excessive cost, Americans are generally rather comfortably housed by most standards. This is the result not of unfettered private enterprise, but of a housing market enmeshed in a protective cocoon of public aid and regulation, which offers something to almost all citizens.

## Housing Transfers: Direct, Indirect, and Regulatory Measures

In contrast to Britain where local government authorities own and maintain about 31 percent of all housing units, publicly owned housing in the United States amounts to less than 1.5 percent of the housing stock.[21] The low proportion of publicly owned units fosters an impression that social welfare measures in the housing sector are limited. This impression arises, in part, because a great deal of public aid takes the form of hidden subsidies and, in part, because a considerable portion of this aid goes to middle-class home owners who do not conform to the conventional image of "social welfare recipients."

Assistance for housing is provided through a wide range of policy measures, which knit public and private activities together in a complex network of social transfers. These measures fall under three headings.

DIRECT EXPENDITURE

Construction and management of public housing

Rent supplements and housing vouchers to low-income tenants

Rent subsidies for designated housing units

INDIRECT EXPENDITURE

Subsidized private purchase and improvement of units through tax expenditures

Hard-to-measure credit subsidies, insurance subsidies, and contingent liabilities related to loan guarantees

REGULATORY MEASURES

Health, safety, zoning, and building codes regulating construction standards

Diverse state and local measures controlling the level of rents and conditions of tenure for tenants

Banking and securities regulations affecting arrangements to finance housing

## *Direct Government Expenditures*

Direct expenditures on housing take several forms. Up through the 1960s federal funds went mainly for the construction of housing units owned and managed by public authorities. By 1985 there were approximately 1.3 million public rental housing units, relatively few of which had been built or acquired during the last two decades.[22] Public housing is, for the most part, old, large scale, congested, and plagued with intense physical and social problems. Of public housing residents, half are elderly, an especially vulnerable group frequently victimized by other residents. As the landlord, government agencies become effectively liable for the physical deficiencies of its public housing projects and for many of the numerous mishaps and catastrophes that occur on their premises. In New Orleans, for example, where about 10 percent of the population resides in public housing, the local public housing authorities were sued an average of three times daily in 1986.[23]

Since the 1970s, housing assistance has focused on providing income supplements to individuals and rent subsidies tied to newly constructed or substantially rehabilitated units. Under the Section 8 program of the Housing and Community Development Act of 1974, rent supplements are provided to households earning up to 80 percent of the median family income in their community (or about 200 percent of the poverty line). After 1981, eligibility was limited to families with incomes below 50 percent of the median in their communities, adjusted for family size. Households participating in this program are required to pay between 15 and 25 percent of their income for rent and must reside in dwellings that meet certain minimum standards. Housing assistance payments to these families are portable. In 1985, Congress authorized a housing voucher demonstration program that is similar to the Section 8 rent supplement with some modifications. In addition to providing rent subsidies for existing quarters, the Section 8 program also encourages the development and renovation of new housing through government commitments to subsidize designated units for the difference between their fair market rent and a reduced payment that would be made by low-income tenants participating in the program.

Another important form of direct federal expenditure involves public funding for community development efforts devoted to the physical improvement of neighborhoods. These efforts are financed mainly by the Community Development Block Grant program established in 1974. Rehabilitation of housing is among the major activities conducted within the program's broad objectives, which include helping low-income and moderate-income households, eliminating slums and blight, and meeting other urgent needs of selected localities.

In addition to federal expenditures, housing programs are also financed by a variety of state and local agencies. Funds for housing and community development allocated through direct measures by all levels of government amounted to approximately $27.3 billion in 1987, down from a high of $39.3 billion in 1985 (as shown in Table 7.4). While the 1987 expenditure is about 65 percent above the 1980 figure of $16.6 billion, relative to total spending it remained at the 1980 level of 0.2 percent of all government outlays. It should be noted that a major source

*Table 7.4.* Direct Expenditures for Housing, 1970–1987[a]

| Financial Source | 1970 | 1975 | 1980 | 1985 | 1987 (est.) |
|---|---|---|---|---|---|
| Federal | | | | | |
| Housing Assistance[b] | .50 | 2.06 | 5.63 | 25.26[d] | 12.94 |
| Veterans Housing | .05 | .02 | — | .21 | .13 |
| Community Development[c] | 1.45 | 2.32 | 4.90 | 4.60 | 4.25 |
| State and Local | 2.14 | 3.46 | 6.06 | 9.28[e] | 10.00 |
| Total | 4.14 | 7.86 | 16.59 | 39.35 | 27.32 |
| Direct Housing Expenditure Divided by Total Federal, State, and Local Expenditure (%) | 1.4 | 1.6 | 2.0 | 3.1 | 2.0 |

[a]Given in billions of dollars.

[b]Includes low-income housing (Section 8), public housing, homeownership, and rental (Sections 235 and 236), public housing loans and operating subsidies, and other housing asisistance.

[c]Includes Community Development Block Grants, Urban Development Action Grants, rental rehabilitation rental development, and other programs.

[d]Includes $14.3 billion in one-time amortizaton of Public Housing Authority rehabilitations and acquisitions.

[e]For 1984.

*Sources*: Office of Management and Budget, *Historical Tables: Budget of the U.S. Government, FY 1988* (Washington, D.C.: U.S. Government Printing Office, 1987), Tables 3.3 and 15.2; U.S. Bureau of the Census, *Statistical Abstract of the United States, 1987* (Washington, D.C.: U.S. Government Printing Office, 1986), p. 258.

of public support for housing is not being counted in these figures; that is, federal and state benefit payments under the income maintenance programs (discussed in Chapter 4) of Aid to Families with Dependent Children, Supplementary Security Income, and General Assistance include explicit and implicit allowances for shelter. According to recent estimates, the shelter allowances contained in these welfare payments add at least $10 billion more a year to public transfers for housing.[24]

## *Indirect Expenditures*

In 1985 federal tax expenditures for housing, as shown in Table 7.5, amounted to $41 billion or approximately 12 percent of all tax expenditures. The sum attributed to this category of tax expenditure equaled or exceeded the sum of direct federal spending on housing, depending on the items of expenditure that one includes. The largest item on the list of housing tax expenditures is the mortgage interest deduction on owner-

*Table 7.5.* Tax Expenditures for Housing, 1985

| Recipient | Expenditure[a] |
|---|---|
| *Directly Benefiting Individuals* | |
| Mortgage Deduction on Owner-Occupied Homes | 24.9 |
| Property Tax Deduction on Owner-Occupied Homes | 9.7 |
| Capital-Gains Exclusions and Deferrals on Home Sales | 2.6 |
| *Other Preferences* | |
| Housing Bond Interest Exclusion | 2.8 |
| Accelerated Depreciation on Rental Housing | .8 |
| Investment Credit for Rehabilitation of Structures (Nonhistorical) | .3 |
| Total | 41.1 |

[a]Given in billions of dollars.

*Source*: U.S. Bureau of the Census, *Statistical Abstract of the United States, 1986*, (Washington, D.C.: U.S. Government Printing Office, 1985), p. 310.

occupied homes, which affords a substantial transfer to the middle classes and reduces the effective cost of home ownership by about 20 percent on the average.[25] The amount of indirect expenditures would be considerably higher if the nontaxation of imputed rental income from owner-occupied housing was viewed as a tax expenditure in the United States as is the practice in Britain, France, and Sweden.[26] (Imputed income from housing is seen as a tax expenditure because if one person buys a house for $100,000 and lives in it rent free, that person pays no tax; however, if a second person buys a house for $100,000 and rents that house for $8000, that person must pay tax on this income even though the income is used to purchase another house that he is living in at the time. The first person escapes being taxed on the imputed rental value of his house—say $8000—which he then puts into the purchase of another house. Both parties have invested the same capital in one house, are using the dividends to buy a second house, and are living in one of the two houses; the preferential treatment given the first party can be seen as a tax expenditure.) The mortgage interest deduction on owner-occupied homes covers not only the primary residence but also vacation homes, which include habitable boats and trailers. This deduction accounts for a small fraction of housing tax expenditures, is of greatest benefit usually to those who need it the least, and is likely to be eliminated in future tax reforms.

Credit subsidies represent another indirect form of social assistance for housing. Transfers through credit subsidies are more difficult to trace than tax expenditures. While the federal credit budget—established in 1980—measures direct loan obligations and loan commitments, it does not calculate the cost of federal subsidies inherent in these transactions. A proposal to reform budgeting for credit programs that would incorporate an estimate of the subsidies provided by these programs was under review by Congress in 1987 and is likely to stimulate some adjustments in the federal approach to credit budgeting.

As Glennerster points out, it is difficult to compare public expenditures on housing in England with other countries, "since much of it abroad takes the form of hidden subsidies—low-interest loans."[27] Indeed, these subsidies not only are hidden, but they also operate through several arrangements including direct loans, guaranteed loan commitments, and loan write-offs. Direct loans from federal agencies result in a subsidy to borrowers under any of the following conditions[28]:

Interest rates below commercial levels

Longer maturities than private loans

Deferral of interest

Allowance of grace periods

Waiver or reduction of loan fees

Higher loan amounts relative to property value than available through private loans

Availability of funds to borrowers for purposes for which the private sector would not lend

Estimates of the subsidies provided by federal direct-loan programs for housing reveal a benefit to borrowers of at least $175 million in 1986. This figure includes $97 million for the elderly and handicapped, $61 million for veterans, and $17 million for home weatherization loans. An additional $578 million in credit subsidies was furnished through disaster loans under the Small Business Administration and loans from the agriculture credit insurance fund, a substantial part of which was devoted to housing. It should be noted that the estimated cash value of these subsidies to borrowers is higher than the direct cash costs to government, because government can always borrow money at a lower rate than the private sector.[29]

Federal loan guarantee programs afford financial benefits to borrowers, which are similar to direct loan subsidies. The subsidies derived from these programs are based on the difference between interest rates available when a loan is guaranteed by federal agencies and the rates that borrowers would have to pay in the absence of such guarantees. In the cases in which loan guarantees are available from private insurers—as for example with private mortgage insurance—the subsidy is calculated according to the difference between fees charged by federal agencies and those charged by a private insurer to provide an identical loan guarantee. Most of the subsidies attributable to federally guaranteed loan commitments related to housing flow out of programs under the Department of Agriculture, Housing and Urban Development, and the Veteran's Administration. The total subsidy for housing from these sources amounted to approximately $6.1 billion in 1986. In general, the calculations of federal credit subsidies probably underestimate their true value. This is because the supply of federal credit for housing is so large that, to compete for borrowers, private lenders may have to charge less than the market would otherwise bear if federal credit were not available.[30]

The several conditions just noted, under which direct and guaranteed federal loans result in a transfer to borrowers, can be thought of as planned subsidies. In contrast, when borrowers default on these loans they often receive what might be termed an unplanned subsidy. These unplanned subsidies run into rather high sums, because federal loans tend to embrace a clientele that is riskier than private lenders are willing to carry. In 1986, direct-loan write-offs and guaranteed-loan terminations for default in housing-related credit programs amounted to more than $4.5 billion. Surveying these figures, the OMB notes "a growing awareness that losses in both direct and loan guarantee programs are higher than reported."[31]

## Regulatory Measures

Housing regulation is a diverse and complicated activity conducted by many public bodies at different levels of government. Until recently, this activity was focused mainly on the safety and quality of individual dwellings and the neighborhood milieu. As the scope of regulation has expanded, housing costs have climbed and developers have experienced greater difficulty in gaining access to local housing markets. Currently, the myriad of health, safety, zoning, environmental, and public amenity-related regulations add considerably to the cost of placing a new unit on the market. In Connecticut, for example, at least 110 towns regulate the minimum size of a house; to meet the minimum size in East Hampton would add approximately $16,500 to the price for those seeking to build a modest-sized two-bedroom house of 1026 square feet.[32] Regional environmental regulations have emerged as frequent hurdles in the course of housing development. In the San Francisco area, for example, between 1971 and 1975 environmental lawsuits challenged plans for 29,000 housing units, about two-thirds of a year's normal housing production for this area.[33]

Beyond the promotion of health and safety, several measures involve public regulation of private enterprise in a manner that begets social transfers. Cities such as Boston, Santa Monica, Jersey City, and San Francisco permit large-scale development only if builders reserve a certain proportion of space for low-income families, provide day-care facilities, or contribute to unrelated projects. It is hard to calculate the extent to which these transfers are directly subsidized by the developers accepting a lower rate of profit or are shifted to middle-income and upper-income consumers by charging a higher purchase price for their units. In either case, certain consumer groups—low-income residents and those with children—receive benefits below what they might cost in the absence of local regulations.

Rent control is another regulatory measure that results in social transfers under which some people pay less for housing than it would otherwise cost if the local market were unregulated or if they were to rent comparable dwellings in a similar community without rent control. Originally instituted in a few localities to cope with wartime and other housing emergencies when geographic mobility was limited and new construction minimal, rent control measures now exist in approximately 200 cities throughout the country.[34] Among the most controversial regulatory measures, rent control often affects local property owners who are small-scale middle-class entrepreneurs. For example, 60 percent of the landlords in New York City own only one building and the majority have incomes of between $10,000 and $40,000. With few exceptions, there are no requirements that occupants of regulated units be financially qualified for special treatment or show that they are unable to afford the higher rents that would be charged in the absence of local controls. Indeed, affluent families often occupy rent-controlled units that are let at a fraction of market value. In a magnificent building overlooking Central Park, for example, Mia Farrow, Carly Simon, and other celebrities pay up to $2200 a month for huge rent-controlled units that could command $5000 to $10,000 a month in the absence of regulation.[35]

Even if some form of income test were applied, there is good reason to argue (as discussed later) that the burden of poor tenants should be borne by the public as a whole rather than by particular landlords. As for other consequences, there is a tendency for rent control to decrease the supply and inhibit the movement of local rental housing. Entrenched tenants are financially motivated to stay put and reap the benefits of below-market rents. Developers see little advantage to building new units. And homeowners would rather sell than lease existing units.

Rent control measures range from mild constraints to draconian restrictions that border on the confiscation of property. Implemented through local initiatives, these measures have been continuously subject to judicial review at the state and federal levels. In the most recent case with national implications, the U.S. Supreme Court upheld a rent control law in San Jose, California. The challenge to this law was based largely on a "tenant hardship" provision, which stipulates that if a tenant's income is below a certain level, the hardship to that tenant incurred by a rent increase greater than 8 percent may be considered as one of seven criteria used to determine the reasonableness of the proposed increase. For a family of four, the income level at which the hardship provision may be applied goes as high as $32,400 a year. In upholding this law the Court did not pass judgment on the constitutionality of the "tenant hardship" provision. It ruled instead that an opinion on this clause would be premature because there was no evidence that the "hardship" criterion had ever been employed by a hearing officer to reduce a tenant's rent below the level at which it would have been set according to the other criteria in the law.[36]

In a dissenting opinion, Judge Scalia observed that the "hardship" provision did not deal with the availability of reasonably priced housing, but addressed instead the problem of some renters being too poor to afford even reasonably priced housing. That problem, he explains, "is no more caused or exploited by landlords than it is by the grocers who sell needy renters their food, or the department stores that sell them their clothes, or the employers who pay them their wages, or the citizens of San Jose holding higher paying jobs from which they are excluded." A particular landlord who happens to rent to a tenant who is currently poor or whose circumstances decline into the "hardship" category cannot be held responsible for this condition. "The traditional manner," Scalia argues, "in which American government has met the problem of those who cannot pay reasonable prices for privately sold necessities—a problem caused by society at large—has been the distribution to such persons of funds raised from the public at large through taxes, either in cash (welfare payments) or in goods (public housing, public subsidized housing, and food stamps)."[37] While rent control represents mainly local efforts to impose housing transfers through public measures that often restrict free-market transactions, on the national level housing policy has moved toward greater consumer choice and encouragement of market-oriented solutions.

## Commercialization of Housing Policy

In both the United States and Britain, the trend toward market-oriented measures has dominated policy reforms dealing with public provisions for housing. During the last decade, the most dramatic development along these lines occurred in Britain where, since 1979, the Conservative government has promoted the sale of council houses to tenants, setting prices well below market value and varying them by the length of tenancy.[38] In the private sector, from 1960 to 1981, the proportion of rental units declined from 31 percent to 13 percent of all housing in England and Wales.[39] This contraction of rental units took place, in part, because of strict public regulations that set rents substantially below market levels and require many landlords who wish to reclaim their property to win a court-ordered eviction. Following the general trend toward the commercialization of housing, efforts to revive private renting, are high on the political agenda. In 1987, for example, the minister of housing advanced a proposal under which new rentals would be allowed to charge market rents and tenants would receive security of tenure only for the period of their lease.[40] Overall, as Robinson points out, between 1979 and 1985 public expenditures on housing in Britain declined substantially less than political rhetoric would have one believe. Rather, it was the composition of expenditures, including a large increase in mortgage interest tax relief, that was transformed to encourage market-oriented housing initiatives.[41]

Housing policy in the United States has moved in a similar direction toward market-oriented reforms, but along somewhat different paths. From the mid-1930s through the 1960s, federal housing assistance to the poor was delivered almost exclusively through grant-in-aid programs for the construction and maintenance of public housing. In the 1960s, additional programs were enacted to subsidize the development of privately operated low-income to moderate-income housing through below-market mortgage rates. These subsidized rates were available to housing developers who agreed to set their rents at levels below the market value for up to twenty years. The effectiveness of these efforts to augment the supply of low-cost housing increasingly came under question. By the early 1970s, the escalating costs of housing construction and maintenance coupled with the unmanageable density of social problems lodged in the large-scale housing projects forced policymakers to reconsider the federal strategy of subsidized construction.

During this period, a major congressional review of government policy resulted in the Housing and Community Development Act of 1974. This act introduced the Section 8 housing program, setting in motion a new approach to federal aid. As initially crafted, the Section 8 program included assistance in the form of rent subsidies for leasing existing units as well as funds for the construction of new units and the substantial rehabilitation of deteriorated housing. In both cases, the subsidized units are owned and managed by private landlords.

From 1977 to 1980, new construction and substantial rehabilitation accounted for the majority of assisted units under Section 8. This mix was reversed in 1981 as Congress encouraged the greater use of existing units. Among the several reasons that influenced this important shift in policy was that a unit of housing could be subsidized for considerably less by the leasing of existing structures than by the construction of new ones. Also, it was believed that the supply of adequate housing in most areas was sufficient to meet the needs of low-income tenants. In 1982, existing housing accounted for 88 percent of the units subsidized under the Section 8 program; in 1983 this proportion increased to 92 percent.[42] Following the reduced construction of federally subsidized housing and the increased reliance on the use of existing units, a voucher demonstration program was established under the Housing and Urban Recovery Act of 1983, which moved federal efforts farther in the direction of a market-oriented approach to housing assistance for the poor.

While both programs take avail of housing in the private sector, the voucher demonstration program differs from the Section 8 use of existing units in several important dimensions. Operating on a contractual basis between government and landlords, the Section 8 program directly compensates landlords for a portion of the fair-market rent charged to low-income tenants on units that meet minimum housing standards. The voucher demonstration provides assistance directly to low-income tenants, thereby eliminating government's role in the tenant–landlord transaction and enhancing consumer choice. Along the same lines, the voucher provides a strong incentive for consumers to shop for units with lower rents. The Section 8 subsidy is based on the difference between the actual rent paid up to the fair-market levels in local markets (established by the Department of Housing and Urban Development [HUD]) and 30 percent of the tenant's income. Introducing a shopper's incentive, the voucher is computed as the difference between the fair-market rent and 30 percent of the tenant's income, which allows tenants to pocket the difference when their actual rent is below the fair-market level. Finally, unlike Section 8, the voucher program permits recipients to live in units that charge more than the fair-market rent prescribed by HUD for their community; although the amount of the voucher subsidy remains limited to the difference between the fair-market rent and 30 percent of the tenant's income, a larger selection of units is thereby available to program participants, increasing the range of choice while holding public cost stable.

The voucher demonstration was designed drawing heavily upon the experiences of the Experimental Housing Allowance Program (EHAP). A social experiment of unprecedented scale, the EHAP involved tests of vouchers in twelve sites across the nation for more than a decade, at the cost of approximately $200 million. Findings from these studies suggest that, if funds were available to serve all who are eligible, only about 50 percent of the qualified population would ultimately participate in the voucher programs. On a more positive note, other findings alleviated the long-standing concern that a housing allowance would lead to rent increases in the low-income market. The absence of program-induced price changes in two highly saturated experimental localities was partly because the majority of recipients qualified for assistance in the units they were currently renting. This support of existing arrangements reflects the vouchers' central function as an income enhancement program aimed at reducing rent burden rather than increasing the supply of low-income housing.[43]

By 1988, the move to reduce construction of new public housing was joined with proposals to sell existing public housing units to tenants at a discounted price, a recommendation put forth by the Presidential Commission on Privatization.[44] At that time, public housing covered about 22 percent of the 6.5 million households receiving direct federal housing aid, with the remainder supported by vouchers and Section 8 subsidies.[45]

In addition to the shift in policy with respect to direct assistance for low-income households, the commercialization of social transfers for housing has also advanced through several changes in the Community Development Block Grant (CDBG) program. Since 1981, for example, private profit-oriented enterprises engaged in economic development have become eligible for funding under the CDBG program. At the same time, the vast reduction of federal requirements has increased local control over CDBG activities. This decentralization allows states and localities greater flexibility in responding to community needs, but no longer assures that CDBG benefits will be directed to low-income groups. The trend away from neighborhood and housing rehabilitation and toward the encouragement of commercial activity is most clearly exemplified in various proposals for the creation of enterprises operating in depressed areas. In reducing government impediments to entrepreneurial activity, these proposals embody the free-market approach to community development.[46]

Even indirect transfers, such as credit subsidies, have come under increasing pressure to accommodate the commercialization of housing policy. The Federal Housing Administration (FHA), for example, insures about 25 percent of all mortgages written each year. By protecting lenders from the threat of loss in the event of a default, this insurance program allows cash-short home buyers to assume a mortgage for as little as 3 percent of the purchase price. Not only does the borrower receive credit at more favorable terms than are normally available in the private market, but the cost of FHA insurance is also lower than private mortgage insurance. Since the early 1980s, the Reagan administration has sought to level the playing field for the private mortgage insurance industry by various proposals to change the terms of the FHA program. In 1988, provoked by studies showing that in recent years a substantial portion of FHA-insured loans went to borrowers with household incomes of $40,000 or more, the administration urged that down-payment requirements for families in this upper-income category be increased to the level regularly set by the private mortgage insurance industry. Other proposals were also put forth to bring the FHA mortgage insurance premium and closing-cost policies more closely into line with those of private insurers.[47]

Similar measures have been recommended to reduce the competitive edge of the Government National Mortgage Association (Ginnie Mae), the Federal Home Mortgage Corporation (Freddie Mac), and the Federal National Mortgage Association (Fannie Mae), three federally sponsored corporations that support the huge secondary-mortgage market. Created by Congress, and affectionately known in the housing trade as Ginnie Mae, Freddie Mac, and Fannie Mae, these corporations buy mortgages from lenders and repackage them as securities for sale to investors, thus increasing the supply of capital available for housing loans. Because of government sponsorship, they enjoy lower credit costs than their fully private counterparts. While continuing to maintain a lively presence in the mortgage market, by the late 1980s these corporations emerged as targets of a continuous stream of proposals to limit or privatize their activities.[48]

Overall, during the last three decades public involvement in the area of housing has moved away from the provision of benefits in kind and toward the provision of cash through direct allowances, tax expenditures, and credit subsidies. Thus, the role of the state in the public–private relationship has been fashioned around the partial financing of low-income and middle-income consumers, leaving production, maintenance, and the remainder of financing to the private sector. In the joint public–private venture, the part played by government programs has increasingly followed the charge of the 1981 President's Commission on Housing to develop "options that strengthen the ability of the private sector to maximize opportunities for home ownership and provide adequate shelter for all Americans."[49] In this role, the enabling state has served well the housing needs of middle-income groups. Low-income groups, however, remain financially squeezed by housing costs. Existing measures in the form of vouchers and credit subsidies could help to meet the housing needs of the poor, if benefits are aimed more sharply at this group and adequately financed.

## Notes

1. Kathleen Proch and Merlin Taber, "Helping the Homeless," *Public Welfare,* 45:2 (Spring 1987), pp. 5–9.

2. Peter Rossi, Gene Fisher, and Georgianna Willis, *The Condition of the Homeless in Chicago* (Amherst, Mass.: University of Massachusetts, Social and Demographic Research Institute, 1986), p. 56. For an interesting account of the reception to this study's findings, see Peter Rossi, "No Good Applied Social Research Goes Unpublished," *Society,* 25:1 (November–December 1987), pp. 73–79.

3. Paul Applebaum, "Crazy in the Streets," *Commentary,* 83:5 (May 1987), p. 37.

4. E. Fuller Torrey, "Fiscal Shell Game Cheats Mentally Ill," *Wall Street Journal,* November 3, 1987, p. 32.

5. Ibid.; Applebaum, "Crazy in Streets."

6. James D. Wright, "The Worthy and Unworthy Homeless," *Society,* 25:5 (July–August 1988), p. 69.

7. Rossi et al., *Condition of Homeless in Chicago,* pp. 79, 156–158.

8. Richard First, Dee Roth, and Bobbie Arewa, "Homelessness: Understanding the Dimensions of the Problem for Minorities," *Social Work,* 33:2 (March–April 1988), pp. 120–24.

9. Thomas J. Main, "The Homeless Families of New York," *The Public Interest,* 85 (Fall 1986), p. 16.

10. Timothy Smeeding, *Alternative Methods for Valuing Selected In-Kind Transfer Benefits and Measuring Their Effects on Poverty,* U.S. Bureau of the Census, Technical Paper No. 50 (Washington, D.C.: U.S. Government Printing Office, 1982).

11. Peter Salins, "Toward a Permanent Housing Problem," *The Public Interest,* 85 (Fall 1986), pp. 22–33.

12. Vincent Carroll, "Origin of a Housing Squeeze," *Wall Street Journal,* October 13, 1986, p. 14.

13. Ibid.; also see Lew Sichelman, "Home Prices Jump 10% in 1986," *San Francisco Chronicle,* March 8, 1987, p. F-2.

14. Christopher Jencks, "The Hidden Prosperity of the 1970s," *The Public Interest,* 77 (Fall 1984), p. 70. A similar conclusion is drawn in John Tuccillo with John Goodman, Jr., *Housing Finance: A Changing System in the Reagan Era* (Washington, D.C.: The Urban Institute, 1983), p. 22.

15. James Hughes and George Sternlieb, *The Dynamics of America's Housing* (Rutgers, N.J.: Rutgers University, Center for Urban Policy Research, 1987), p. 59 and 206.

16. U.S. Bureau of the Census, *Statistical Abstract of the United States, 1987* (Washington, D.C.: U.S. Government Printing Office, 1986), p. 712.

17. Hughes and Sternlieb, *Dynamics of Housing,* pp. 139–142.

18. General Accounting Office (GAO), *Housing Allowances: An Assessment of Program Participation and Effects* (Washington, D.C.: U.S. Government Printing Office, 1986), p. 20; Michel McQueen, "Low-Income Housing Demand to Reach 'Crisis-Level' in Near Future, Study Says," *Wall Street Journal,* June 3, 1987, p. 10.

19. Irving Welfeld, "Poor Tenants, Poor Landlords, Poor Policy," *The Public Interest,* 92 (Summer 1988), p. 112.

20. Hughes and Sternlieb, *Dynamics of Housing,* pp. 182–83.

21. The structure of the British housing stock is analyzed by Richard Rose, "The Dynamics of the Welfare Mix in Britain," in *The Welfare State East and West,* eds. Richard Rose and Rei Shiratori (New York: Oxford University Press, 1986), pp. 85–88.

22. U.S. Bureau of the Census, *Statistical Abstract of the United States, 1987* (Washington, D.C.: U.S. Government Printing Office, 1986), p. 171.

23. William Celis, "Crumbling Projects," *Wall Street Journal,* December 15, 1986, pp. 1, 22.

24. Sandra Newman and Ann Schnare, *Subsidizing Shelter: The Relationship Between Welfare Reform and Housing Assistance* (Washington, D.C.: The Urban Institute, 1988), p. 8.

25. William Hellmuth, "Homeowner Preferences," in *Comprehensive Income Taxation,* ed. Joseph Pechman (Washington, D.C.: The Brookings Institution, 1977), pp. 167–68.

26. Organisation for Economic Co-operation and Development, *Tax Expenditures: A Review of the Issues and Country Practices* (Paris: OECD, 1984).

27. Howard Glennerster, *Paying for Welfare* (Oxford: Basil Blackwell, 1985), p. 198.

28. OMB, *Special Analysis, Budget of the United States Government, FY 1988* (Washington, D.C.: U.S. Government Printing Office, 1987), p. F-32.

29. Ibid., p. F-35. These subsidies are calculated by comparing the terms and conditions available under direct federal loans to those available for financing a loan through the private sector.

30. Ibid., pp. F-37-38.

31. Ibid., p. F-39.

32. Andrew Brooks, "Can a Town Regulate the Minimum Size of a House?" *The New York Times,* May 3, 1987, p. 6.

33. Carroll, "Origin of Housing Squeeze," p. 14.

34. "Founders vs. Rent Control," *Wall Street Journal,* March 9, 1987, p. 22.

35. Welfeld, "Poor Tenants, Landlords, Policy," pp. 112–14.

36. *Pennell et al.* v. *City of San Jose et al.,* 86-753 U.S. (1987).

37. Ibid.

38. Glennerster, *Paying for Welfare,* p. 204.

39. Rose, "Dynamics of Welfare in Britain," pp. 85–88.

40. Nicholas Wood, "Patten Pledges Move to Revive Private Lettings," *The Times,* March 21, 1987, p. 1.

41. Ray Robinson, "Restructuring the Welfare State: An Analysis of Public Expenditure 1979/80–1984/85," *Journal of Social Policy,* 15:1 (January 1986), pp. 1–23.

42. Raymond Struyk, Neil Mayer, and John Tuccillo, *Federal Housing Policy at President Reagan's Midterm* (Washington, D.C.: The Urban Institute, 1983), pp. 69–71.

43. GAO, *Housing Allowances: Program Participation,* pp. 72–76.

44. *Presidential Commission on Privatization,* March 1, 1988 (Washington, D.C.: U.S. Government Printing Office).

45. OMB, *Budget of the United States, FY 1988, Supplement* (Washington, D.C.: U.S. Government Printing Office, 1987), pp. 5–126.

46. Struyk et al., *Housing Policy at Reagan's Midterm,* pp. 85–87.

47. OMB, *Budget of U.S., FY 1988, Suppl.,* pp. 5–61, 5–62; Michel McQueen, "Mortgage Insurer's Survey Faults FHA," *Wall Street Journal,* December 2, 1987, p. 29.

48. For a more detailed analysis of these developments, see Tuccillo and Goodman, *Housing Finance: A Changing System,* pp. 35–83. A sample of the recent efforts to curb

these credit programs has been reported on in several articles by Michel McQueen, see "HUD Rescinds Increase in Fee Charged by Ginnie Mae for Securities Guarantees," *Wall Street Journal*, March 9, 1987, p. 18; "U.S. Sets Limits of $75 Billion on Freddie Mac," *Wall Street Journal*, March 5, 1987, p. 5; "Fannie Mae to Shun Home Equity Loans in Step that Could Limit Their Growth," *Wall Street Journal*, March 17, 1987, p. 5; "Broad Housing Bill Opposed by Reagan is Cleared by House," *Wall Street Journal*, June 12, 1987, p. 48.

49. U.S. President's Commission on Housing, *Report* (Washington, D.C.: U.S. Government Printing Office, 1982), p. XV.

# 8

# *The Enabling State:*
# *Public Support for*
# *Private Responsibility*

Since the 1960s there has been a marked change in the mix of public and private activities devoted to the finance and production of social welfare. As illustrated in previous chapters, the focus of public activity has shifted away from production toward the use of direct and indirect measures for financing benefits provided through the private market. This trend is among the clearest indicators of the commercialization of social welfare and is most evident in housing and personal social services. While the signs of commercialization are also revealed in health and income maintenance benefits, there is one traditional area of social provision that remains somewhat immune to the interplay of public and private measures that animates contemporary welfare capitalism.

## Education: A Sector Ripe for Change

Unlike housing, the overwhelming majority of which is produced and owned privately, education in primary and secondary schools is almost a public monopoly; in contrast to private housing, the vast majority of which is in relatively decent condition, public education is in shambles.

While proprietary agencies have gained an increasing share of the market in the delivery of other social provisions, private involvement in primary and secondary education has remained limited to about 10 percent of this market and is relegated mainly to nonprofit organizations, which account for about 90 percent of the private schools in this field.

In 1955, private schools enrolled about 13 percent of all children in the elementary and secondary grades. This rate of enrollment declined to 10 percent by 1975 and then moved up to approximately 11 percent in 1985, a level that projections suggest will remain stable through the early 1990s.[1] The relatively small change in rates of private enrollment, however, portrays an image of stability that masks some rather large swings in the enrollment distribution within the private sector. In 1965, for example, Catholic schools accounted for almost 90 percent of the students in the private sector. Between 1965 and 1983 enrollment in these schools fell by 46 percent. During this period, enrollment in Protestant fundamentalist, Jewish, and independent (secular) schools registered substantial increases, altering the basic composition of the private system.

Many influences shaped these changes. The precipitous drop in Catholic school enrollment derived, in part, from a declining birth rate and migration to the suburbs. Also, as the Protestant influence on public schools dwindled, the public sector became more congenial to Catholics at the same time that it was losing appeal to fundamentalist Protestant groups.[2]

Whereas the public sector continues to serve almost 90 percent of children in elementary and secondary school, the quality of this service has come under increasing criticism. In 1982, a highly publicized study by Coleman, Hoffer, and Kilgore reported that, after controlling for race and socioeconomic status, the academic achievement of students in private schools was higher than that of public school students.[3] These findings stirred much debate. Analyses of the study methods and re-calculations of the data by others raised serious doubts about the extent of the achievement gap attributable to private education.[4] Although its results were disputed, the study's message that private schools offered a likely solution to the problems of public education struck a receptive chord. The message arrived just as misgivings about the deteriorating education of American students had reached an urgent level of national concern.[5] From 1967 to 1982, for example, the national averages for verbal and math scores on the Scholastic Aptitude Test dropped from 446 and 492 to 426 and 467, respectively. These scores increased slightly between 1982 and 1985, but remained well below the 1967 levels.[6] International comparisons lend further testimony to the deficiencies of educational achievement in the United States. Tests conducted in 1986 reveal that American students fare poorly in physics, chemistry, and biology relative to their counterparts in England and Japan.[7]

By the late 1980s, the reform of elementary and secondary education emerged as a lively topic of political debate. One of the most controversial issues in this debate concerns the method and extent of government involvement in promoting private educational alternatives. It is an issue that signals the dramatic change surrounding private education since the case of *Pierce* v. *Society of Sisters* in 1925, when the Supreme Court ruled that parents had the right to use private schools as alternatives to public education in meeting compulsory attendance requirements.[8] While private schools won the right to exist, they had to do so largely on their own resources. Fear that private schools would deepen social divisions along with traditional support for the separation of church and state have served to restrain public aid for private education at the elementary and secondary levels, where the vast majority of private schools are affiliated with religious groups.

However, private schools are not entirely without public aid. They benefit from indirect transfers in the form of exemptions from property and income taxes. Charitable donations to nonprofit private institutions, including schools, are also deductible from the donor's taxable income. Additionally, direct government subsidies are provided through both cash and in-kind provisions. More than half of the states offer in-kind provisions such as bus transportation, textbook loan programs, health services, instructional materials, psychological testing, remedial instruction, and guidance and counseling to private school students.[9]

On the federal level, direct support for private school students from all sources was estimated at $606 million in 1981, $279 million of which came from the Department of Education.[10] Federal aid to private school students was first introduced under Titles I and II of the Elementary and Secondary Education Act of 1965; these provisions were later incorporated into the Education Consolidation and Improvement Act of 1981. Supporting compensatory programs for educationally disadvantaged children, Title I is probably the most important source of direct federal aid to private education. This program finessed political objections to federal support for religious schools by focusing on children rather than institutions as the units of aid.

While federal aid to private education is limited in scope, acceptance of the principle established a political foundation upon which federal activity in this area might expand. Growing concerns about the quality of public education and a general resurgence of faith in the benefits of competition, consumer choice, and the market mechanism have lent impetus to proposals for government intervention that would enhance private alternatives in the educational marketplace. Public discussion of these alternatives has focused mainly on vouchers and tuition tax credits.

The modern debate about educational vouchers was initiated by Milton Friedman in 1955, although it did not gain serious consideration until the mid-1960s. His proposal was straightforward. Rather than paying for public schools, government would divide the funds among parents in the form of vouchers, which they could use to purchase education for their children at any school of their choice. Parents could supplement these vouchers with their own funds, if the school they selected charged more than the average cost of public education. His proposal placed no restrictions on parents or schools, giving free rein to competition and consumer choice.[11] A more restrictive proposal for educational vouchers was designed by Jencks and his associates in 1970. Not content to leave the distribution of educational benefits completely to market forces, the Jencks proposal includes a series of regulations governing admissions policies, incentives for enrollment of poor students, and the supply of information about programs to enhance the exercise of choice.[12] A voucher demonstration based on this restrictive approach was tested by the Office of Economic Opportunity (OEO) in the early 1970s at the Alum Rock Elementary School District in San Jose, California. As it was implemented, however, the Alum Rock version of educational vouchers deviated substantially from the original voucher concept; participants included only thirteen of the district's twenty-four public schools and none of the private schools, demand was restricted by enrollment ceilings, and one-third of the voucher payments went for centralized administrative services. Finally, the cutting edge of competition was blunted by assurances that no jobs would be lost if programs were unsuccessful in attracting consumers.

Though hardly a test of a genuine voucher scheme, the Alum Rock demonstration introduced a degree of consumer choice and diversity beyond that normally operating in the school district. Thus, the results of this experiment are at best suggestive of what might be expected under an authentic voucher system. On the matter of consumer choice, geographic proximity appeared to be the predominant consideration for most parents, with more than 80 percent sending their children to the nearest school. Furthermore, in choosing among different miniprograms within schools, the majority of parents favored the traditional curricula.[13] As for the extent to which competition and choice result in greater educational achievement, comparisons between voucher and nonvoucher programs revealed negligible differences in student performance.[14]

Although the Alum Rock demonstration was federally subsidized, educational vouchers are more appropriately instruments of states rather than federal government. State and local sources finance more than 90 percent of the cost of public school education. At the state level, a 1979 voucher proposal by Coons and Sugarman received a fair amount of public encouragement in California.[15] A judicious and well-crafted voucher design, this proposal failed to qualify for the state ballot in 1980; if it had qualified, however, public opinion polls at the time suggested that the vote to adopt a voucher system in California would have been rather close.[16]

In the 1980s, tuition tax credits have gained considerable attention, perhaps even more than vouchers, as instruments for reform of educational financing that would increase the choice among private options. These schemes are not an invention of the 1980s. Seven proposals for tuition tax credits passed the Senate between 1967 and 1978; since 1955, Minnesota has allowed tax deductions for education expenses, currently up to $700 for students in grades seven to twelve. Throughout the 1980s, various tuition credit schemes have been proposed by the Reagan administration and others. While Congress has yet to agree on these proposals, the general idea of tuition credits enjoys substantial interest. A 1982 nationwide survey of 1200 households reports, for example, that 23.5 percent of the parents claim that they would be very likely or somewhat likely to transfer their children to private schools with a tuition tax credit of only $250; with a credit of $500, 32 percent of the respondents indicate that they would move their children. There are reasons to believe that these responses greatly overestimate the extent to which tax credits would actually result in transfers to private schools.[17] Nevertheless the findings reflect favorable perceptions of educational tax credit schemes by a broad segment of the population.

A number of issues surround educational reforms aimed to increase competition and choice, particularly through vouchers and tax credits that can be applied to private schools. Generally, those opposed to vouchers and tax credits argue that these instruments would violate separation of church and state, further weaken an already shaky public system, and exacerbate racial and economic segregation. On the separation of church and state, as already noted, the distinction between public subsidy of students and direct aid to the private institutions they may attend was used to justify federal support to students in private schools under the Elementary and Secondary Education Act. Moreover, tax deductions for charitable contributions to nonprofit private educational institutions include those sponsored by religious groups. Thus, the partition between church and state in the educational sector has been breached by measures that might easily be extended to vouchers and tuition tax credits.

The impact of government support for private school students on the system of public education depends on the precise form these measures would take, particularly the size of the subsidy and the conditions attached to it. It is unclear, for example, exactly how many families might switch their children to private schools if tuition tax credits were available. If relatively few families exercised this option, the credit would serve more to reduce the tax burden on those with children already enrolled in private schools than to promote greater parental choice. Evidence from the Minnesota experience suggests that the state income tax deductions exercised relatively little influence on parent schooling choices. However, the dollar value of these deductions was small and only those who itemized their tax returns could receive benefits.[18]

Proponents of vouchers and tuition tax credits argue that these measures, properly designed, will stimulate greater competition in the educational sector, under which the strongest schools, public and private, would thrive. Indeed, there is some evidence that in other areas of municipal service, competition from private providers has a bracing affect on public agencies.[19] But the salutary effects of competition are most likely to emerge on a level field where all the teams play under the same rules. In education, however, private schools have certain advantages. They enjoy considerable latitude in arranging how to govern themselves, setting the conditions of staff employment and retention, selection and discipline of students, and curriculum design. Public schools, in comparison, are constrained by federal and state regulations.[20] Increasing public subsidies to private schools—even indirectly through student aid—without some accompanying regulation would leave private schools with a competitive edge, particularly telling in the area of student selection. The tension between quality and access in education is well recognized. Three disruptive students in a class of twenty can seriously undermine the quality of the educational experience for all. Private schools tend either to exclude or expel such "educationally costly" students. Public schools are obliged to educate them.

Assuring access to private programs is one of the central issues in the design of voucher and tax credit plans. Many of these plans contain incentives for accepting students from low-income families and regulations pertaining to admissions that must be met by private schools in order to participate; however, regulations that reduce a private school's control over the composition of its student body also impinge on an aspect of private education that contributes to the academic quality of its program and attracts many of its consumers in the first place. The trade-off between access and quality presents a regulatory dilemma whenever public financing is provided for the delivery of private social services, the results of which derive in part from client characteristics.[21]

Regulation is a delicate process that, if carried too far, can interfere with the presumed efficiencies of a competitive market. The Netherlands, for example, offer an interesting case in point. Their educational system is marked by generous public support coupled with stringent regulation of private education. Under the Dutch system, private education is almost completely financed by public funds. As few as fifty parents may form a nonprofit association to organize a private school that qualifies for government support. At the same time teachers' salaries, credential requirements, and conditions of tenure are set by the central government. The student–faculty ratio of approximately 31 : 1 is also centrally prescribed. Because teachers' salaries account for 80–90 percent of school expenditures, limited budgetary discretion remains in the hands of local authorities, public or private. Educational results are determined through curriculum requirements and uniform national exams that all students must take at the end of elementary and secondary school. By regulating educational inputs and outputs the Dutch system narrows the scope of decision for the allocation of resources within schools, which results in the kinds of inefficiency of production that some advocates for vouchers and tuition tax credits in the United States would hope to reduce by expanding the role of private education.[22]

In addition to vouchers and tuition tax credits, several other policies to promote parental choice have been suggested in recent years. One approach involves need-based assistance that would open more options to poor families. Along these lines, the Reagan administration advanced a plan to assist low-income parents through "minivouchers" that could be used to pay for public or private educational services. Another approach envisions charging tuition at public schools or perhaps user fees for extracurricular activities, thereby diminishing the public system's competitive edge; this approach would have to be accompanied by a large reduction in local property taxes and means-tested subsidies for those who could not afford tuition.[23] Tuition charges are highly unlikely to be imposed at public schools, but a few public systems have introduced user charges for special activities and nonrequired courses.[24]

The appropriation of user charges, however, has stirred public controversy and legal contradictions. The "free-school" guarantee in the California Constitution, for example, was used to challenge the imposition of student fees for extracurricular activities such as cheerleading, madrigal singing, and athletics. In 1984, the California Supreme Court ruled that these fees violated the constitutional guarantee, even though the activities involved were not required for graduation. The "free-school" clause was interpreted not as a guarantee to "free education" but to the school and its entire product.[25] In 1988 a similar ruling was handed down forbidding public schools to charge students a fee for transportation, which was seen as a vital component of the school service.[26] Several months later, in contrast to the California ruling, a decision by the U.S. Supreme Court upheld the right to charge state-mandated school bus transportation fees in North Dakota. According to this decision, the U.S. Constitution's guarantee of "equal protection of the laws" did not extend any special protection to poor people against paying the same fees as charged to everyone else for access to education and other basic services.[27]

Finally, there is the public choice approach, which argues that instead of increasing access to private schools, parental choices may be enlarged by expanding the range of educational options within the public sector. This could be achieved through various arrangements such as open enrollment, decentralization of school governance, development of schools or minischools specializing in different themes, and contracting out parts of the educational program to private providers.[28] Experiments in public choice are under way. In 1988, for example, Minnesota passed an open-enrollment law that allows students to switch public schools both within and between school districts, with state aid of up to $3600 per student following them. About one-third of the public school districts, which encompass almost half the students in the state, participate in this program; the remainder are expected to join as the program gains experience and public pressures for participation increase. The choose-a-school program includes regulations to preserve desegregation plans and allows students in grades eleven and twelve to enroll in college courses at the state's expense.[29]

Whether one favors vouchers, tuition tax credits, decentralization, open enrollment, specialized minischools, or contracting out, the general consequence of these measures is to introduce market signals into the financing and delivery of educational services. The aim is to imbue the public system of education with competition, choice, and flexibility of response. In this sense, the various measures for educational reform represent an essential feature of the enabling state's role in the provision of social welfare.

## A Functional Model of the Enabling State

Without the reforms just mentioned, the educational sector resembles, more closely than other areas of social provision, the conventional welfare state model in which government controls the finance and production of benefits. However, the conventional welfare state model captures neither the full range of social transfers nor the functional orientation of public activity that has emerged in the realm of social welfare during the last few decades, particularly in the United States. As suggested in the previous chapters, a new model for financing and producing social welfare has evolved—that of the enabling state. The enabling state can be distinguished from the conventional welfare state along several dimensions, but foremost in its relations to the corporate sector. The enabling state's orientation toward private enterprise state porates none of the emnity often expressed between the welfare state and the market economy.

In contrast to the welfare state's direct financing of publicly produced benefits, the enabling state emphasizes private production and employs a range of measures for both direct and indirect financing. Subsidizing private activity that supports a market-oriented approach to social welfare is one of the four main functions of the enabling state. The other functions involve regulating private welfare activity through appropriate standard-setting measures, addressing normative expectations about individual and family responsibility, and providing an adequate level of aid and social protection for those in need. These four functions provide a tentative blueprint for understanding how the enabling state operates, its broad tendencies, and inherent tensions.

## *Subsidizing Private Activity*

In underwriting a market-oriented approach to social welfare, the enabling state confronts a long-standing debate on whether social welfare benefits should be given in cash or in kind.[30] The classic argument favoring benefits in kind claims that they are less costly and more effective than the cash alternative. According to this view, economies of large-scale production, standardization of the product, and the absence of advertising costs reduce the overall price of in-kind benefits manufactured by government. To provide a pair of shoes for every child in the nation, for example, a few large state-controlled factories presumably can do the job at the lowest cost by using the same materials purchased in massive quantities and producing one style of durable quality distributed without charge through a government store in each city. This approach supposedly eliminates many of the wasteful attributes of competition in the economic market. Assistance in kind is also seen as more effective than cash subsidies because it ensures that the benefit serves the purpose intended by the state.

The classic argument favoring benefits in cash claims that they are less costly and more effective than the in-kind alternative. This position suggests that, without the spur of competition, government bureaucracies manufacturing in-kind benefits become bloated and their products are more costly. Judged from this perspective, cash benefits stimulate consumer demand in response to which private enterprise is likely to generate innovations that in the long term lower product costs. As for effectiveness, it depends on how this is measured. In-kind benefits are to be preferred if the criterion is to meet the state's objectives that certain people receive specific provisions. However, if the objective is to maximize welfare as defined by the beneficiary rather than the state, assistance in the form of cash better allows for consumer sovereignty and the satisfaction of individual needs.

The enabling state favors social welfare transfers in the form of cash over in-kind provisions, where possible, leaving the production of benefits to the private market. Following this general tendency, the enabling role in the finance and production of social welfare proceeds along several avenues:

> Financing private consumption of goods and services through direct transfers of cash grants, such as social security, AFDC, and housing assistance payments, or cash equivalents such as vouchers
>
> Financing private consumption of goods and services through indirect transfers of cash with tax expenditures and credit subsidies
>
> Encouraging private enterprise to finance social welfare goods and services through partial public subsidies reflected, for example, in the tax-exempt treatment of health insurance and other fringe benefits of employment
>
> Encouraging voluntary financing of nonprofit welfare providers through tax deductions for charitable contributions and other tax benefits for voluntary agencies
>
> Financing the private production of social welfare goods and services through purchase-of-service arrangements

As these measures suggest, at the same time that the public sector supports social welfare transfers through direct and indirect subsidies, one of the major functions of the enabling role is to stimulate private sector responsibility for the production of welfare goods and services. This market-oriented approach transforms the traditional mix of public and private contributions to the welfare system. However, the enabling state serves as more than just a vehicle for the commercialization of social welfare. In regard to both the market and the family, it performs several other important functions.

### Regulating Private Activity

Greater reliance on the market for the delivery of social welfare goods and service necessitates more careful attention to the regulation of these provisions, especially where (as noted in Chapter 2) the most vulnerable beneficiaries are concerned. In assessing this function of the enabling state, it is important to distinguish between two types of regulatory measures: redistributional and standard-setting.

Redistributional measures employ the state's legal authority to compel private enterprise to subsidize social provisions. These measures include, for example, requirements that commercial developers build and maintain day-care facilities in their projects, and price-setting initiatives, such as rent control, that force the seller to make goods and services available at prices below their market value. Regulatory measures of this sort often impede the normal operations of the market and can result in unanticipated consequences such as a decline in rental units and commercial building. In regard to redistributional measures, Bardach and Kagan note, "it has been apparent that out-and-out deregulation is a good policy."[31]

In the production of social welfare, however, standard-setting or protective regulations are more common than redistributional measures. Between the mid-1960s and the late 1970s, the scope of federal protective measures broadened considerably with the creation of half a dozen new government bureaucracies such as the Environmental Protection Agency, the Occupational Safety and Health Administration, and the Equal Employment Opportunity Commission. At the same time, Congress extended the legal powers of existing agencies such as the Food and Drug Administration and the Federal Trade Commission. The growth of these protective regulatory programs is embodied in the *Federal Register* where, for example, the amount of space devoted to regulations of higher education multiplied almost tenfold, from 92 to more than 1000 pages, between 1965 and 1977.[32] From 1976 to 1980, the total number of pages in the *Federal Register* increased from 65,604 to 87,012. After 1980 this figure declined, falling to 47,718 pages in 1986.[33]

However, as regulatory programs expanded so did their unanticipated consequences, which affected particulars ranging from employee pensions to children's pajamas. More than 10,000 companies eliminated their pension plans in the wake of the Employee Retirement Income Security Act. These plans were dropped, according to testimony given the Senate Small Business Committee, when many small firms found prohibitive costs attached to compliance with the act's regulatory provisions. In response to the Flammable Fabrics Act, the Consumer Product Safety Commission in 1972 ordered that all children's sleepwear be protected with a flame-retardant chemical. More than 40 percent of these garments were treated with the chemical Tris, which was banned five years later as a carcinogenic substance. Whereas the social benefits were not always as beneficial as intended, the economic costs imposed by regulations were often quite high. By the late 1970s, a public backlash developed, railing against the "bureaucratic excesses" of regulatory programs. As Vogel observed, "government regulation was no longer seen as a solution to the problem created by business; it had become a problem in its own right."[34]

The backlash against government regulation emerged as the commercialization of social welfare was gaining momentum. By the mid-1980s, an increasing reliance on the market for the delivery of social welfare provisions was accompanied by a growing hesitancy to regulate these activities. Although much of government regulation may be rigid or intemperate, consumer protection cannot be left to private enterprise and the market mechanism. As an editor emeritus of the *Wall Street Journal,* a publication little given to sympathy for government intervention, explains,[35]

> Tourists to the ruins of Pompeii see an early version of the bureau of weights and measures, a place where the townsfolk could go to be sure they weren't cheated by local tradesmen. Unfortunately a little larceny is too common in the human species. So regulation in some form or other is one of the prices we pay for our complex civilization.

The choice for the enabling state is not whether or not to regulate, but what form and degree regulation should take. There are several major alternatives; for example, regulation may be achieved through litigation, disclosure of information, and direct oversight. Regulation by litigation substitutes judicial ruling for legislative requirements and bureaucratic oversight. The strength of this approach is succinctly expressed in "the difference between a million-dollar verdict and a $500 fine."[36] The $500 fine refers, of course, to the modest sanctions typically exercised by public regulatory agencies. In contrast, the threat of a multimillion-dollar liability suit poses a mighty incentive for private enterprise to ensure the safety of its services and products. This incentive also extends to the insurance industry, which generates a significant stimulus to corporate product safety efforts. Under certain circumstances where, for instance, risk assessment is relatively accurate and the court's representatives are qualified to judge the merits of technical scientific evidence, the liability mechanism offers a viable substitute for direct regulatory measures.[37]

However, there are limits to which regulation through litigation can effectively protect social welfare consumers. Marginally profitable services to low-income and moderate-income consumers often are unable to absorb the costs of liability insurance. Following several horrifying cases of sexual abuse in day-care centers, for example, the increased rates for liability insurance have forced a number of these facilities to choose among operating uninsured, closing shop, or raising fees beyond levels reasonably within reach of their consumers.

Litigation is expensive and time-consuming. A large number of social welfare recipients possess neither the resources nor personal energy necessary to initiate legal actions; even when such suits are brought, the problems of proof are formidable in many of the personal social services, such as nursing home care, foster care, and psychosocial therapy. Finally, as Bardach and Kagan point out, the deterrence effect of regulation by litigation assumes that private enterprise operates according to profit-maximizing calculations that will respond to a sufficient threat of financial loss with adequate preventive measures; however, even under these conditions, accidents occur due to error and slippage in preventive routines, which can be reduced by setting standards, conducting periodic inspections, and other direct regulatory efforts.[38]

Another indirect approach to regulation is through the use of information, which heightens the consumer's ability to appraise product risks and quality in light of costs.[39] In nursing homes, for example, dimensions of service such as cleanliness, nutritional value and presentation of meals, staff training, fire safety, private space and comfort of living quarters, recreational facilities, and the like could be graded along a quality-of-care continuum from minimally acceptable to highly satisfactory. Supplied with these data, consumers then may purchase the combination of service qualities best suited to their preferences.

This approach to empowering consumers was built into the Alum Rock voucher demonstration project, which included an independent evaluation unit to provide parents with information that would enhance the intelligent exercise of choice. For most parents, however, what information they received about the programs came directly from the schools, and the majority gained only a superficial knowledge of how the program operated.[40] This suggests one of the basic limits of regulation through the use of information; there is no way to assure how well the information will be processed by those on the receiving end. Even for highly motivated consumers, the costs of processing information may limit its utility. Anyone who has read the charts, graphs, tables, and text of the annual ratings of *Consumer's Guide* appreciates the expense of time and effort incurred in this process.

Most complaints against the excesses of public regulation center upon direct command and control protective measures. These measures address the palpable qualities associated with the production of social provisions—physical facilities, social inputs, and administrative procedures. In these areas, stringent direct regulations may increase the costs, curtail the supply, smother in "red tape," and have other unintended side effects on the production of social welfare services without appreciably benefiting their quality and safety.[41] However, there are various ways to invest direct regulation with greater flexibility.[42] Regulatory practices may be designed with procedures for granting exemptions for those cases in which the costs of compliance would greatly exceed social benefits. And uniform regulations may be carefully tailored to different classes of activity; for instance, day-care center standards might vary by the size of the facility, whether the program provided a temporary respite service or daily care for children of working parents, and the extent to which care involved supervision or educational objectives. As private enterprise increasingly engages in the production of social services, the task of framing regulatory measures that protect consumers without stifling the market's creative energies is a pressing order of business for the enabling state.

## Shaping Normative Expectations

As an instrument contributing to both private activity and its regulation, the enabling state promotes social welfare through interaction with the market economy. However, the enabling role goes beyond these concerns for the private production of social welfare. It seeks to promote individual responsibility and self-help, sustaining a moral dimension of welfare capitalism that complements the public altruism of unilateral social transfers. As Ryerson explains, "Since maintaining oneself is the precondition for assisting others, as well as a positive good in itself, surely it deserves a formal place in our moral categories alongside the polarized simplicities of selfishness and altruism."[43] In order to foster individual responsibility and self-help, the enabling state is expressly attentive to the ways social welfare policy may influence behavioral expectations.

Explicit regard for the normative influences of social welfare policy has gained serious consideration in recent years. Typically, policymakers want to know how much money will be spent and what benefits will be secured in return. This cost–benefit approach to policy focuses mainly on program outcomes that are proximate, concentrated in the populations served, and empirically verifiable. However, in assessing the consequences of social welfare policies, there is another class of outcomes—less immediate, more pervasive, and difficult to document—that rarely enters into conventional cost–benefit equations. This class of outcomes addresses the relation between social welfare policy and societal norms. What normative messages are conveyed about the nature of civic responsibilities that should accompany the rights to various forms of welfare transfer? By clarifying and endorsing these responsibilities the enabling state seeks, as James Q. Wilson puts it, to "induce private virtue through public policy."[44]

The normative effects of social welfare policies are difficult to gauge in part because they often appear as unanticipated consequences. These policies are ordinarily designed to meet pressing needs, not to mold social norms. Moreover, welfare policies constitute only one of the many forces that may shape normative behavior. Although the degree of influence cannot be measured with precision, one can judge the direction, a point illustrated in the following examples of normative issues arising from policies in Denmark, Sweden, and California.

How ill should one be to stay home from work and draw sick pay? Since the mid-1960s, Denmark's system of sick-leave benefits has been growing increasingly generous, culminating in the 1976 reforms that provided replacement of earnings up to 90 percent of the average industrial wage. Between 1966 and 1977, the number of periods for which Danish workers reported being sick, including those who went to work despite the illness, more than doubled. During a three-month period in 1977, more than 25 percent of the workers aged twenty to twenty-nine were sufficiently ill to receive sick pay. In the same period, sick pay was drawn by about only one-half that proportion of workers between the ages of sixty and sixty-six. What accounts for the startling increase in rates of illness? Are younger workers really ill twice as often as older workers? Part of the difference can be attributed to the increase in the number of working mothers with small children. However, even after controlling for these variables, rates of illness for the young are still higher than for older workers. Examining these data, Logue finds no evidence of increased malingering. "What seems to be happening," he suggests, "is that the threshold for considering oneself sick—at least as far as going to work is concerned—has been progressively lowered. Ailments ignored in the past (and hence not registered in the 1966 survey as 'going to work despite being sick') have become grounds for staying home." The norm concerning illness and work has changed. According to Logue, this has occurred because, as social welfare benefits have been generalized and minimum levels raised, the tie between obligations to contribute and rights to benefits have weakened, a circumstance that "has encouraged the use of benefits and the avoidance of obligations."[45]

Between the provinces of family and state, where should responsibility for the daily care of young children rest? In Sweden, 83 percent of the married women with children under age seven work, mainly because the average Swedish family cannot get by on the salary of one wage earner. The single-earner married couple with two children and an average production worker's salary returns 62 percent of their income to the government. These taxes finance a host of state-produced social welfare benefits, including day-care provisions subsidized annually by as much as $9000 a child. The Swedish family cannot choose between this "free" day-care service and, for example, a tax rebate equal to the cost of this service. The absence of such a choice creates a compelling financial inducement to shift responsibility for the care of children from the family to the state. Traditional family obligations are neither sustained nor encouraged by these measures.[46] In almost one generation, the elaborate well-subsidized day-care system has modified social expectations and individual behavior in the realm of child care. Reporting on a similar experience in Denmark, Logue notes the extent to which this change is embodied in the official idiom of Danish day-care statistics, where children are categorized "as 'taken care of in day care institutions' or 'taken care of by (approved) day nurses,' and 'not taken care of,' that is, left to their mother."[47]

While day care remains popular in Sweden, there is some indication of growing public support for family care, at least in the first few years of childhood. A 1987 poll of Swedish citizens reveals that in lieu of investing more resources in the expansion of state-run day-care centers, more than 60 percent of the women surveyed would prefer a child care allowance to assist parents who wanted to stay home with their children or to purchase care privately.[48] In a similar vein, recent proposals in the United States suggest that the child care tax credit should be available to all families, including those in which mothers care for their own children at home. This would send a message that parents who remain at home to care for their children are as socially valued as those who enter the labor force; it would also afford a more balanced distribution of welfare transfers, which are currently available to two-earner families whose incomes are on the average 50 percent higher than that of the two-parent, one-earner families who are ineligible for child care tax relief.[49]

Who should be responsible for preventing the abuse of young children? In 1984, the California state legislature passed the Child Abuse Prevention Training Act, which allocated $10.4 million annually for special instruction to children beginning at the preschool level. (While this act gave California the most extensive program of early education, similar efforts are under way in almost every state in the nation.) Most of the preschool programs run from one to three sessions, each lasting about a half hour. Focusing mainly on sexual abuse, these programs teach three- to five-year-olds to distinguish the feelings aroused by being touched on different parts of the body and what they should do about them. A "bad touch" is one that makes the child uncomfortable. Among the examples typically offered are wet or yucky kisses, tight hugs, and contact with the child's "private parts." Children are told to avoid strangers and informed that sexual assaults can be committed by family members, particularly fathers, stepfathers, and uncles. One of the most widely used curricula in the country also teaches physical self-defense:[50]

> You can kick them. Even if they try to pick you up you can kick them. But you have to remember not to kick them too high or you can fall over. (Dolls demonstrate kick.) You can stomp on their foot. (Demonstrate stomp.)

These lessons contain deep flaws. Children are taught to discern "bad touches" by listening to their feelings about physical contact on any part of their body. However, even adults have a hard time sorting all this out. How many adults are seduced every day by false promises and gentle touches? Leaning heavily on the intuitive powers of three- to five-year-olds, these lessons assume a remarkable confidence in chil-

dren's abilities to deal with complex emotional responses. In their inno-
cence, perhaps, children's intuition is more penetrating than that of their
elders. However, the evidence on this score is hardly compelling. Although many parents may find lessons on "stranger danger" reassuring, one would not expect them to harbor much enthusiasm for having
their children taught about "daddy danger" or that they should be
prepared to protect themselves against sexual assault by family members. And all that can be said about lessons on self-defense for three-
year-olds is that they exhibit a severe deficiency in good judgment.
Beyond these issues, however, a more fundamental question has been
raised. "That is, should young children be expected to protect themselves? Preschool children need care and security. At a time in their
lives when it is important to feel that parents will nurture and protect
them, should children be taught that they must evaluate the boundaries
of appropriate adult behavior?"[51] These programs convey a social expectation that four-year-olds must take charge to control the dangerous
outside world. It is a normative message that downplays the responsibilities of family and community for the protection of young children.
However, path-breaking social policies in California do not always
deliver messages quite as incogitant as those of the preschool sexual
abuse prevention services. For example, with the passage of AB
1820—the "Human Corps" bill—California became the first state in
the nation to adopt a formal policy encouraging community service by
college students. Although the bill does not make community service
mandatory, it transmits a clear statement that students are supposed to
provide at least thirty hours of service each year, investing a normative
appeal for volunteerism with the full weight of public expectation.

The normative impact of welfare policy is, perhaps, of greatest consequence in the realm of family life. Following Wilson's theme of
"inducing private virtue through public policy," Margaret Thatcher
counsels politicians and community leaders to advance measures that
encourage the good in people and discourage the bad. She notes,
however:[52]

> They can't create the one or abolish the other. They can only see that the
> laws encourage the best instincts and convictions of the people—instincts
> and convictions which I am convinced are far more deeply rooted than is
> often supposed.
>
> Nowhere is this more evident than in the basic ties of family life which
> are at the heart of our society and are the very nursery of civic virtue. It is

on family that we in government build our own policies for welfare, education, and care.

Under the Reagan administration, formal expression of concern for the impact of social welfare programs on family life was announced in Executive Order 12606, which called for assessing policies through questions such as: Does this action by government strengthen or erode the stability of the family and particularly the marital commitment? Does this action strengthen or erode the authority and rights of parents in the education and supervision of their children? What message, intended or otherwise, does this program send to the public concerning the status of the family?[53]

## Providing Aid and Social Protection

As evidenced throughout this book, welfare transfers in every area of social provision benefit citizens from all classes in society. In executing these transfers, the enabling state endorses private activity, appropriate forms of social regulation, and norms of personal responsibility. Reviewing these functions of the enabling role, the question remains: What about the poor?

Along with encouraging market-oriented initiatives and civic duties, the enabling state assumes the communal obligation to protect and care for its least fortunate members. Among the several functions of the enabling role, this is the one most closely associated with the traditional pursuit of social welfare. Performance in this area is generally judged by progress against poverty as defined according to official measures. In this regard, welfare transfers have worked to reduce poverty since the mid-1960s. In 1965, 17.3 percent of the population lived on income below the official poverty line; by 1985, the level of poverty had declined to 14 percent. These figures improve when income is adjusted for the cash value of in-kind benefits (discussed in Chapter 4), with the rate of poverty falling from 16.8 percent in 1965 to 11.8 percent in 1985. While the overall trend during this period registers a decrease in the rate of poverty, a closer look at the data reveals a fluctuating pattern in which the official rates fell to a low of 11.1 percent in 1973, moving up to a high of 15.2 percent in 1983 and edging down to about 14 percent in 1986. The rise in poverty since the late 1970s is attributable to a halt in the growth of real cash and in-kind transfers after 1978, the recession from the late 1970s to the early 1980s, and demographic changes such as the increases in the number of elderly and female-headed families.[54]

Another way to express the dimensions of poverty involves a measure of the total dollar amount required to lift all of the poor up to the official poverty line. This measure of the "poverty gap" (in 1982 dollars) increased from $31.8 billion in 1965 to $45.6 billion in 1983. Subtracting the market value of in-kind benefits, the poverty gap in 1982 amounted to $25.9 billion.[55] Though not a trivial sum, this amount equaled about 16 percent of the minimum and 10 percent of the maximum figure for welfare tax expenditures in 1985 and 70 percent of the tax expenditures on housing in that year (see Table 1.3), which were welfare transfers that in most instances subsidized people who were not poor. Private charitable expenditures in 1986 would have filled the 1982 poverty gap with an overflow of about $9 billion; the 1985 federal farm subsidies would have covered about two-thirds of the poverty gap. In each of these cases, of course, the wholesale shift of welfare transfers from programs aimed largely at people who were not poor to direct subsidies for the poor is politically inconceivable and, in any event, would be fraught with undesirable side effects. A more plausible approach would be to fine-tune the transfer system by shaving a few percentage points here and adding a few there. Through a relatively small reduction in indirect transfers to the middle class, direct transfers to low income groups could be materially increased without changing the overall costs of the transfer system. For example, a 3 percent decrease in the overall 1985 social welfare tax expenditures amounts to almost 30 percent of the 1982 poverty gap. The point here is not to compose specific recommendations for reform, but to illustrate how the synoptic view of modern welfare capitalism set forth in the previous chapters opens a range of policy alternates for refining the system of social transfers.

However, an encompassing view of the social transfer system supplies only part of the vision needed to administer better aid and social protection for the poor. Neither those suffering from serious hardships and deprivation, nor those seeking to alleviate these conditions are well served by current definitions of poverty as diagnostic categories for judging the effects of social policy.[56] The economic potential and life circumstances of "land-poor" farmers and low-income elderly homeowners are quite different from those of other officially designated poor people. Several studies show, for instance, that the number of poor elderly would be reduced by 32–35 percent if the annuitized value of their net worth were added to their cash income.[57] In a country as vast as the United States, the meaning of uniform national poverty measures is confounded by large regional cost-of-living differences, particularly urban/rural disparities, in regard to which estimates reveal a mean figure for a "minimum adequacy" budget in the largest urban areas that is 41 percent greater than for rural areas.[58] Whether poverty is perceived in relation to a decent standard of living or as a matter of relative deprivation (assessed against the circumstances of one's neighbors), more precise measures of this phenomenon are required to direct public efforts in aid of the truly disadvantaged.

## Constructive Tensions: Accommodating Public and Private Initiatives

There are inherent strains among the four central functions of the enabling role. Public regulation habitually collides with privatization. Too tightly formulated, regulation constricts the playing field and dulls the initiative of private enterprise; too loosely employed, it furnishes loopholes through which private enterprise is ever ready to press the advantage. Providing communal aid and social protection sometimes runs contrary to encouraging individual responsibility. What one might call the "dilemma of the helping hand" suggests that making public aid readily available to those in need mitigates the press of traditional familial obligations to care for dependent members.[59]

Impelled by these countervailing forces, the degree of emphasis on public versus private solutions to social welfare problems shifts as the societal context in which the enabling state functions inclines toward one or the other spheres of action. There are various theories as to how frequently these alternations occur. Several analyses suggest that American politics is characterized by a cyclical movement between liberalism and conservatism or the pursuits of public purpose and private interests, with each phase lasting from fifteen to twenty years.[60] Following this line of thought, one detects the distant echo of current trends in the critical views expressed at the 1927 National Conference on Social Work to the effect that "the dismantling of the regulatory commissions and the handing over of important parts of the machinery and powers of government to predatory interests; the attempt to decry public management of almost everything out of which private gain could be made even though at the public expense are all in full sway."[61]

As to why such cycles occur, Hirschman elaborates an intriguing theory that traces swings between the pursuit of private interests and involvement in public affairs to several disappointments, which invariably attend both the consumption of private goods and participation in public life. He believes that these alternations between public-oriented and private-oriented activities are useful and desirable, if not carried to an extreme. As often as not, however, these matters are distinguished by the lack of moderation. "Western societies," Hirschman concludes, "appear to be condemned to long periods of privatization during which they live through an impoverishing 'atrophy of public meanings,' followed by spasmodic outbursts of 'publicness' that are hardly likely to be constructive."[62] As a philosophical treatise on cyclical tendencies, his analysis raises an important question about the course of modern welfare capitalism.

Since the early 1970s, intellectual activity and policy initiatives around the private-oriented functions of the enabling state have advanced at a rapid pace, while efforts to promote public aid and social protection have remained somewhat idle. The movement toward the commercialization of social welfare lends impetus to the private production of welfare benefits and reinforces personal responsibilities that accompany the rights to these benefits. At the same time, it has spurred deregulation and contributed to a reduced sense of collective responsibility for protecting the destitute and most vulnerable members of society. Thus, by the late 1980s, the tensions among competing functions of the enabling role were reconciled mainly in favor of private-oriented activities.

While there is much to commend in these activities, there is also reason to regard them with caution. They represent not an abnegation of state support for social welfare so much as a change in the way it is carried out and who benefits. The emerging emphasis on public support for private responsibility has been conducive to indirect social transfers that benefit working-class and middle-class groups. Tax expenditures and credit subsidies, for example, help homeowners, farmers, and retirement pension holders to accumulate assets.[63] At the same time, there is a tendency for this movement to dilute protection and aid for the weakest, most disadvantaged members of the community. To temper the increasing concern for private responsibility with greater tolerance for public purpose is no simple task. During the next decade, the enabling state must grapple with this task if it is to invest the social fabric of modern welfare capitalism with resiliency and compassion.

As a first step, the time has come to reform the conventional model of social accounting. In recent years, a growing body of information has become available with which to construct a new ledger on social welfare, one that covers the full range of direct and indirect social transfers flowing to homeowners, employees, retired workers, veterans, college students, and farmers, as well as the disabled, poor, and dependent. An annual report that draws together this information, perhaps as a supplement to the federal budget, would contribute to a fuller public understanding of who benefits from the diverse activities of the enabling state.

## Notes

1. U.S. Bureau of the Census, *Statistical Abstract of the United States, 1987* (Washington, D.C.: U.S. Government Printing Office, 1986), p. 114.

2. These trends are discussed by Donald Erickson, "Choice and Private Schools: Dynamics of Supply and Demand," in *Private Education: Studies in Choice and Public Policy,* ed. Daniel Levy (New York: Oxford University Press, 1986), pp. 82–93.

3. James S. Coleman, Thomas Hoffer, and Sally Kilgore, *High School Achievement: Public, Catholic and Private Schools Compared* (New York: Basic Books, 1982).

4. See for example, Richard Murnane, "Comparisons of Private and Public Schools the Critical Role of Regulations," and "Comparisons of Public and Private Schools: What Can We Learn?", in Levy, ed., *Private Education: Studies,* pp. 138–69; A. S. Goldberger and G. G. Cain, "The Causal Analysis of Cognitive Outcomes in the Coleman, Hoffer, and Kilgore Report," *Sociology of Education,* 55 (April 1982), pp. 103–22.

5. A highly publicized report by the National Commission on Excellence in Education, *A Nation at Risk* (Washington, D.C.: U.S. Department of Education, 1983), warned that the educational system was awash in "a rising tide of mediocrity."

6. U.S. Bureau of the Census, *Statistical Abstract, 1987,* p. 135.

7. T. Neveille Postlethwaite, *Science Achievement in 17 Countries: A Preliminary Report* (Oxford: Pergamon Press, 1988).

8. *Pierce* v. *Society of Sisters,* 268 U.S. 510 (1925).

9. Mary-Michelle Upson Herschoff, "Public Policy Toward Private Schools: A Focus on Parental Choice," in Levy, ed., *Private Education: Studies,* pp. 33–37.

10. Mark Kutner, Joel Sherman, and Mary Williams, "Federal Policies for Private Schools," in Levy, ed., *Private Education: Studies,* p. 58.

11. Milton Friedman, "The Role of Government in Education," *Economics and the Public Interests,* ed. Robert Solo (New Brunswick, N.J.: Rutgers University Press, 1955).

12. Christopher Jencks et al., *Education Vouchers: A Report on Financing Elementary*

*Education by Grants to Parents* (Cambridge, Mass.: Center for the Study of Public Policy, 1970).

13. David Cohen and Eleanor Farrar, "Power to Parent? The Story of Education Vouchers," *The Public Interest,* 48 (Summer 1977), pp. 72–97.

14. For a discussion of the evidence on achievement, see P. Barker, "Preliminary Analysis of Metropolitan Achievement Test Scores, Voucher and Title 1 Schools," in *A Public School Voucher Demonstration: The First Year at Alum Rock, Technical Appendix,* ed. D. Weiler (Santa Monica, Calif.: Rand Corporation, 1974), pp. 120–30; Paul Wortman and Robert St. Pierre, "The Educational Voucher Demonstration: A Secondary Analysis," *Education and Urban Society,* 9 (August 1977), pp. 471–91; R. Crain, *Analysis of Achievement Test Outcomes in the Alum Rock Voucher Demonstration, 1974– 75,* Technical Report WN-9593-NIE (Santa Monica, Calif.: Rand Corporation, 1976).

15. John E. Coons and Stephen Sugarman, *Education by Choice: The Case for Family Control* (Berkeley: University of California Press, 1978).

16. E. G. West, "Choice or Monopoly in Education," *Policy Review,* 15 (Winter 1981), pp. 103–17.

17. Kutner et al., "Federal Policies." pp. 68–76.

18. Sheila N. Kirby and Linda Darling-Hammond, "Parental Schooling Choice: A Case Study of Minnesota," *Journal of Policy Analysis and Management,* 7:3 (Spring 1988), pp. 506–17.

19. Louis Uchitelle, "Public Services Found Better If Private Agencies Compete," *The New York Times,* April 26, 1988, p. 1, C6.

20. Upson Herschoff, "Public Policy," pp. 38–40.

21. Murnane, "Comparisons of Private and Public Schools," pp. 147–48.

22. For a revealing analysis of the Dutch experience, see Estelle James, "Public Subsidies for Private and Public Education: The Dutch Case," in Levy, ed., *Private Education: Studies,* pp. 113–37.

23. Upson Herschoff, "Public Policy," p. 46.

24. See, for example, "Looking Ahead, Town Uses Student Fees, Not Taxes, to Cover School Frills," *The New York Times,* August 31, 1981, p. 10.

25. *Hartzell* v. *Connell,* 35 Cal. 30, 904–913 (1984).

26. *Salazar et al.* v. *Honig et al., California Daily Opinion Service,* 3151 (1988).

27. *Kadrmas* v. *Dickson Public Schools,* 108 S.Ct 2481 (1988).

28. For a rationale and elaboration of the public choice approach, see Henry Levin, "Education as a Public and Private Good," *Journal of Policy Analysis and Management,* 6:4 (Summer 1987), pp. 628–41.

29. Gary Putka, "Choose-a-School: Parents in Minnesota Are Getting to Send Kids Where They Like," *Wall Street Journal,* May 13, 1988, pp. 1, 4.

30. For a general discussion of this issue, see Neil Gilbert and Harry Specht, *Dimensions of Social Welfare Policy* (Englewood Cliffs, N.J.: Prentice-Hall, 2nd edition 1986), pp. 92–98; the case for benefits in kind is ably recommended by Alva Myrdal in *Nation and Family* (Cambridge, Mass.: MIT Press, 1968), pp. 133–53; Milton Friedman and Rose Friedman, in *Free to Choose* (New York: Avon Books, 1979), pp. 110–18, present a forceful view of the other side in favor of cash benefits.

31. Eugene Bardach and Robert Kagan, eds., *Social Regulation: Strategies for Reform* (San Francisco: Institute for Contemporary Studies, 1982), p. 6.

32. Robert Hatfield, "Introduction," in *Bureaucrats and Brainpower: Government Regulation of Universities*, ed. Paul Seabury (San Francisco: Institute for Contemporary Studies, 1979), p. 4.

33. Irwin Stelzer, "Fairy Tales About a 'New America'" *The Public Interest*, 88 (Summar 1987), p. 124.

34. David Vogel, "The Decline and Resurgence of Business Power," presented at the Public Policy Group Seminar, University of California, Berkeley, January 26, 1988, p. 80.

35. Vermont Royster, "'Regulation' Isn't a Dirty Word," *Wall Street Journal*, September 9, 1987, p. 36.

36. William Havender "Assessing and Controlling Risks," in Bardach and Kagan, eds., *Social Regulation: Strategies*, p. 52.

37. For discussion of some of these conditions see Joseph Ferreira, Jr., "Promoting Safety Through Insurance," in Bardach and Kagan, eds., *Social Regulation: Strategies*, pp. 267–88.

38. Eugene Bardach and Robert Kagan, "Liability Law and Social Regulation," in Bardach and Kagan, eds., *Social Regulation: Strategies*, p. 251.

39. See, for example, Michael O'Hare, "Information Strategies as Regulatory Surrogates," in Bardach and Kagan, eds., *Social Regulation: Strategies*, pp. 221–36.

40. Cohen and Farrar, "Power to Parent? Vouchers", pp. 83–89. Wortman and St. Pierre, "Educational Voucher Demonstration."

41. See, for example, Susan Rose-Ackerman, "Unintended Consequences: Regulating the Quality of Subsidized Day Care," *Journal of Policy Analysis and Management*, 3:14 (1983), pp. 14–30.

42. For a more detailed analysis of these alternatives see Timothy Sullivan, "Tailoring Government Responses to Diversity," in Bardach and Kagan, eds., *Social Regulation: Strategies*, pp. 119–38.

43. André Ryerson, "Capitalism and Selfishness," *Commentary*, 82:6 (December 1986), p. 40.

44. James Q. Wilson, "The Rediscovery of Character: Private Virtue and Public Policy," *The Public Interest*, 81 (Fall 1985), pp. 3–16.

45. John Logue, "Will Success Spoil the Welfare State?" *Dissent* (Winter 1985), pp. 96–104.

46. Neil Gilbert, "Sweden's Disturbing Family Trends," *Wall Street Journal*, June 24, 1987, p. 23.

47. Logue, "Will Success Spoil the Welfare State?" pp. 96–104.

48. *Dagens Nyhetar*, April 12, 1987.

49. Douglas Besharov, "The ABCs of Child-Care Politics," *Wall Street Journal*, March 9, 1988, p. 29.

50. Child Assault Prevention Training Center of Northern California, *Preschool Project Training Manual*, Berkeley, Calif., 1983.

51. Neil Gilbert, "Teaching Children to Prevent Sexual Abuse," *The Public Interest*, 93 (Fall 1988), p. 14.

52. Margaret Thatcher, "Thatcher: Sow and Ye Shall Reap for All," *Wall Street Journal*, May 31, 1988, p. 22.

53. *Federal Register*, 52:250 (December 27, 1987), p. 49252.

54. Sheldon Danziger, Robert Haveman, and Robert Plotnick, "Antipoverty Policy: Effects on the Poor and the Nonpoor," in *Fighting Poverty: What Works and What Doesn't,* eds. Sheldon Danziger and Daniel Weinberg (Cambridge, Mass.: Harvard University Press, 1986), pp. 50–77.

55. Ibid., p. 59.

56. For a more detailed discussion of the inadequacy of poverty measures, see Neil Gilbert, *Capitalism and the Welfare State* (New Haven, Conn.: Yale University Press, 1983), pp. 180–83, and Charles Murray, "In Search of the Working Poor," *The Public Interest* 89 (Fall 1987), pp. 3–19.

57. See, for example, Burton Weisbrod and H. Lee Hansen, "An Income-Net-Worth Approach to Measuring Economic Welfare," *American Economic Review,* 8 (December 1968), pp. 1315–29; J. Murray, "Potential Income From Assets: Findings of the 1963 Survey of the Aged," *Social Security Bulletin,* 24 (December 1964), pp. 3–11.

58. Lee Rainwater, *What Money Buys* (New York: Basic Books, 1976), p. 57.

59. Nathan Glazer, "The Limits of Social Policy," *Commentary,* 52 (September 1971), pp. 51–58.

60. Arthur M. Schlesinger, Jr., *The Cycles of American History* (Boston: Houghton-Mifflin, 1986), pp. 23–34.

61. John Lapp, "Justice First," *Proceedings of the National Conference of Social Work, 1927* (Chicago: University of Chicago Press, 1928), p. 13.

62. Albert Hirschman, *Shifting Involvements: Private Interest and Public Action* (Princeton, N.J.: Princeton University Press, 1982), p. 132.

63. For an interesting discussion of social welfare policy and asset accumulation, see Michael Sherraden, "Rethinking Social Welfare: Toward Assets," *Social Policy* (Winter 1988), pp. 37–43.

# 9

# *Implications for the Comparative Study of Social Welfare*

It is almost common knowledge that, in comparing the social welfare efforts of developed nations, Sweden stands among the leaders while the United States and Japan fall near the end of the list. This knowledge derives from that widely used measure of "welfare effort"—the percentage of a nation's gross domestic product (GDP), or gross national product (GNP), spent on social welfare programs.[1] According to this conventional index of welfare effort, Table 9.1 reveals that in the 1980–1981 period Japan, Australia, and the United States lie at the bottom, Ireland, Austria, and Britain are in the middle, and Sweden and the Netherlands place at the top of the scale. The relative standing of these countries closely parallels the findings on welfare effort reported by Wilensky for 1966, although his index used social security spending, which encompasses a more limited range of social welfare programs than the social expenditures covered in the conventional index.[2]

By comparing direct welfare expenditures to GDP, the conventional

This chapter is a revised version of an article by Neil Gilbert and Ailee Moon, "Analyzing Welfare Effort: An Appraisal of Comparative Methods," *Journal of Policy Analysis and Management*, 7:2 (Winter 1988).

index of welfare effort focuses on the transfer of resources to individuals and families that takes place outside the regular channels of exchange in the market economy. There is a sense of proportionality to the concept of "welfare effort," which this index captures in the relative magnitude of resource transfers. However, it conveys only part of the picture and in so doing presents a somewhat distorted view. This distortion stems from several normative and technical assumptions implicit in the index.

The first normative assumption is, simply stated, the more the better; countries that spend a high proportion of their GDP on welfare programs are leaders, and those that do not are laggards. In the absence of any criteria of need, however, this judgment amounts to an implicit indictment of the market economy as a mechanism for allocating resources. Should a country with a relatively small elderly population be regarded as making an inferior welfare effort if it spends a lower proportion of its GDP on social security pensions than a country with a substantially larger group of elderly members? What if the first country spent less as an overall percentage of its GDP, but more per capita on the elderly?

The second normative assumption is that taxes do not count in assessing welfare effort. However, if two countries spend the same percentage of their GDPs on social welfare, and one collects proportionately twice as much in taxes as the other, are their welfare efforts equal? Surely the country with proportionately smaller tax revenues would be making a greater commitment to social welfare at the expense of other governmental expenditures. It is making less effort to collect taxes, but more effort to spend what it collects on social welfare.

The technical assumption is that direct public expenditures represent the only source of transfers used by societies to achieve social welfare purposes. This narrow frame of reference neglects a range of indirect transfers and private and voluntary efforts that considerably supplement the overall level of provision for social welfare in many countries. As noted throughout the previous chapters, the direct public expenditure model of the welfare state yields not so much an incorrect as an incomplete picture of welfare effort. Viewing welfare effort from the broader perspective of the enabling state takes into account transfers through indirect and private channels as well as direct public spending.

Welfare effort is a concept that embodies several dimensions of proportionality. Development of an index that deals with the issues just noted requires that we combine a range of direct and indirect expenditures with measures of national product, taxes, and social need. Going beyond the usual ratio of direct expenditure to GDP, such an index provides an estimate of what a country gives in various forms of welfare transfers relative to social need, compared to what it takes through taxes relative to national wealth. This index not only broadens the conceptual boundaries of comparative analysis but also affords a more penetrating assessment of welfare effort.

## Broadening the Conceptual Scope of Comparative Analysis

While direct public expenditures constitute an essential criterion in defining welfare effort, two other measures must be considered to render a full account of the expenditure component in this concept; these additional measures involve indirect expenditures, and transfers through voluntary and private channels. Ideally, the expenditure component of a comprehensive welfare effort index (WEI) would be calculated as follows:

$$WEI = \frac{\begin{array}{c}\text{Direct Public} \\ \text{Expenditure}\end{array} + \begin{array}{c}\text{Indirect Public} \\ \text{Expenditure}\end{array} + \begin{array}{c}\text{Private–Voluntary} \\ \text{Financing}\end{array}}{\text{Gross Domestic Product}}$$

Indirect transfers derive mainly from credit subsidies and tax expenditures. Credit subsidies (as noted in Chapter 1) are difficult to assess. Estimates are possible in some program areas, but a full accounting of indirect transfers attributable to credit subsidies in the United States has yet to be compiled. Moreover, comparative data on this form of indirect expenditure are not available. Although credit subsidies should be ideally counted among the indirect expenditures in the comprehensive welfare effort index, the limited data on these subsidies preclude their use in current calculations of this index.

As for tax expenditures, not everyone agrees that these measures should be thought of as a form of transfer payment. As Irving Kristol put it, to think of tax concessions as subsidies tacitly assumes that "all income covered by the general provisions of the tax law belongs of right to the government, and what government decides, by exemption or qualification, not to collect in taxes constitutes a subsidy."[3] This observation reflects the conceptual issue of determining what constitutes a "special" deduction for purposes of calculating tax expenditures. Practically speaking, however, tax expenditures cannot be ignored in comparative assessments of welfare effort inasmuch as they produce transfer effects that are similar to those of direct government outlays. For example, a refundable tax credit of $300 for child care expenses in one country and a direct government payment of equal amount in aid for child care expenses in another country would yield the same financial relief to eligible families. The exclusion of tax benefits from an appraisal of social welfare expenditures would result in underestimating the welfare efforts of countries that rely most heavily on "indirect" provisions of social support through the tax system.

The consideration of tax expenditures is also important because it takes into account the impact of different tax treatments on the ultimate dispersal of social welfare benefits. If two countries spend the same proportion of their GDPs on social welfare, but one taxes these benefits and the other does not, are their "welfare efforts" really equal? By adding the government's revenue losses from nontaxation of welfare benefits to the expenditure component of welfare effort, tax expenditures give a deserved edge to the country that does not tax benefits. In recent years, the systematic gathering of information on the extent of tax expenditures has made it possible to deepen empirical inquiry into the spending dimensions of welfare effort.

There remain, however, a number of difficulties in the comparative assessment of tax expenditures. Countries include different kinds of taxes in their tax expenditure calculations. They also employ different methods to estimate the value of these expenditures, such as the "revenue-foregone" and "revenue-gain" approaches as discussed in Chapter 1. Moreover, countries vary in regard to the range of welfare-related expenditure items on which data are available. Although present tax expenditure data are not fully developed for comparative purposes, these indirect transfers play a role too significant to be ignored in measures of welfare effort. Tax expenditure estimates are incorporated into the index of comprehensive welfare effort with full recognition of the tentative quality of these data.

Along with direct and indirect public expenditures, private and voluntary efforts contribute to the transfer of social provisions in the enabling state.[4] Thus, an ideal measure of the expenditure component would also include the value of cash and in-kind benefits that are transferred outside market channels through charitable agencies and informal arrangements with family and friends. The absence of systematic information on the monetary value of private and voluntary provisions and the complexity of their estimates for comparative purposes, however, make it unfeasible to incorporate the costs of these informal supports into the expenditure component of welfare effort. Although the exclusion of private contributions results in an expenditure index that falls short of the ideal, the actual distortion in comparative welfare effort is minimal. Theoretically, a country with a high amount of charitable giving would require less in the way of publicly financed provisions to achieve the same level of welfare effort as a country with a low rate of charitable giving; however, in practice the overall magnitude of philanthropic contributions is generally negligible compared to direct and indirect public expenditures.[5] Moreover, private efforts would not be totally excluded because the untaxed portion of most charitable contributions is entered into the calculation of public spending as an item of tax expenditures.

While the monetary value of private donations could be compared if cross-national data were available, the value of voluntary provisions such as family care of dependent members and organized volunteer activities are least amenable to quantification for comparative purposes. In Japan, for example, 64 percent of those over sixty-five years of age in 1980 lived with relatives, in most cases with their children.[6] In the United States, the proportion of elderly living with their children declined from 38 percent in 1957 to 18 percent in 1975; still, estimates indicate that almost 80 percent of home health services for the elderly in the United States is provided by family members.[7] Beyond family care, about 48 percent of the population fourteen years old and older in the United States did some volunteer work in 1985.[8] Similarly, 20 percent of the Japanese interviewed in a 1982 public opinion poll had done volunteer work, and the Minsei-iin, an elite core of volunteers appointed by the minister of health and welfare, had made approximately 18 million home visits that year.[9] National differences may be large in private and voluntary aspects of welfare effort, but there is no accounting scheme to determine exactly what units to include among these informal transfers or how to estimate their monetary equivalents for comparative purposes.

So far our assessment of welfare effort has focused upon the issue of what to count on the expenditure side of the ledger; on the other side of this ledger is the issue of how much citizens are taxed to achieve different levels of social welfare expenditure. The proportion of tax revenues spent on social welfare varies considerably among countries. This raises a fundamental question as to whether social welfare expenditure relative to GDP alone provides a sufficient criterion for measuring welfare effort. How do we interpret and compare the welfare effort of a country that spends about 33 percent of its GDP on social welfare but collects taxes amounting to nearly 50 percent of the GDP, with that of another country that spends about 20 percent of its GDP on social welfare but has taxes that constitute less than 33 percent of the GDP?

The difference in the relative size of tax revenues among countries deserves consideration in a comparative analysis of welfare efforts. Generally speaking, because a significant part of a person's economic well-being may be measured by his or her disposable income after taxes and transfers, rather than by pretax income, the overall welfare level of people is affected not only by social welfare expenditures but also by taxes. More to the point, the size of tax revenues has a direct bearing on a government's ability to spend on social welfare as well as on other items of public expenditures. As a result, in order to spend the same proportion of their GDPs on social welfare, governments with relatively small tax revenues would have to make greater efforts or commitments to social welfare (at the expense of other governmental expenditures) than those with relatively large tax revenues. There is a high correlation between tax revenues and welfare expenditures (Appendix, Table A.2, rows 3 and 5); in fact, the total tax revenues, as a proportion of GDP, of some countries are even lower than the social welfare expenditures relative to GDP of some other countries. This suggests that failure to take into account the different magnitudes of tax revenue may result in a measure of welfare effort that is largely a function of "tax effort" rather than of public choices about how taxes should be spent.

In addition to controlling for taxes, a meaningful analysis of differential welfare effort requires some fundamental estimate of need against which levels of expenditure can be assessed. To the extent that "welfare effort" implies an attempt to meet human needs through social provisions allocated outside of the market economy, a country with greater need would have to allocate a larger proportion of its resources to achieve a level of welfare equivalent to a country with a lesser magnitude of need. If welfare efforts are made to achieve a desirable social condition, then to compare these efforts without reference to needs would convey the impression that needs are either equal among the countries under comparison or irrelevant to the social condition being sought.

There are a number of variables that might plausibly be used to estimate the magnitudes of need among countries. For example, rates of pretransfer poverty (percentage of poverty before the allocation of social welfare benefits) would offer the best estimate of need. However, these measures are currently beyond our reach for comparative purposes because of the absence of cross-national data on pretransfer poverty rates and the considerable variations among countries in their definitions of poverty. Another approach is to focus upon those groups likely to be nonworking and in need of assistance, such as children, the elderly, single-parent families, and the unemployed, who traditionally constitute the core of social welfare beneficiaries. This approach is conceptually somewhat less proximate to need than the use of pretransfer poverty rates, but the availability of data on these variables make them among the most practical choices for comparative analyses of need. Recognizing that operational definitions of unemployment rates vary among countries, our index of comprehensive welfare effort incorporates the dependency ratio, the percentage of single-parent families, and the unemployment rate to estimate relative magnitudes of need. To analyze social welfare expenditures relative to GDP in the context of taxes and the magnitude of need, the NET (need, expenditure, and tax) index of comprehensive welfare effort will be constructed as follows:

NET Index of Welfare Effort =

$$\frac{\text{Direct Public Expenditures} + \text{Indirect (tax) Expenditures}}{\text{(GDP) (Standardized Tax Burden) (Standardized Need)}}$$

Conceptually, there are three steps by which this index refines the conventional direct expenditure/GDP measure. First, social welfare tax expenditures are added to the basic direct expenditure measure in the calculation of the ratio of welfare effort to GDP. Second, the spending component is divided by a standardized measure of tax burden. Third, the expenditure component, now controlled for taxes, is divided by a standardized need index. (Arithmetically, the last two steps may be combined by multiplying the measures of need and tax burden.)

## Need, Expenditure, and Tax: Constructing the NET Index

The ten major countries selected for analysis of welfare effort cover a wide range of scores as measured by the conventional index. This analysis presents a detailed account of how the expenditure, tax, and need components of a comprehensive index are constructed and how the rank order on welfare effort changes as each of these components are joined to the index. There is a numerical density in this step-by-step approach that does not make for lively exposition. However, it provides insight into some of the complexities of measuring welfare effort and affords an operational sense of how several dimensions of this concept can be pieced together for empirical analysis.

Beginning with the expenditure component, all ten countries devote more than 50 percent of their total direct government expenditures to various social programs, with the Netherlands and France ranked at the top (62.4 percent and 61.4 percent, respectively), the United States, Austria, and Japan in the middle (58.0 percent, 57.3 percent, and 57.0 percent), and the United Kingdom at the bottom (50.6 percent) of the group (see Appendix, Table A.2, row 1). This rank is substantially altered when tax expenditures for social welfare are added to direct expenditures (row 2 in Appendix, Table A.2). Among the nine countries with data available on both direct and tax expenditures, the United Kingdom climbs to the top (77.2 percent), followed by Sweden (74.9 percent), and France and Austria (63.1 percent and 57.6 percent) fall to the bottom of the group.

The proportion of total government expenditures allocated to social programs reveals the extent of government involvement in the provision for social welfare relative to other state functions. However, this is, at best, a weak indicator of a country's welfare effort in relation to its overall national resources. Using the GDP, rather than total government outlay, as the base for comparison creates an entirely different picture of social expenditures (compare rows 1 and 3 in Appendix, Table A.2). Major changes are evident for Australia, Japan, Sweden, and the United States. With direct social welfare expenditures ranked as a percentage of GDP, Sweden moves up from eighth to second on the list, while Australia and the United States fall to ninth and eighth from the third and fourth, respectively; Japan drops from the sixth place to tenth at the bottom of the list. These shifts reflect the sizeable differences among countries in the amount of total government spending relative to GDP. Total government expenditures in Sweden, for example, equal 61.1 percent of its GDP, which is nearly double the rate of that in the United States (35.7 percent). Thus, while the proportion of total government expenditure devoted to social welfare in Sweden (53.2 percent) is somewhat lower than that of the United States (58 percent), Sweden spends a much higher proportion of its GDP on social welfare (32.5 percent) than the United States (20.7 percent).

Turning to the other main variable in the expenditure component, the data show large variations in tax expenditures. The magnitude of tax expenditures relative to direct social welfare expenditures ranges from 52.6 percent in the United Kingdom and 40.8 percent in Sweden to less than 10 percent in Australia, Austria, and France. For more than half the countries in our sample, tax expenditures play a significant role in the provision of social welfare. This does not necessarily imply that the addition of tax expenditures will produce sweeping changes in the rank order of welfare states based on their direct expenditures only. In fact, the degree of change is negligible; most of the countries remain at the same ranks or move one step up or down.

The values of most tax expenditures vary according to the taxpayers' marginal tax brackets. Thus, whether a country's rate of tax expenditure is more an artifact of its tax level than of the government's explicit policy choice to emphasize indirect spending is open to question. While a low correlation between tax revenue and tax expenditure rates would indicate explicit policy choices operating independently of tax levels, a high correlation is more difficult to interpret, because it is not implausible for high tax rates to be coupled with an explicit policy emphasis on indirect social spending.

When direct expenditures are added to tax expenditures, the resulting overall level of social welfare spending is highly correlated ($r = .84$) with total tax revenues (Appendix, Table A.2, rows 4 and 5). Sweden and the Netherlands rank very high on both overall expenditure and total tax revenue, while Canada, Australia, and the United States are at the bottom of the list. Except for Ireland, the data suggest that a country is more likely to achieve a high level of social welfare provision at the expense of the taxpayer than by the sacrifice of expenditures for other governmental functions.[10]

How would the countries' ranks on the expenditure component

change if we were able to control for relative tax burdens? In exploring this issue, we must introduce a tax component into the welfare effort index. To assemble this component (see row 6 in Appendix, Table A.2), the differences in tax revenues are standardized by measuring the ratio of the tax revenue of each country as percentage of its GDP to the average percentage of all the ten countries (37.23 percent). Using the average as the standard, the index indicates the revenue level of each country in relation to the mean. For example, Sweden's index score of 1.327 suggests that its tax revenue level is nearly one and one-third times the average tax/GDP ratio for the ten countries, while Japan's score of .720 implies that its revenues are less than three-fourths of the average ratio.

The index is then used to adjust the overall social welfare expenditures for the differences in tax revenue levels.[11] This is done by dividing the percentage of GDP spent on social welfare by the standardized tax burden index score for each country, because social welfare expenditures and taxes are inversely related on the scale of welfare effort. That is, the higher the expenditures and the lower the taxes, the greater the welfare effort. The rationale for the method just described can also be understood by the notion of "controlling" for the variations in tax revenues. Thus, the results represented in Appendix, Table A.2, row 7, can be interpreted as an estimate of how much the social welfare expenditures as percentage of GDP would change if the tax revenues were fixed hypothetically at the same percentage of GDP for each of the ten countries, given the actual ratio of the expenditures to the tax revenues of individual countries. For example, because Australia and Sweden spend 20.6 percent and 45.7 percent of their GDPs on social welfare when their tax revenues amount to 31.1 percent and 49.4 percent of the GDP, they would spend 24.67 percent and 34.44 percent of GDP, respectively, if both countries taxed at the group average of 37.23 percent of GDP.[12]

Ranked according to the adjusted percentage of GDP spent on social welfare after accounting for the differences in tax revenues, Ireland and the United Kingdom are at the top, Canada and the United States place in the middle, and Austria and Japan are at the bottom. This represents modest changes in these countries' positions compared to their ranks based on the overall expenditures relative to GDP alone. The positions of seven countries change by two ranks, while Japan remains unchanged at the bottom in both measures and Austria moves to the ninth from the sixth. Although Japan's tax revenue level is the lowest of the ten countries, equivalent to 72 percent of the average, this does not compensate for having the lowest welfare expenditure, which comes to 56.6 percent of the average. Japan's low tax revenue, however, does account for its increase in welfare effort from 17.3 percent of GDP before adjusting for taxes to 24.03 percent after the adjustment. It should be noted that the overall expenditures for Japan include only direct outlays, because of the absence of data on its tax expenditures. Japan's position would probably rise by several steps if its tax expenditures were included in the measure of welfare effort, because it is separated from the two countries immediately higher in rank by an index score of less than 1 percent.

The overall expenditures adjusted for taxes are approximately the same for Australia and Austria (24.67 and 24.57 percent of GDP) even though the latter allocates a 6.6 percent higher proportion of its GDP to social welfare before the adjustment (20.6 and 27.2 percent). This is mainly due to the substantial difference in their tax revenue levels (31.1 and 41.2 percent of GDP). Ireland comes out at the top on adjusted expenditures because of its relatively high social expenditures joined with a level of tax revenues that is close to the average. It spends about 20 percent more than the average on social welfare while maintaining a tax level of 3 percent less than the average.

The final component in the comprehensive NET index of welfare effort involves a measure of need. As shown in Appendix, Table A.3, estimates of the magnitude of need for social welfare expenditures are based on the sum of the dependency ratio, the unemployment rate, and the percentage of single-parent families. The three variables are given equal weight in determining the overall magnitude of need. That the dependency ratio scale, which varies between 69.5 and 48.1 percent, is somewhat higher in absolute terms than those of the other two variables is unimportant for the purpose of this analysis. What becomes crucial for a comparative analysis is the range of variability and the extent to which the dependency ratio of a country is higher or lower than that of another, rather than the size of the dependency ratio per se.

Ranked according to the overall magnitude of need, Sweden and Ireland are at the top, France and the United States place in the middle, and the Netherlands and Japan are at the bottom of the group. By applying the same method used on tax revenues, we standardized the need magnitude of each country based on the average of the ten countries (73.66 percent). As shown in Appendix, Table A.2, row 8, the standardized need index goes from a high of 1.154 for Sweden to a low of .756 for Japan. The need index range (1.154 − .757 = .397) is considerably lower than that of tax burden index (1.327 − .720 = .607). In addition, except for the Netherlands and the United States, the rank order of the other countries based on their need scores closely parallels their rank order on social welfare expenditures. Thus, as with tax burden, welfare expenditure and need tend to be related.

It remains to be seen how the levels of social welfare expenditures are finally arrayed after holding constant both tax burden and need. These outcomes are measured by the NET index of welfare effort (Appendix, Table A.2, row 9), which lists the adjusted overall social welfare expenditures as a percentage of GDP after accounting for the differences in tax revenues and the magnitude of need. The NET index score is obtained by dividing the overall expenditures as percentages of GDP adjusted for taxes by the standardized need index score of each country. This procedure assumes that if two countries tax the same proportion of GDP overall, but one has greater need for social welfare expenditures than the other, the former must devote a higher proportion of its GDP to social welfare in order to achieve an equivalent level of welfare effort. Thus, welfare effort is operationally defined relative to both resources and needs. Adding the need component to complete the NET index of welfare effort alters the positions of five countries by at least two ranks; the largest changes are evident for Japan, the Netherlands, and Sweden. Japan moves from the bottom to fifth place and the Netherlands move from the fourth position to the top; Sweden falls from third to sixth place (Appendix, Table A.2, rows 7 and 9).

## Ranking Welfare Effort: Alternative Measures

Which countries excel and which lag behind in their level of welfare effort? The answer, as illustrated in Table 9.1, varies with the index used. In comparing the conventional index of social welfare expenditures to GDP with the more comprehensive NET index, the ranks of six countries change by three or more steps. On the decline, Austria falls from fifth to tenth, France from third to ninth, and Sweden from second to sixth place. Moving up, Canada climbs from seventh to fourth, the United Kingdom from sixth to second, and Japan from tenth to fifth place. Again, in the absence of tax expenditure data on Japan, the index may underestimate its relative position on welfare effort, particularly because the third- and fourth-ranked countries score only two percentage points higher than Japan.

Looking more closely at some of this movement we find that, even though France's direct social welfare expenditure as a proportion of GDP is higher than those of seven countries, its welfare effort based on the comprehensive NET index is next to the lowest on the list. This is mainly due to both low tax expenditures and high tax revenues. Similarly, while Sweden spends a larger proportion of its GDP on direct social welfare provisions than the United Kingdom, its tax burden and magnitude of need (especially the percentage of single-parent families) are far higher. Thus, in applying the NET index, the rank-order positions of these countries change direction.

Given the tentative quality of tax expenditure data and the absence of these data on Japan, we have also calculated the NET index excluding tax expenditures. Several notable changes in welfare effort emerge when ranks on the conventional index are compared with the NET index minus tax expenditure; most conspicuous is the reversal of positions between Sweden and Japan. Weighed down with the highest tax burden and level of need, Sweden drops from second place on the conventional index to tenth place, while Japan buoyed by the lowest tax burden and level of need climbs from tenth place to second place in the adjusted NET index. For similar reasons, but to a lesser degree, Canada and the United States also improve their positions moving from the lower to the upper half of the group.

Finally, in assessing the NET index of welfare effort, an additional calculation is offered based on a modified measure of the need component. Under this modified NET index, the "percentage of single-parent families" is excluded from the construction of the need component (see Appendix, Table A.3, Standardized Need Index II). While the percentage of single-parent families is a credible indicator of need, this alternative measure is presented for two reasons. First, our data on single-parent families (Appendix, Table A.3, row 3) are in three cases more than ten years old, which surely underestimates the need score for those countries on this variable. Second, the unusually high proportion of single-parent families in Sweden may be somewhat misleading in light of the increasing trend toward cohabitation outside of marriage in this country. As illustrated in Table 9.1 (last column), the exclusion of

*Table 9.1.* Rank on Welfare Effort by Alternative Indices

| Country (year) | Indices of Welfare Effort | | | |
|---|---|---|---|---|
| | Conventional (score) | NET | NET Excluding Tax Expenditures | NET Modified for Need |
| Netherlands (1980) | 1 (35.5) | 1 (40.02) | 1 (34.07) | 2 (35.79) |
| Sweden (1980) | 2 (32.5) | 6 (29.84) | 10 (21.22) | 1 (35.80) |
| France (1980) | 3 (28.3) | 9 (24.51) | 5 (23.92) | 10 (24.18) |
| Ireland (1981) | 4 (27.8) | 3 (33.77) | 4 (25.95) | 6 (29.50) |
| Austria (1980) | 5 (27.1) | 10 (23.01) | 8 (22.92) | 8 (25.67) |
| United Kingdom (1981) | 6 (23.5) | 2 (34.07) | 9 (22.31) | 4 (33.12) |
| Canada (1980) | 7 (21.0) | 4 (33.68) | 3 (26.49) | 3 (33.68) |
| United States (1981) | 8 (20.7) | 7 (28.40) | 6 (23.70) | 5 (31.01) |
| Australia (1981) | 9 (18.9) | 8 (22.35) | 7 (23.26) | 9 (25.30) |
| Japan (1981) | 10 (17.3) | 5 (31.79) | 2 (32.79) | 7 (28.54) |

*Source*: See Appendix, Tables A.2 and A.3.

single-parent families from the need component alters the rank order on welfare effort. The most conspicuous change is Sweden's rebound from sixth to first place.

What are the implications of these findings? Some may accept the NET index or its modified version as a better standard against which to calibrate welfare effort than the conventional direct expenditure/GDP ratio. Others will no doubt argue with the accuracy of tax expenditure estimates, choice of need indicators, consideration of tax levels, and the equal weights given the several variables in the NET index. As we have noted, the various measures used in the NET index are not without flaws. The criticism of imperfect measures may be applied as well to the conventional index. Official estimates of GDP, for example, do not include what is thought to be a large amount of production that takes place in the "gray" or "off-the-books economy." But the criticism of imperfect measures can be brought to bear on most comparative analyses. Cross-national studies often draw tentative comparisons. Indeed, the more interesting the phenomena under examination, the more tentative are the comparative measures.

Certainly, there is room for refining measures and improving the comparability of cross-national data in the appraisal of welfare effort. But first it is necessary to identify the salient variables and how they fit into a framework for comparative analysis. The NET index clarifies and broadens this conceptual framework. On the expenditure side, this index brings an analytic perspective to focus on a range of measures used to accomplish social transfers in the enabling state. Although comparative data currently are not available on all of these measures, by incorporating tax expenditures and controlling for taxes and need, the NET index mitigates the conventional bias of equating welfare effort with direct expenditures and sets forth a more rigorous standard for comparative judgments. It is a standard that should encourage more probing analysis and reevaluation of societal arrangements to promote the commonweal.

# Notes

1. This index is reported with minor variations and occasional qualifications in most comparative discussions of welfare effort. See, for example, Harold Wilensky, *The Welfare State and Equality* (Berkeley: University of California Press, 1975); Leonard Miller, "The Structural Determinants of Welfare Effort," *Social Service Review*, 50:1 (March 1976), pp. 57–79; Ramesh Mishra, *Society and Social Policy* (London: Macmillan Press, 2nd edition, 1981), pp. 104–5; J. F. Sleeman, *The Welfare State* (London: George Allen and Unwin, 1973), p. 136; Ian Gough, *The Political Economy of the Welfare State* (London: Macmillan Press, 1979), p. 79; Winifred Bell, *Contemporary Social Welfare* (New York: Macmillan, 1983), pp. 38–39. The measure of "welfare effort" must not be confused with that of "welfare outcome." Theoretically, we would expect higher welfare efforts (e.g., expenditures controlled for need and taxes) to result in higher welfare outcomes (e.g., reduction of poverty and improvement of other social conditions); however, that remains an empirical question, which among other things depends on the actual distribution of welfare benefits, how efficiently they are delivered, and their unanticipated consequences for the well-being of recipients.

2. Wilensky, *Welfare State and Equality.*

3. Irving Kristol, *Two Cheers for Capitalism* (New York: Basic Books, 1978), p. 194.

4. For a discussion of the voluntary alternatives, see Neil Gilbert, *Capitalism and the Welfare State* (New Haven, Conn.: Yale University Press), pp. 91–136.

5. According to Lampman's estimate, philanthropic transfers amounted to 0.6 percent

of the GNP in 1978. See Robert Lampman, *Social Welfare Spending: Accounting for Changes from 1950 to 1978* (Orlando, Fla.: Academic Press, 1984), p. 15.

6. Shinya Hoshino, "Perspectives on the Japanese Welfare State," a report prepared for the 2nd Conference of the International Study Group on Social Welfare Trends, McCormack Institute of Public Affairs, University of Massachusetts, September 22–26, 1986.

7. Abraham Monk, "Family Supports in Old Age," *Social Work,* 24:6 (November 1979), p. 536; National Center for Health Statistics, U.S. Department of Health, Education, and Welfare, "Home Health Care for Persons 55 and Over," *Vital and Health Statistics Publication Series,* 10:73 (1972).

8. U.S. Bureau of the Census, *Statistical Abstract of the United States, 1988* (Washington, D.C.: U.S. Government Printing Office, 1987), p. 359.

9. Japanese Ministry of Health and Welfare, *Annual Report On Health and Welfare for 1983* (Tokyo: Japan International Corporation of Welfare Services, 1984), pp. 108, 276.

10. It should be noted that the overall welfare expenditures for Ireland appear to exceed its total tax revenues shown in Appendix, Table A.2. This does not mean that Ireland spends more on social welfare than it collects in taxes; it just reflects the way tax expenditures are treated in the analysis. The costs of tax expenditures are already absorbed in tax revenues in the form of revenue losses. They are added to direct expenditures to arrive at overall expenditures because, as mentioned earlier, revenue losses caused by special tax provisions are similar to direct expenditures in terms of both function and fiscal implication. These revenue losses are treated as "expenditures," even though they are not shown in government outlays. As a result, the overall expenditures may exceed revenue figures as in the case of Ireland.

11. In adjusting for tax burden, we are emphasizing proportional differences between taxing and spending over absolute differences among expenditure/GDP ratios. This is because we would not want to say that if two countries spend the same proportion of their GDPs on social welfare but one collects proportionately twice as much in taxes as the other, they are both making an equal welfare effort. Clearly, the country with the proportionately smaller tax burden would have to make a greater commitment to social welfare at the expense of other governmental expenditures. Thus, our index emphasizes proportional equality controlling for taxes. In other words, to claim that two countries achieve the same level of welfare effort, they would have to demonstrate the equality in their ratios of expenditure/tax rather than expenditure/GDP. On the other hand, at some point of extreme absolute difference between expenditure/GDP ratios, one would argue that proportional equality does not necessarily imply equivalent welfare effort. As a hypothetical example, if one country collects 5 percent of its GDP in taxes and spends 5 percent of its GDP on social welfare, while proportionately equal to a country that collects 40 percent of its GDP in taxes and spends 40 percent on social welfare, the extreme difference in absolute commitments to welfare spending cannot be ignored. While absolute differences among the ten countries in our sample are not that extreme (the largest difference in expenditures is 25 percent between Australia and Sweden or 18 percent between Japan and Sweden if tax expenditures are excluded), at some point in addition to controlling for tax burden, one would want to weight the index to adjust for very large absolute differences. This admits that at some point tax effort and welfare effort overlap. In the extreme case, one could argue that the choice not to collect or to collect a very low level of

taxes is in part a choice not to have funds directly available for social welfare spending. It is possible, as in the case of Ireland, for a government's social welfare spending to exceed its total tax revenues when tax expenditures are included in the expenditure component. It must be noted, however, that even if one chooses to weight the index, the decision on what weighting method to be used and how much weight to be assigned to absolute differences in the expenditure/GDP ratio remain largely arbitrary.

12. The introduction of tax levels raises an interesting question of how to handle a country with a low level of taxation and a high level of deficit spending. One might argue that this country achieves a favorable rating on the welfare effort index simply by shifting the tax burden to the next generation. However, it is unclear that deficit spending must eventually require higher taxation. Instead of tax revenues, we could have controlled for total government expenditures, which would have absorbed deficit financing into the measure, but lost the comparative dimension of what government takes from people (affecting their income position) to achieve welfare expenditures. In any event, the financial balance of the ten countries in the years under study varied from a surplus of 0.3 percent of nominal GNP in France to a deficit of 4.8 percent in the Netherlands.

# Appendix

*Table A.1.* Revenue Loss Estimates for Selected Tax Expenditures, 1985

| Sources | Revenue Loss Estimates[a] |
|---|---|
| *Nonwelfare Tax Expenditures—Total 84,360* | |
| International Affairs—Subtotal 2,250 | |
|     Exclusion of Income Earned Abroad by U.S. Citizens | 1,405 |
|     Deferral of Income of Domestic International Sales Corporations | 470 |
|     Deferral of Income from Controlled Foreign Corporations | 375 |
| General Science, Space, and Technology—Subtotal 5,330 | |
|     Expensing of Research and Development Expenditures | 3,690 |
|     Credit for Increasing Research Activities | 1,640 |
| Energy—Subtotal 3,480 | |
|     Expensing of Exploration and Development Costs, Oil and Gas | 2,030 |
|     Excess of Percentage over Cost Depletion, Oil and Gas | 1,120 |
|     Residential Energy Credits Supply Incentives | 330 |
| Natural Resources and Environment—Subtotal 2,330 | |
|     Excess of Percentage over Cost Depletion, Nonfuel Minerals | 380 |
|     Tax Incentives for Preservation of Historic Structures | 325 |
|     Capital-Gains Treatment of Certain Timber Income | 355 |
|     Interest Exclusion on Industrial Development Bonds (IDBs) for Pollution, Sewage, and Waste Disposal Activites | 1,270 |
| General Commerce—Subtotal 70,970 | |
|     Excess Bad-Debt Reserves of Financial Institutions | 810 |
|     Investment Credit, Rehabilitation, Energy Property, Reforestation Expenditures | 23,900 |

*(continued)*

*Table A.1 (Continued)*

| Sources | Revenue Loss Estimates |
|---|---:|
| Accelerated Depreciation on Buildings Other than Housing | 8,060 |
| Accelerated Depreciation on Machinery and Equipment | 20,185 |
| Safe-Harbor Leasing Rules | 2,340 |
| Dividend Reinvestment in Public Utility Stock | 450 |
| Reduced Rates on First $100,000 of Corporate Income | 5,000 |
| Corporate Tax Credit for Income Related to Doing Business in U.S. Possessions | 1,440 |
| Interest Exclusion on Public Purpose State and Local Debt | 8,785 |

*Welfare Tax Expenditures Directly Benefiting Individuals—Total 163,030*

Housing—Subtotal 38,030
| | |
|---|---:|
| Exclusion of Employee Meals and Lodging (Nonmilitary) | 795 |
| Deductibility of Mortgage Interest on Owner-Occupied Homes | 24,925 |
| Deductibility of Property Tax on Owner-Occupied Homes | 9,725 |
| Capital-Gains Deferral on Home Sales | 1,780 |
| Capital-Gains Exclusion (up to $125,000) on Home Sales by Persons 55 or older | 805 |

Employment—Subtotal 9,245
| | |
|---|---:|
| Tax Credit (up to $4800) for Child and Dependent Care Expenses | 2,195 |
| Deduction for Two-Earner Married Couples | 6,745 |
| Earned Income Credit | 305 |

Health—Subtotal 24,675
| | |
|---|---:|
| Exclusion of Employer Contributions for Health Insurance and Care | 21,245 |
| Deductibility of Certain Unreimbursed Medical Expenses | 3,430 |

Education—Subtotal 1,775
| | |
|---|---:|
| Exclusion of Scholarship and Fellowship Income | 655 |
| Parental Personal Exemption for Students 19 and older | 1,120 |

Income Security—Subtotal 89,305
| | |
|---|---:|
| Partial Exclusion of Social Security Benefits Including Medicare | |
|   Disability Benefits | 1,165 |
|   Retirement Annuities | 12,830 |
|   Dependent and Survivor Benefits | 3,780 |
| Exclusion of Railroad Retirement System Benefits | 450 |
| Exclusion of Benefits, Allowances, and Disability Benefits to Military Personnel | 3,635 |
| Exclusion of Workmen's Compensation Benefits | 2,325 |
| Exclusion of Public Assistance Benefits | 520 |
| Partial Exclusion of Unemployment Insurance Benefits | 1,605 |
| Partial Exclusion of Pension Contributions and Earnings Employer Plans | 44,205 |

*Table A.1* *(Continued)*

| Sources | Revenue Loss Estimates |
|---|---:|
| Individual Retirement Accounts | 12,050 |
| Keoghs | 1,585 |
| Exclusion of Certain Employee Benefits (Group Term Life Insurance Premiums) | 2,055 |
| Extra Exemption for the Elderly | 2,665 |
| Deductibility of Unreimbursed Casualty Losses | 435 |

*Partial and Indirect Welfare Tax Expenditures—Total 93,235*

Income Enhancement—Subtotal 68,495

| | |
|---|---:|
| Deferral of Interest Taxation on U.S. Savings Bonds | 770 |
| Dividend Exclusion (First $100) | 505 |
| Deductibility of nonBusiness State and Local Taxes Other than on Owner-Occupied Homes | 22,520 |
| Reduced Tax Rates on Capital Gains | 19,895 |
| Carryover Basis of Capital Gains at Death | 4,355 |
| Interest Deductibility on Consumer Credit | 14,625 |
| Exclusion of Life Insurance Policy Income | 3,915 |
| Investment Credit for Employee Stock Option Plans | 1,910 |

Agricultural Income Enhancement—Subtotal 1,280

| | |
|---|---:|
| Expensing of Certain Capital Outlays | 670 |
| Capital-Gains Treatment of Certain Income | 610 |

Housing and Community Development—Subtotal 6,895

| | |
|---|---:|
| Interest Exclusion on State and Local Housing Bonds for Owner-Occupied Housing | 1,850 |
| Interest Exclusion on State and Local Debt for Rental Housing | 910 |
| Accelerated Depreciation on Rental Housing | 775 |
| Investment Credit for Rehabilitation of (Nonhistoric) Structures | 345 |
| Investment Exclusion on Industrial Development Bonds | 3,015 |

Health—Subtotal 3,450

| | |
|---|---:|
| Interest Exclusion on State and Local Debt for Private Nonprofit Health Facilities | 1,640 |
| Deductibility of Charitable Contributions for Health | 1,810 |

Education—Subtotal 1,565

| | |
|---|---:|
| Interest Exclusion on State and Local Student Loan Bonds | 375 |
| Deductibility of Charitable Contributions for Education | 1,190 |

Employment—Subtotal 415

| | |
|---|---:|
| Targeted Jobs Credit | 415 |

Other Charity—Subtotal 11,135

| | |
|---|---:|
| Deductibility of Charitable Contributions Other than for Health and Education | 11,135 |

[a]In millions of dollars; for year ending September 30; all tax expenditures of $300 million or more.

*Table A.2.* Comparative Welfare Effort Statistics of Ten Countries

| Equation | Australia (1981) | Austria (1980) | Canada (1980) | France (1980) | Ireland (1981) | Netherlands (1980) | Sweden (1980) | United Kingdom (1981) | United States (1981) | Japan (1981) |
|---|---|---|---|---|---|---|---|---|---|---|
| (1) DE/G[a] | 60.9(3)[l] | 57.3(5) | 52.6(9) | 61.4(2) | 53.9(7) | 62.4(1) | 53.2(8) | 50.6(10) | 58.0(4) | 57.0(6) |
| (2) DE + TE/G[b] | 66.5(7) | 57.6(9) | 67.0(6) | 63.1(8) | 70.6(4) | 73.3(3) | 74.9(2) | 77.2(1) | 69.5(5) | — |
| (3) DE/P[c] | 18.9(9) | 27.1(5) | 21.0(7) | 28.3(3) | 27.8(4) | 35.5(1) | 32.5(2) | 23.5(6) | 20.7(8) | 17.3(10) |
| (4) DE + TE/P[d] | 20.6(9) | 27.2(6) | 26.7(7) | 29.0(5) | 36.5(3) | 41.7(2) | 45.7(1) | 35.9(4) | 24.8(8) | 17.3(10)[m] |
| (5) TR[e] | 31.1(8) | 41.2(4) | 32.0(7) | 42.5(3) | 36.2(6) | 45.8(2) | 49.4(1) | 36.5(5) | 30.8(9) | 26.8(10) |
| (6) STI[f] | .835(8) | 1.107(4) | .860(7) | 1.142(3) | .972(6) | 1.230(2) | 1.327(1) | .980(5) | .827(9) | .720(10) |
| (7) DE + TE/P/STI[g] | 24.67(8) | 24.57(9) | 31.05(5) | 25.39(7) | 37.55(1) | 33.90(4) | 34.44(3) | 36.63(2) | 29.99(6) | 24.03(10)[m] |
| (8) SNI-I[h] | .973(7) | 1.068(4) | .922(8) | 1.036(6) | 1.112(2) | .847(9) | 1.154(1) | 1.075(3) | 1.056(5) | .756(10) |
| (9) NET Index[i] | 25.35(8) | 23.01(10) | 33.68(4) | 24.51(9) | 33.77(3) | 40.02(1) | 29.84(6) | 34.07(2) | 28.40(7) | 31.79(5)[m] |
| (10) SNI-II[j] | .975(4) | .957(7) | .922(9) | 1.050(3) | 1.273(1) | .947(8) | .962(6) | 1.106(2) | .967(5) | .842(10) |
| (11) Mod. NET Index[k] | 25.30(9) | 25.67(8) | 33.68(3) | 24.18(10) | 29.50(6) | 35.797(2) | 35.8(1) | 33.12(4) | 31.01(5) | 28.54(7)[m] |

[a] Direct Social Welfare (SW) expenditures/total direct government expenditures for all purposes × 100.
[b] Direct SW expenditures/tax expenditures for SW/total direct government expenditures for all purposes × 100.
[c] Direct SW expenditures/GDP × 100.
[d] Direct SW expenditures + tax expenditures for SW/GDP × 100.
[e] Total tax revenues/GDP × 100.

$$\text{f Standardized tax burden index} = \frac{\text{tax revenues/GDP}}{\text{Average tax revenues as percentage of GDP of the ten countries}}.$$

g SW Direct and tax expenditures as percentage of GDP adjusted for tax revenue index $= \frac{(4)}{(6)}$.

h See Appendix; Table A.3 for detailed information.

$$\text{Standardized Need Index I} = \frac{\text{Dependency ratio} + \text{unemployment rate} + \text{percentage of single-parent families}}{\text{The ten-country average of the sum of dep. ratios, unempl. rates and single-parent rates}}.$$

i NET Index of welfare effort $= \frac{(7)}{(8)} = \frac{(4)}{(6) \times (8)} = \frac{\text{SW expenditures as percentage of GDP adjusted for the differences in tax revenues and need among the ten countries.}}{}$

j See Appendix, Table A.3 for detailed information.

$$\text{Standardized Need Index II} = \frac{\text{Dependency ratio} + \text{unemployment rate of individual countries}}{\text{The ten-country average of the sum of dependency ratios and unemployment rates}}.$$

k Modified NET index of welfare effort $= \frac{(7)}{(10)} = \frac{(4)}{(6) \times (10)}$.

m The estimation for Japan is based on its direct social welfare expenditures because of the lack of data on tax expenditures.

l The figures in parentheses indicate ranks.

Sources of Data:

Direct expenditures, total direct government expenditures, and GDPs: OECD, Social Expenditure 1960–1990, Problems of Growth and Control (Paris: OECD, 1985).

Tax expenditures: OECD, Tax Expenditures: A Review of the Issues and Country Practice, Report by the Committee on Fiscal Affairs (Paris: OECD, 1984); Paul R. McDaniel and Stanley S. Surrey, eds., International Aspects of Tax Expenditures: A Comparative Study, Series on International Taxation No.5 (Deventer, The Netherlands: Kluwer Law and Taxation Publishers, 1985).

Tax revenues: OECD, Revenue Statistics of OECD Member Countries 1965–1984 (Paris: OECD, 1985).

211

Table A.3. Comparative Index of Need

| | Australia | Austria | Canada | France | Ireland | Nether-lands | Sweden | United Kingdom | United States | Japan |
|---|---|---|---|---|---|---|---|---|---|---|
| (1) Dependency Ratio (%)[a] | 53.1 | 55.8 | 48.1 | 57.0 | 69.5 | 51.1 | 56.0 | 55.3 | 50.8 | 48.6 |
| (2) Unemployment Rate (%) | 5.7 | 1.9 | 7.5 | 6.3 | 7.3 | 6.0 | 2.0 | 11.4 | 7.5 | 2.2 |
| (3) Single-Parent Families (%)[b] | 12.9 | 21.0 | 12.3 | 13.0 | 5.1[c] | 5.3[d] | 27.0 | 12.5 | 19.5 | 4.9 |
| Total (1 + 2 + 3) | 71.7 (7) | 78.7 (4) | 67.9 (8) | 76.3 (6) | 81.9 (2) | 62.4 (9) | 85.0 (1) | 79.2 (3) | 77.8 (5) | 55.7 (10) |
| Standardized Need Index I = $\dfrac{(1 + 2 + 3)\text{ of individual countries}}{\text{Average of the sum of }(1 + 2 + 3)\text{ of the ten countries}}$ | .973 | 1.068 | .922 | 1.036 | 1.112 | .847 | 1.154 | 1.075 | 1.056 | .756 |
| Standardized Need Index II = $\dfrac{(1 + 2)\text{ of individual countries}}{\text{Average of the sum of }(1 + 2)\text{ of the ten countries}}$ | .975 | .957 | .922 | 1.050 | 1.273 | .947 | .962 | 1.106 | .967 | .842 |

[a]The dependency ratio is the sum of the ratio of the population aged 0–14 years and that of the population aged 65 years or older to those aged 15–64 years.

[b]Single-parent families as percentage of all families with children younger than 18 except for Ireland and the Netherlands.

[c]Single-parent families as percentage of all families with children younger than 14 in 1966.

[d]The figure is the sum of divorce rate in 1970 (3.3%) and illegitimate births as percentage of total births in 1974 (2.0).

Sources of Data:

*Dependency ratio:* OECD, Department of Economics and Statistics, *Labor Force Statistics, 1963–1983* (Paris: OECD, 1985).

*Unemployment rate:* OECD, *Main Economic Indicators* (Paris: OECD, September 1982); OECD, *Labor Force Statistics 1963–1983.*

*Single-parent families:* For Ireland and the Netherlands, OECD, Centre for Educational Research and Innovation, *Child and Family: Demographic Developments in the OECD Countries* (Paris: OECD, 1979); for Japan, Statistics Bureau, Management and Coordination Agency, *Statistical Yearbook of Japan 1985* (Tokyo: Statistics Bureau, 1985), p. 48, Table 2-19; for Austria, Rainer Munz, personal communication; for the remaining six countries, Alfred J. Kahn and Sheila B. Kamerman, *Income Transfers for Families with Children: An Eight-Country Study* (Philadelphia: Temple University Press, 1983), p. 59.

212

# Index